Our Material Blind Spot

Since Our Invention of Words

TERRY MOLLNER

The Love Skill Publishing

Copyright © 2019 by Trusteeship Institute, Inc.

Published and distributed in the United States by THE LOVE SKILL Publishing
PO Box 631 Shutesbury, MA 01072
www.theloveskill.com, www.chrysalisnation.org

All right reserved. No part of this book may be used or reproduced by any mechanical, photographic or electronic process, or in the form of an audio recording; nor may it be stored in a retrieval system, transmitted or otherwise be copied for public use, other than for fair use as brief quotations embodied in articles and reviews without prior written permission of the author.

Cover design: Greg Caulton
Interior layout: Frances Lassor

Printed by Kindle Direct Publishing

Our Mutual Blind Spot Since Our Invention of Words / Terry Mollner

ISBN-13: 9781704079592

Printed in the United States of America

Any views expressed in this book, *Our Mutual Blind Spot Since Our Invention of Words,* are my own and do not necessarily reflect those of Calvert Funds, Calvert Investment Management, Inc., Eaton Vance, Inc., nor those of Stakeholders Capital, Inc..

$19.95 US

To all those who achieve
mutual mature love
and enjoy Eldering

CONTENTS

NOTE TO READERS

This book is also available on our website, www.chrysalisnation. org. We are doing that so people around the world will have easy access to the information in it. We want the knowledge, skills, and organizations described herein to come alive in as many communities around the world as possible and as quickly as possible. It is our hope you will enjoy supporting us in this effort through the purchase of this book, particularly once you have read it. Thank you.

If you prefer to get into these ideas through the stories of how I discovered them little by little throughout my seventy-four years, first read *Chapter 4: How I Backed into the Discovery of Mutual Mature Love.*

The main purpose of this book is to have you become aware of the layers of maturity of the skill of human self-consciousness. Once you have achieved the Teen layer, the last three can only be the result of free choice by you. They are an inside job. If you conclude you have not achieved full maturity in this most important skill for each of us to learn, I hope you experience yourself supported in completing that task as a result of reading this book.

All proceeds from the sale of our books go to our educational organization, Trusteeship Institute, Inc., to support the development of the organizations described herein, particularly the broader Maturation Movement we hope this book stimulates into existence.

Do earnestly answer the 7 questions in the first pages of *Chapter 1: The 7 Questions.* The rest of this book is based on the discovery of your answers to them by giving priority to keeping your power, all of it, and using it to primarily study your direct, present, and repeatable by choice experience to find the answers. As you will discover, this is exercising your ability and right of mature free choice.

"An individual has not started living until he can rise above the narrow confines of his individual concerns to the broader concerns of all of humanity."

Dr. Martin Luther King, Jr.

INTRODUCTION

When I was a sophomore in high school something dramatic happened that had me realize I had no idea why to do one thing rather than another. I was only reacting to things. This resulted in making a vow with myself to discover the "meaning of life," why to do one thing rather than another. It was the first of three vows in my life, and I tell the stories of how they happened in this book. Each was a commitment, like the first one, to learn something I did not know.

I am now 74 years old and I believe I have found the answers to all three questions. Herein, I present what I have discovered for you to determine if you agree.

In 2000, I stepped in and was part of orchestrating the purchase of Ben & Jerry's ice cream company by Unilever with a contract that has allowed it to remain a socially responsible company forever, with me on its board of directors. Suddenly, I was part of a $51 billion multinational corporation with 161,000 employees and factories in over 50% of the nations on Earth.

I quickly realized there was no way a person could graduate up the hierarchical management system of the company to become the CEO without being committed to the priority of maximizing profits for a few people, the shareholders. I also realized this was an immoral contract supported by national governments. Throughout history we have at least intuitively known loving behavior, also known as moral behavior, is consistently giving priority to the common good of us all. And it is always this *priority* that is most important in all we do.

This had me realize Earth is in big trouble. Any individual or organization not giving priority to the common good, to our ability to mature into managing Earth well, is undercutting the ability of the rest of us to do it. If sufficiently widespread, this could lead to the destruction of our ability to sustain life on Earth.

When I got to know them, there was also no question the managers in Unilever had the best of primary intentions. Therefore, they, and us all, had to be operating on a *mutual blind spot*. There had to be something we did not know that was necessary to correct this self-destructive course of humanity.

Stop for a moment and think about this. Currently, most people assume it is natural for each part of the universe to give priority to its self-interest with competition, therefore, being the fundamental process in nature. If we extend this assumption to its natural conclusion, when there are only two parts left, they will either destroy each other, in an effort to be the only one left, or one will win the battle and be the only one left. If the latter happens, it will then have no reason to exist because there is no other left with which to compete. Ultimately, the only two options are self-destruction or no reason to exist. Yet, it is self-evident there is always a reason to do one thing rather than another, such as when driving to Boston to turn right when leaving my driveway. Therefore, the self-interest of my physical body cannot be the natural highest priority of it and competition can't be the fundamental process in nature. As you will discover, both are part of the process of learning a human language and, as a result, being self-conscious. However, as I think you will also discover, when we achieve full maturity in the skill of human self-consciousness the self-interest of our physical bodies is not our natural highest priority and competition is not the fundamental process in nature.

My third vow was to discover our mutual blind spot that had all in Unilever, and nearly all in our current corporate communities and societies, comfortable with this immoral priority. I believe I have now also discovered the answer to this now global capitalism riddle. The answers to the questions of all three vows are described in this book.

The main insight that is the foundation of all you will read is this: since our invention of words we have had a mutual blind spot. As with most blind spots, what is being missed is in plain sight.

The second main insight is there are smaller skills that define the layers of maturity of the skill of human self-consciousness. There are only seven main ones, and most people on Earth have already mastered the first four or five. Once we discover the knowledge of the smaller skill of each next layer, we can't ever fool ourselves into thinking we do not know it. It then naturally, effortlessly, freely, and permanently becomes knowledge we have, a skill to consistently honor that knowledge, a habit, and part of who we are. Therefore, the way to mature capitalism is not by primarily developing a new economic theory. It is assisting all the people involved, from the boards of directors to the CEOs to the employees to the customers to achieve full maturity in the skill of human self-consciousness.

When we know the next layer of maturity of the skill of human self-consciousness, we can't ever fool ourselves into thinking we do not know it. That maturation is permanent, and in every moment going forward it will be present in our every action. People operating at the higher layers of maturity of the skill of human self-consciousness will not be able to stop themselves from not only maturing capitalism into common good capitalism but also maturing every other area of their personal and organizational lives.

Our blind spot is like the mutual blind spot we had until 1492 when Christopher Columbus sailed to America. Until then most people thought the Earth was flat. Yet one could watch a boat disappear from the bottom up when it sailed out to sea. Also, when standing on the shore of an ocean or large lake and looking at where it meets the sky, the line looks flat. However, if we looked fully to the left and right and take the entire 180 degrees of the horizon into view what is flat is a perfect half circle. Both of these were fully and easily visible since human beings have been on Earth. Yet it was not until 1492 that people began to entertain the obvious fact, in plain sight, the Earth is round.

Since everyone in 1492 assumed the Earth was flat, it was very difficult for anyone to discover, much less convince others, of this *mutual* blind spot.

We have the same situation today.

Nearly all of us assume the universe is separate parts and we are each one of them. For instance, we each assume we are only our physical bodies. As you will discover in *Chapter 1: The 7 Questions*, it is obvious in plain sight the universe operates as an indivisible whole, the opposite of as separate parts. This means we are each first the indivisible universe that will not die and secondly our physical bodies that will die, a very different self-definition.

What has had nearly all of us assume it operates as separate parts until 2019 is we are unaware that to invent the first words of a human language we had to also invent the assumption the universe is separate parts. Only then could we invent the sound and symbol "tree" for a tree, "rock" for a rock, and a word for every other part of the universe that is different from all the others.

It was not necessary for us to be aware we had unconsciously (without choice) invented the assumption the universe is separate parts to invent words. As a result, we have been giving priority to words ever since we invented them and unaware that in doing so we are sustaining the assumption the universe operates as separate parts. This is our mutual blind spot.

To this day nearly all of us think it is wise to choose the most fundamental belief to guide our thinking from the smorgasbord of *beliefs in words* we come upon. We are unaware that when doing this we are also sustaining the assumption the universe is separate parts when it isn't separate parts.

Words are themselves separate parts we invented. There are over 6,000 human languages on Earth. Each is invented agreements on sounds and symbols for each part of the universe. By giving priority to a belief in words we are two layers of illusions from direct experience. Words are a mutually agreed upon illusion tool we invented, and the assumption the universe is separate parts is another mutually agreed upon illusion tool we invented.

These are both extremely valuable illusion tools! Arguably our two most brilliant inventions! It is these two inventions that allow us to be the self-conscious parts of the indivisible universe.

Herein we will define "self-conscious" as our ability to know what we are doing while we are doing it and to exercise individual free choice.

Thus, instead of just reacting, as do lions, tigers, and bears, we can *choose* how to respond to a situation. This gives us the option to respond in a way that honors how the universe operates or in a less mature way.

What has made it difficult for us to discover this mutual blind spot is there are layers of maturity of the skill of human self-consciousness. It is not a simple skill like learning to use a straw to drink water or a fork to eat food. It is a complex skill like riding a bicycle or driving an automobile. There are a number of smaller skills we need to learn in the natural progression to master the full skill.

On top of this, we know from observation, and now also from neuroscience, our brains are not sufficiently developed to master the last two smaller skills until the teenage years. If as teenagers we are not eldered into the mastery of the last two of the seven smaller skills, we, and all in our society, can remain stuck at one of the lower layers. We are still operating on the assumption necessary to become self-conscious parts of the individual universe: the assumption the universe is separate parts.

Regardless of its content, we do this when we sustain choosing the most fundamental belief to guide our thinking from the smorgasbord of *beliefs in words* we come upon. In doing so, what we are unaware we are doing is unconsciously (without choice) sustaining the relationship pattern of childhood where we did not have our power. Our parents had it. To survive, our only choice was to obey them.

We have been unconsciously (without choice) sustaining this relationship pattern, the only pattern of relationship we know up to our teenage years, by giving our power to a parent-substitute, today usually not another person or group but our freely chosen *belief in words* (herein described as an "outside belief" we have chosen from the smorgasbord of fundamental beliefs in words we come upon).

Again, regardless of its content, once this is done our only option of relating with it is obedience. We do not have our power any longer. It is where we believe we have given it: to our outside belief, something we are unconsciously (without choice) assuming is another separate part.

This obedience is in conflict with our awareness from the teenage years on we have the ability and right to exercise individual free choice. However, most of us are unaware of this inner conflict: we believe we exercised individual free choice when freely choosing our fundamental outside belief.

Therefore, we are unaware by giving priority to an outside belief we no longer have our ability and right to exercise individual free choice. This is the unknown inner conflict as a result of this blind spot. We want to simultaneously do both and can't simultaneously do both: obey where we have given our power and exercise individual free choice.

The ending of this unknown inner conflict is knowing the difference between *individual free choice* and *mature free choice*.

The latter is determining our most fundamental belief about the operation of the universe in the same way we were able to confirm the Earth is round. It is *keeping our power, all of it, and giving priority to studying our direct, present, and repeatable by choice experience* to identify the most fundamental belief we will use to guide our thinking (herein using this approach to identify our most fundamental belief is labeled an "inside belief," *something determined to be true in direct experience*).

This is the exercise of *mature free choice*. It is not giving our power to a second thing, a parent-substitute. This is keeping our power, all of it, and using our skill of human self-consciousness as a *sixth sense* to discover *in direct experience* how the universe operates, as an indivisible whole. Only this allows us to continue to keep our power and, in the future, execute our ability and right to exercise individual, now mature, free choice.

Like the use of our other five senses, we use our skill of human self-consciousness as a sixth sense to discover this fact *in direct experience*. Once we repeatably know something is true in direct experience, in our thinking it becomes knowledge we label as "true," then "a skill" to continuously honor it as true, "a habit," and "part of who we are." This does not qualify our ability and right in the future to exercise individual, now mature, free choice. Herein this activity is labeled being a "personal scientist."

Only this process can result in natural confidence. We can in any moment turn our attention to our direct experience to confirm our inside belief is accurate.

Truths or facts, such as rocks are hard and fire is hot, are the same for everyone. Consistently relating with these truths as truths are *skills* that become habits and part of who we are no longer in need of our primary attention. Skills, unlike beliefs, are also the same for everyone: the skills of relating with rocks as hard and fire as hot are the same for everyone. Also, we each either remain balanced on a bicycle or we fall off of it. Truths and skills are the same for everyone.

Outside beliefs are not the same for everyone. They can represent anything accurate or inaccurate. Being two steps removed from knowing truths in direct experience, an outside belief cannot *in any moment* be confirmed as accurate by giving priority to turning our attention to our direct experience to confirm it is accurate, like touching a rock or getting close to a fire.

This leaves us vulnerable to being pulled in the direction of the best marketing. All of our outside beliefs are equally illusions. They primarily exist in words. They are two layers of illusions from knowledge discovered in direct experience, inside beliefs.

Like learning the complex skill of riding a bicycle, learning the complex skill of human self-consciousness is the learning of a number of smaller skills in a natural progression. Each time we learn the next smaller skill we integrate the lower ones we know with it into one skill. Ultimately, when we have learned all the smaller skills, we achieve full maturity in the complex skill of riding a bicycle or human self-consciousness.

The smaller skills of the seven layers of maturity of the complex skill of human self-consciousness are described in this book. You probably already know the first five of them. Today, most societies on Earth know them and teach them to their children. You probably do not know the last two. To learn them you must discover this mutual blind spot and replace your outside beliefs with inside beliefs.

Full maturity in the skill of human self-consciousness results in the natural, effortless, freely chosen, and permanent habitual skill of it that, like any skill, is the same for everyone. Also, like relating with rocks as hard and fire as hot, no effort, force, or discipline is necessary.

This is the value of each of us giving priority to identifying truths in direct experience, by exercising mature free choice. This results in inside beliefs that are the same for everyone. They are accurate knowledge that can be confirmed as accurate in any moment by again turning our attention to being a personal scientist. This is keeping our power, all of it, and studying our direct, present, and repeatable by choice experience to confirm in direct experience it is accurate knowledge.

As you hopefully will discover as you read this book, nearly all of us have been assuming it makes sense to choose our most fundamental belief from the smorgasbord of outside beliefs we come upon. Since inventing words, this is the result of giving priority to words instead of direct experience. Choosing from among the outside beliefs we come upon is the exercise of individual free choice. Only understanding the wisdom of *giving priority to direct experience instead of the choice of an outside belief* has us keep our power, all of it, and in the future continue to have our ability and right to continue exercising what is herein labeled "mature free choice."

This ends the usually unknown inner conflict between obeying our freely chosen outside belief and exercising individual free choice.

Primarily being a personal scientist and achieving full maturity in the skill of human self-consciousness results in the *experience* of natural confidence, the *effortless choice* of moral and loving behavior, and, as a result, the consistent *feeling* of contented joy, the most enjoyable joy. Socially, it results in *freely and consistently giving priority to cooperation for maturation,* participation in the fundamental process in nature. Now our most important task is the maturation of us all to full maturity in this skill that is the same for everyone.

This widespread mutual blind spot, like until 1492 assuming the Earth is flat, has continued until 2019.

The only solution is ending it by discovering it. There is no other solution.

As long as we are not aware of it, the experience of natural confidence and the feeling of contented joy are not possible, the experiences of mastering the last two smaller skills of the seven layers of maturity of the skill of human self-consciousness.

Our maturation out of our current self-destructive course of humanity, and the maturation of capitalism into common good capitalism, will be the result of more people each day becoming personal scientists by exercising mature free choice. Just as today nearly all children on Earth are born into societies that know the Earth is round, someday all children will also be eldered into primarily being personal scientists by the end of their teenage years.

The *skill* of being a personal scientist, and using it to master the smaller skills of the last two of the seven layers of maturity of the skill of human self-consciousness, will be discovered by all to be the same for everyone. Therefore, it is this that will result in both personal and social contented joy.

A friend of mine read a draft of this book and suggested I give some reasons in this *Introduction* why I think it would be wise for you to read it. I thought that was a good idea. Here are two.

Let's start at the biggest level, the global level.

It is this mutual blind spot that could have the US and China end up in a military conflict rather than cooperation for maturation, giving priority to the actual fundamental process in nature. This would be the second time there would be direct military conflict between two nuclear powers. A war between India and Pakistan was the first time this occurred and that may also be ready to happen again. The purpose of the Cold War was to avoid this.

In the early 1930s, prior to World War II, Joseph Stalin killed nearly four million people and we did nothing about it. We considered ourselves fully separate from them and information about such things did not instantly flow around the world as it does now. Such a holocaust would probably be known today and fully unacceptable to most people around the world. Action in response would be demanded.

If we do not uncover and correct this mutual blind spot, immature people can easily do immature things as Stalin did. And as we all know the democratically elected Adolph Hitler did. We do not like to think about the obvious possibility three people could get pilot licenses, hijack three commercial airplanes, and fly them into the two World Trade Centers and the Pentagon, but immature people can comfortably do such things. Thus, we almost never read articles about the possibility of these things. We do not want to admit their possibility in the hope they won't happen. However, they can happen and not planning for the possibility is immature behavior.

Today, do we know where all the nuclear bombs are around the world? Do we know no one would be able to get ahold of one and detonate it in a major city? Of course, we do not like to even think about such things, but the question is, "Are we giving high priority to making sure such a catastrophe can't happen?" More important, "Are we also making sure all of our children on Earth are educated into knowing of this blind spot and eldered up the layers to full maturity in the skill in human self-consciousness before the end of their teenage years so no one would ever want to do such a thing?"

Today, any determined immature person is capable of horrendous harm to others, as we have witnessed in the now many mass murders and terrorist attacks. We are now a global village. Like in any village, *the highest priority of our elders* is the education of every child into full maturity in the skill of human self-consciousness by the end of their teenage years. Ultimately, only this ends these horrendous actions by any one person. Only this ends a nation choosing military war, or any kind of war, rather than reaching agreements that work for all.

All wars begin and end in peace. All wars are mutually destructive. Mature people skip the war part and live with each other based on freely chosen agreements that give priority to the common good, that we now know is cooperation for maturation of the indivisible universe.

The second reason for reading this book is a more immediate and personal reason.

Our romantic relationships can be a consistent experience of contented joy. They should not be some kind of unconscious (without choice) agreement where in exchange for having someone with whom we can consistently have sex we will have children or *vice versa*, or to commit to one to have companionship, and/or for social acceptance.

Every couple wants to primarily be together because they are primarily experiencing love, the eye-to-eye-consistent-and-enjoyable-experience-of-love. This is mature romantic love.

This is only possible when the mutual blind spot of being separate parts is replaced with the accurate assumption the universe operates as an indivisible whole. Until then we are unconsciously (without choice) primarily experiencing ourselves as a separate part and calculating if the tradeoffs are worth it, *primarily* a business deal not the *everyday experience of love.* Only when we know the latter can the experience of love naturally, effortlessly, freely, and permanently be the container experience of all other experiences in our romantic relationship and potentially in all the areas of our lives. Knowing how to achieve this in our romantic relationship is a second reason for reading this book.

As I think you will agree as you read further, cooperation for maturation, the assumption we all have of the relationship among the parts inside our skins, is the fundamental process in nature everywhere because it is obvious in plain sight the universe operates as an indivisible whole.

I like to get up in the early morning and sit in the hot tub on our deck from where I can easily watch the sunrise. I then do my form of meditation. I listen for information directly from the universe that is always being downloaded into words in my thinking. It is the opposite of beginning, processing in, and ending my thinking with words. It nearly always provides me wise information about the issues in my thinking.

This morning, as is sometimes the case, a mosquito began to bother me. My entire life I have swatted them away or waited until it landed and then tried to kill it with a smack. A few weeks ago, I discovered if I a few times splashed water toward them they left. There is nothing they hate more than ending up in water because they will die.

I am now seventy-four years old and just discovered this better way to get rid of mosquitos when in the hot tub! Guess what? Ever since I weeks ago discovered this better method, I have been consistently using it instead of swatting at them because *my direct experience consistently confirmed it works better*. It is now new knowledge that is accurate (a truth), a skill, and a habit in only a few weeks.

As I think you will discover, cooperation for maturation is the-fundamental process in nature and can't be escaped or stopped, even when seventy-four years old. As long as you are in your teenage years or older, you can self-elder yourself into replacing this mutual blind spot the universe operates as separate parts with the accurate one it operates as an indivisible whole. I hope you find this book to be helpful in this self-eldering task.

By the way, and as I will point out a few times in this book, you and all of us will still have our belief that answers the fundamental question inside us, "Why is the universe structured the way it is structured?" Our answer to this question is usually a religious, philosophical, or scientific belief we each choose. The mastery of the *skill* of human self-consciousness, or any skill, will always be secondary in importance to our choice of the answer to that question.

This book is solely about mastering the *skill* of human self-consciousness, relating skillfully with the way the universe (nature) operates using self-evident truths. There will be no effort to answer this most fundamental question inside all of us and for which we each have our chosen belief. This is an important distinction to maintain in your thinking as you read further.

Herein we are solely focused on mastering the *skill* of human self-consciousness.

It is important to emphasize when we are a teenager, or older, we know we have the ability and right to exercise individual free choice. Therefore, we are each the only person who can elder ourselves up the last two layers of maturity to achieve full maturity in the skill of human self-consciousness. It is an inside job. Also, mastering the last two smaller skills is only possible when we have discovered the importance of being a personal scientist, of using our skill of human self-consciousness as a sixth sense to exercise mature free choice. They are skills we must freely choose to master as a result of discovering them in direct experience.

Please give this book a read and tell me what you think. I hope you conclude a deep consideration of these thoughts and skills are worthy of your attention. I am looking for fellow personal scientists to join me in maturing our personal and social course of humanity. Hopefully you will discover you too are looking for fellow personal scientists.

Even though it was obvious in plain sight, we were not able to entertain the idea the Earth is a huge round ball until 1492 because it looked flat from where we were each standing. Now, even though it is obvious in plain sight, until now we have not been able to entertain the idea the universe operates as an indivisible whole because it looks huge from where we are each standing. This is the result of most of us still unconsciously (without choice) operating on the assumption we were unaware we had to also invent to invent words and be self-conscious parts of it, the assumption the universe is separate parts.

It is 2019. It is time for all of us to become aware of this mutual blind spot.

CHAPTER 1

The 7 Questions

Allow me to begin this book by asking you seven questions.

While you are answering them, there is one thing I would like to ask of you. Instead of looking for the answers in words, give priority to a study of your direct and present experience to find the answers. Then represent in your thinking in words what you discover there. Words will always be present. That is normal and fine. Just choose to give *priority* to the study of your direct and present experience to find the answers, the way you discovered rocks are hard and fire is hot.

There are no trick questions, and you will not have difficulty finding the answers to all seven. The answers are obvious and self-evident. It is the result of discovering them in your direct and present experience that I want you to experience.

Here is the first question.

"Have you been breathing since you came out of your mother's womb?"

Giving priority to words, the obvious answer is "yes." But give priority to experience instead of words. If you turn your attention to your physical body, is it obvious that you are breathing and are continuously breathing? Do that study now for a few seconds. Then read the next paragraph.

It is surely obvious in your direct and present experience that you are breathing, or you would not be able to be reading this book. It is also obvious you could not be breathing now if you have not also been breathing since you came out of your mother's womb. Therefore, from a study of your *direct and present experience* you can easily conclude that the answer to the first question is, "Yes, I have been continuously breathing since I came out of my mother's womb."

Here is the second question.

"Did you choose to breathe when you came out of your mother's womb or have you been naturally and effortlessly breathing?"

I think you will agree you did not have the ability to sit up and *choose* to keep breathing when you came out of your mother's womb. It is obvious and self-evident by turning your attention to your physical body right now that you were then and are still naturally and effortlessly breathing. Do not trust that conclusion in words. Instead, before you read the next paragraph, turn your primary attention to a study of your direct and present experience of your physical body. Determine if it is true that you are now *naturally and effortlessly breathing* and, therefore, have been naturally and effortlessly breathing since you came out of your mother's womb. Do that for a few seconds now. Then read the next paragraph. Is it obvious that you have been naturally and effortlessly breathing?

Let's now use the remaining five questions to discover who or what has been doing your breathing since you came out of your mother's womb.

Here is the third question.

"If we took the lungs out of your physical body and put them on a nearby table, would you be able to breathe?"

The obvious and self-evident answer in words is "No." However, turn your attention to your breathing, imagine that your lungs were fully separated from your physical body, and put on a nearby table. Then, turn your attention to your physical body without your lungs. Would you be able to breathe? Take a few seconds to study this before you read the next paragraph.

It is, indeed, obvious that your lungs need to be in your body and your body has to be at least healthy enough for you to be breathing for you to breathe.

Here is the fourth question.

"If the air was not around your physical body at all times, would you be able to breathe?"

The obvious answer in words is "No." However, again turn your attention to your present experience to find the answer. From that study, do you also conclude it is obvious that if the air is not around your physical body at all times you would not be able to breathe? Before reading the next paragraph, take a few seconds to turn your attention to your physical body's relationship with the air around you to determine if this is true.

Therefore, I think you have concluded your lungs need to be in your body, your body needs to be healthy enough to breathe, and the air has to be around you at all times to be able to breathe.

Here is the fifth question.

"If the Earth did not have the atmosphere it has, if it had the atmosphere of Jupiter or Mars, would you be able to breathe?"

From what we know of Jupiter and Mars, the obvious answer in words is "No." However, again turn your primary attention to your physical body's relationship with the air around you, the Earth's atmosphere, and your knowledge of the atmosphere on Jupiter and Mars to decide if it is obvious in your direct and present experience it is true that the Earth needs to have the atmosphere it has for you to breathe. Ignore how big or small is the Earth, its atmosphere, and the universe. Here we are only interested in your *relationship* with them. We are only concerned with your judgment from a study of your direct and present experience if you would be able to breathe if the Earth did not have the atmosphere it has. Before reading the next paragraph, take a few seconds to turn your attention to your experience to find your answer to this question: "If the Earth did not have the atmosphere it has, if it had the atmosphere of Jupiter or Mars, would you be able to breathe?"

From a study of your direct and present experience I think you have concluded that your lungs need to be in your body, your body needs to be healthy enough to breathe, the air has to be around you at all times, and the Earth has to have the atmosphere is has to be able to breathe.

Here is the sixth question.

"If the Earth was not in the particular relationship it has with the rest of the universe, if it had the relationship of Jupiter, Mars, or Venus, would you be able to breathe?"

Again, the answer is obvious in words, "No." However, choose to give priority to your experience of your physical body in relationship with the air around you, the Earth's atmosphere, and where it is in relationship to the Sun and the rest of the universe to find your answer to this question. Is it true in your direct and present experience that if the Earth was not in its particular relationship with the rest of the universe you would not be able to breathe? Take a few seconds to do this. Then read the next paragraph.

If you experience this to be true, then it is your lungs being in your physical body, your physical body being healthy enough to breathe, the air being around you, the Earth's atmosphere being what it is, and the Earth being in the particular relationship it is in with the rest of the universe that is doing your breathing.

Here is the seventh and last question.

"If, for a half hour, we took any of those five things away, for instance the air being around you or the Earth's atmosphere being what it is, would you be able to breathe?"

The obvious answer in words is "No." However, again turn your attention to your direct and present experience for a few seconds.

Imagine any one of those five things not being present for a half hour. Would you be able to breathe? Then read the next paragraph.

Therefore, it is obvious and self-evident from a study of your direct and present experience that all five things have to *always* be doing what they are doing and *always* in full cooperation with each other for you to breathe. This means the universe operates as an indivisible whole.

Is this true from a study of your direct and present experience? For a few moments, turn your attention to your physical body and its relationship with all five things on that list—your lungs, physical body, the air around you, the Earth's atmosphere, and the Earth being in its particular relationships with the rest of the universe.

From *keeping your power, all of it, and primarily studying your direct and present experience,* is it true they *always* have to be doing what they are doing, and *always* in full cooperation with each other, for you to be breathing? Close your eyes and take a few moments to turn your attention to studying your direct experience to answer this question.

Take as much time as you like; then turn to the next page.

If you gave priority to a study of your direct and present experience in answering the above seven questions, you now know, in the same way you know rocks are hard and fire is hot, *the universe operates as an indivisible whole.* You know from a study of your direct, present, and repeatable by choice experience this is true. You will now never be able to fool yourself into thinking you do not know this fact. You can always double check to be sure this is accurate by again keeping your power, all of it, and primarily using it to study your direct, present, and repeatable by choice experience to confirm it is accurate by again asking yourself these 7 questions.

Here is a good way to ground this fact.

Normally we do not see the air that is present; yet we *know* it is here or we would not be able to breathe. We also do not see the oneness of nature that is present; yet, in the same way, we now *know* it is here or we would not be able to breathe.

This fact is not mysterious, unknowable, or unable to be directly known and experienced. This is the most fundamental fact in physics, and, as you will discover, it can be directly experienced.

First, you just witnessed this knowledge as true in direct experience.

Now, in the same way you know the air is always present, you now know the oneness of nature is always present.

Secondly, when with a friend and the two of you choose do the exercise in *Chapter 8: Mutual Mature Love Experience,* you will discover you can also mutually know with another person a *sustained direct experience of it as the container of all else in your relationship.* That exercise will only be for the purpose of you knowing it is a possible skill and choice in a direct experience with another. Mutually and consistently knowing this skill in one's romantic relationship is the base camp we all want to have in our lives. It took me 72 years to find it. Now my lover, Lucy, and I know this skill as the container experience of everything else we experience.

If it is true the universe operates as an indivisible whole, as we just observed to be obvious and in plain sight, why is nearly everyone who is reading this, and nearly all of humanity, still operating on the self-definition, "I am my physical body"? From the study we just did of our direct experience, we just discovered our accurate self-definition is this: "I am first the indivisible universe that will not die and secondly my physical body, a part of it that will die."

The following is the most important statement in this book.

Up until now nearly all of humanity has been operating on that immature self-definition. We also now know why. Up until now an understanding of the relationship between the oneness of nature and our human languages has not been widely understood. We now know it.

Fasten your seatbelts. This mature self-definition is probably going to change everything in the current way most readers think. In the rest of this chapter, I am going to walk you into understanding the main changes in your thinking that will now naturally and effortlessly begin to occur as a result of you knowing from a study of your direct experience the universe operates as an indivisible whole.

I am putting it all in this chapter so you can experience it as a whole and understand how all the parts fit together inside it. For many of you, this will be too much information too fast. That is fine. Take your time. Come back and read it again as often as you find that valuable to do. My goal, by having it all in one place, is to have it serve as a place to return to at any time to understand how all the pieces fit together into a whole.

There are five main changes in our thinking that begin to occur from knowing the universe operates as an indivisible whole:

Five Main Changes in Our Thinking From Knowing the Universe Operates As an Indivisible Whole

1. We primarily use our skill of human self-consciousness as our *sixth sense*, as we just did, to discover and know in direct experience truths about relationships between and among the parts of the universe; the most important one is the universe operates as an indivisible whole.

2. We now know in our thinking the *accurate fundamental inside belief* on how the universe operates: it operates as an indivisible whole.

3. We have a new self-definition, *"I am first the indivisible universe that will not die and secondly my physical body that will die."*

4. We add to our thinking process the *oneness pattern of thinking* and, while using both, give it priority over the separate parts pattern of thinking.

5. We are now aware that competition between and among the illusory separate parts with the priority of each being its separate part's self-interest is not the fundamental process in nature. *We now know cooperation of all the parts of the indivisible universe for maturation is the fundamental process in nature.*

Since our invention of human languages, we have had a mutual blind spot. We have been unconsciously (without choice) operating on the assumption we were not aware we invented necessary to invent words, the assumption the universe is separate parts. As a result, we have also been exercising free choice but not aware we are not exercising mature free choice. Let me explain this.

If you did as I suggested and gave priority to studying your direct experience to find the answers to the 7 questions, you may have for the first time used your skill of human self-consciousness in the mature way it can to be used, as a way to know truths *about relationships among the parts of the universe* from a study of direct experience. This is the way you discovered rocks are hard and fire is hot, *in direct experience.*

When you had many experiences of a rock being hard, it became *knowledge* in your thinking that you knew was true. In then became a *skill* to always relate with rocks as hard. It then became a *habit*: it was something you automatically did without having to have your primary attention on it. Ever since you have naturally, effortlessly, freely, and permanently acted as if rocks are hard. Since it is true rocks are hard, nothing has pulled your attention into reconsidering this truth.

By giving priority to experience, this truth became part of who you are. You are now walking, talking, and breathing the truth rocks are hard. This is the process and result when we learn a truth in direct experience. Inside, in our thinking with regard to rocks being hard, our experience is natural confidence: natural, effortless, freely chosen, and permanent confidence. No effort, force, or discipline is necessary. This is the value of identifying truths in direct experience.

This is how we use our first five senses to discover truths in experience. We use our sense of touch to discover the truth rocks are hard and fire is hot. We use our sense of hearing to discover the truth bells can ring. We use our sense of smell to discover the truth lilacs have a delightful fragrance. We use our sense of seeing to discover the truth the sky can be cloudy or clear. We use our sense of tasting to discover Ben & Jerry's Chocolate Fudge Brownie ice cream is delicious (the best!). We use our first five senses to discover truths in direct experience. Once known, these truths become a permanent part of who we are. In relationship to them we have what we will herein label "natural confidence." We know at any time we can again confirm they are true simply by turning our primary attention to direct experience in relationship with any of them. Yet, this almost never happens because, since they are true, in fact mutually known to be true with all other human beings, nothing ever suggests we turn our primary attention to confirm they are true.

In relationship to them, we experience permanent natural confidence.

If you gave priority to experience when answering the 7 questions, you were using your skill of human self-consciousness as a sixth sense, as a sixth way to discover truths in direct experience. It differs from the first five in one important way: it was discovering in direct experience a truth *about relationships between and among the parts of the universe.*

The other five senses only give us information about particular parts of the universe: rocks, bells, lilacs, sky, and ice cream. In answering the 7 questions by giving priority to experience to discover it is the universe that is doing your breathing and, therefore, it behaves as an indivisible whole, you were using your skill of human self-consciousness as a sixth sense, as a sixth way to discover and know truths *in direct experience.*

Since the invention of human languages few of us have been using it as a sixth sense. Since then we have been giving priority to words, particularly to *beliefs in words*. We have mainly been choosing beliefs from the smorgasbord of beliefs, outside beliefs, we come upon in our lives, sometimes switching from one to another.

As will be explained below, a belief is two steps removed from direct experience. Therefore, giving priority to an outside belief will never allow us to have the experience of natural confidence.

Words are our most brilliant invention. They allow us to be self-conscious parts of the indivisible universe: to know what we are doing while we are doing it and exercise individual free choice. Without being near them, and able to point and motion what we want, we can use words to talk with another person about how we could use rocks and some limbs from trees to build a damn at a particular spot in a small river.

However, what we were not aware we were doing when we invented words is that we needed to assume the universe is separate parts.

As described earlier, only then could we give the name "rock" to rocks, the name "tree" to trees, and the name "river" to rivers. To invent words, we needed to assume the universe is separate parts so we could invent a sound and symbol for each part of the universe that was different from the sound and symbol we invented for each of the other parts.

However, as we just discovered by studying our direct experience, the universe operates as an indivisible whole. It is not separate parts. As you will see later, the only way we could have invented the first word was by using the experience of oneness. When doing this we unconsciously (without choice) also invented the assumption necessary to do it, the assumption the universe is separate parts.

Most of us are still unconsciously (without choice) operating on this assumption as if it is the accurate fundamental assumption about how the universe operates. It isn't. However, since we all do this until our early teenage years and most of us are skill doing it, it has been difficult to discover we are nearly all still doing it.

This is clearly evidenced by us thinking we are each only our physical bodies. We just discovered that is not true. We are each first the indivisible universe that will not die and secondly our physical bodies that will die. (There are many theories about the universe, and it certainly changes; but I witness no evidence, nor am I aware of any creditable evidence, the universe will cease to exist.)

This is a very different self-definition.

We could be entering a new era in human history. It will be defined by our discovery of the mature way to use our skill of human self-consciousness. It is using it as our sixth sense to give priority to studying *direct experience* to identify the truths *about the relationships between and among the parts of the universe.* This will allow us the consistent experience of natural confidence in relationship with these truths.

Everything you will read in the rest of this chapter will be an extension of this mature understanding in physics, that the most fundamental fact is the universe operates as an indivisible whole.

At this point, it is important I make the following distinction also made in the *Introduction.*

You and all of us will still have our belief that answers the fundamental question inside us, "Why is the universe structured the way it is structured?" Our answer to this question is usually a religious, philosophical, or scientific belief we each choose. The mastery of the *skill* of human self-consciousness, or any skill, will appropriately always be secondary in importance to our choice of the answer to that question.

This book is solely about mastering the *skill* of human self-consciousness, relating skillfully with the way the universe (nature) operates using self-evident truths. There will be no effort to answer this most fundamental question inside all of us and for which we

– 37 –

each have our chosen belief. This is an important distinction to maintain in your thinking as you read further.

Herein we are solely focused on mastering the *skill* of human self-consciousness.

What you just discovered by giving priority to a study of experience—your direct, present, and repeatable by choice experience—when answering the 7 questions is the most fundamental fact about the relationship among all the parts of the universe: they cooperate with each other as parts of an indivisible whole. About this fact we do not have choice. This is the most fundamental fact about the relationship of all the parts with each other.

The next thing we can discover, from answering the 7 questions by using self-consciousness as a sixth sense, is you were exercising *mature free choice*.

There are three layers of maturity of exercising choice:

Three Layers of Maturity of Exercising Choice

1. Choice,

2. Individual free choice, and

3. Mature free choice.

As a child, we exercise choice by choosing from the options presented to us by others, for instance when asked to choose chocolate, vanilla, or strawberry ice cream. As a young teenager, our brains are sufficiently developed to where we realize we could invent the options of choice, for instance should I try out for the basketball team or the swim team? Or should I be a Buddhist or Catholic? This is exercising individual free choice. We are still unconsciously (without choice) operating on the assumption the universe is separate parts. Or we could keep our power, all of it, and use it as our sixth sense to study our direct, present, and repeatable by choice experience to identify the relationships among all the parts of the universe, as you just did, to identify the most important truth we will use to guide our thinking.

Only the later, the exercise of mature free choice, results in natural confidence. The other two do not.

Up until now you have probably been primarily using your skill of human self-consciousness to pick your most important beliefs from the smorgasbord of beliefs you have come upon, perhaps sometimes switching from one to another. They all exist in words, something two steps removed from direct experience. Let's take a closer look at this.

First, they are operating on the assumption there are separate parts when there aren't separate parts. Secondly, they use words, sounds and symbols, that are not what they are representing.

These are both mutually agreed upon illusion tools that are two layers of illusions removed from direct experience.

By giving priority to studying *direct experience* to find the answers you were using your skill of human self-consciousness as a sixth sense to discover truths about the relationship among the parts of the universe. If you did this when answering the 7 questions, you will now never be able to fool yourself into thinking you do not know the universe operates as an indivisible whole. Like knowing rocks are hard and fire is hot, you can confirm it is true by simply again using the 7 questions to study your direct experience to confirm it is true. After doing this a few times you will not judge there is a need to do it again just as you don't experience a need to double check rocks are hard and fire is hot.

Your relationship with this fact will then be natural confidence.

You achieved this not by using your skill of human self-consciousness to freely choose among beliefs in words, a shallow use of your ability and right to exercise individual free choice. You used this skill as a sixth sense. You kept your power, all of it, and used it to study your direct, present, and repeatable by choice experience to identify the relationship among all the parts of the universe. You were exercising mature free choice. You have kept your power, all of it, and will continue to have it.

No other exercise of individual free choice is true free choice, herein labeled "mature free choice."

Understanding these things is going to eventually change the thinking of us all. It is a maturation of the way we think. Once we know how to walk, we do not go back to crawling. Once we know how to ride a bicycle, we do not go back to riding a tricycle. Once we know how to use a computer, we do not go back to using a typewriter.

As described earlier, once we know a more mature way to do something, it naturally, effortlessly, freely, and permanently becomes *knowledge* we know is more mature, a *skill* to honor that knowledge as more mature, a *habit*, and *part of who we are*. As we will see below, this is because *maturation*, not competition between and among illusory separate parts, is the fundamental *kind of cooperation* that is the fundamental process in nature.

First, and before studying this further, in this book we will define all things as "conscious." Because everything is attached to everything else in an indivisible universe, they respond to what is around them. The response of animals is more substantial than planets and their response is more substantial than rocks. However, they are all connected to each other and respond to what is around them, whether we are talking about the planets and stars, the parts within an atom, and anything in between.

Human beings are also able to be "self-conscious."

This is the ability to know what we are doing while we are doing it and exercise individual or mature free choice. It includes the ability to analyze the past, develop a plan for the future, and consistently execute it in the present, alone or through agreements with others. It also allows us to define "self." Finally, it allows us to be a personal scientist, to keep our power, all of it, and give priority to studying our direct, present, and repeatable by choice experience to identify the fundamental truths we will use to guide our thinking. This is using our skill of human self-consciousness as a sixth sense. This is being a personal scientist.

Professional scientists study experiences to find truths and then share them with us in words. *Personal scientists*, as described above, keep their power, all of it, and study their direct, present, and repeatable by choice experience so they naturally, effortlessly, freely, and permanently *become the knowledge, skills, and habits they discover.* They become walking and talking self-consciously known truths.

You will notice I always write "all of it" after "keeping your power." This is to emphasize we can't divide our power, our ability to choose where to focus our attention, into parts. The universe is not divisible into parts except in our thinking using words. We, the indivisible universe through each of us, is either looking East or West, turning right or left, or getting out of bed or remaining in bed. Our primary attention is indivisible. In each of the above examples, we can only have our full primary attention in one or another place. We can be simultaneously executing many habits, but our *primary attention* can only be focused on one thing at a time.

Yes, we can play the piano with our left hand playing the rhythm and the right hand playing the melody, but those are secondary to us having our attention on playing the piano rather than taking the trash out to the curb to be picked up the next morning. In the illusions we invented of times and places (separate parts), we can only have our primary attention focused on one thing at a time. Therefore, when we keep our power and use it to study our direct experience, we do not want to allow for the illusion we can have our *primary attention* on more than one thing at a time. We want to always know we are using all of our power wherever we are focusing our attention. *Habits will be riding along*, like playing the rhythm with our left hand and melody with our right hand, but *our primary attention* can only be focused on one thing at a time. This is the nature of self-consciousness.

Since the invention of human languages, we have been giving priority to words. This makes sense. It is words that allow us to be self-conscious. As we will see, each time we discover the smaller skill of the next layer of maturity in mastering the skill of human self-consciousness we give it *priority* every moment until we have turned it into a habit, have discovered the smaller skill of the next layer, and are then giving *priority* to mastering it. Whether or not we are aware of it, they are given priority because mastering the skill of human self-consciousness is the only path to natural confidence and the feeling of contented joy that is our natural priority since being on this adventure of mastering it as a skill when a toddler. More on this later.

Humanity is now ready to mature into giving priority to exercising mature free choice, to, as personal scientists, study direct experience to identify the truths we will use to guide our thinking. Below, this will be described as the first step of maturation into the "Elder layer" of maturity in the skill of human self-consciousness.

This is only possible when we understand the relationship between the oneness of nature and human languages. This has only recently become widely known. This is similar to, in 1492, it began to become widely known the Earth is round.

There is much to present here for this to be fully understood, and I will get to the other important aspects of it below. The important thing to bring attention to at this point is the fundamental truth upon which everything in this book is based. Up to now nearly all of us have been using our skill of human self-consciousness in an immature way. We have been using it to choose from among the smorgasbord of *beliefs in words* we come upon in our lives to decide which ones to give priority in our thinking, herein referred to as "outside beliefs." This is giving our power to a second thing we now know does not exist, beliefs in words. If the universe is an indivisible whole, there is not a second thing to receive our power. This is the exercise of individual free choice. It is not the exercise of the mature free choice.

There are two kinds of beliefs in words we could choose to guide our thinking: outside beliefs and inside beliefs. Here is a more detailed description of each.

Outside beliefs are two steps removed from direct experience. First, words were only able to be invented by assuming the universe is separate parts. When talking with each other, each needs to have a different sound and symbol to be representing it than the names for each of the other parts. To do this, when inventing a human language, we unconsciously (without choice) assumed the universe is separate parts. This is the second step removed from direct experience.

However, as you just discovered, it is not separate parts. It operates as an indivisible whole. Separate parts are a *mutually agreed upon illusion tool* we invented that allow us to invent words. They, in turn, allow us to be self-conscious. Therefore, this tool of operating on the assumption there are separate parts is one of our most valuable inventions. It allows us to invent human languages and they allow us to be self-conscious parts of the indivisible universe. There are over 6,000 human languages on Earth. Each is a set of two mutually agreed upon illusion tools, called the assumption of separate parts and words, that allow us to be self-conscious parts of the indivisible universe.

Secondly, words are formed into beliefs. When we give priority to an outside belief in words, we are giving our power to a second thing that does not exist *except in the mutually agreed upon illusion tool of human languages.* Therefore, as mentioned above, in the future we are not able to exercise individual free choice. We no longer have our power. We have given it to beliefs in words, outside beliefs, and we now obey where we believe we have given it.

Rather than experiencing natural confidence, we experience conflict. Each moment we want to give *priority* to both exercising individual free choice and our freely chosen outside belief. That is not possible. They are opposites. We are stuck in inner conflict, may not even know it as that, and frustration, exasperation, confusion, and depression are often the result. The choice of an addiction to escape this unknown inner conflict is a possibility.

The use of *inside beliefs* is different. When we keep our power, all of it, and use it to primarily study our direct, present, and re-peatable by choice experience to observe the truths about relation-ships we will use to guide our thinking, *we have not given it away to a parent-substitute and unconsciously (without choice) sustained the relationship of obedience to it, the only pattern of relationship we know until our teenage years.* This is using our skill of human self-consciousness in the mature way, as our sixth sense. Like the other five senses, it is a sixth way we can know truths *in direct expe-rience*, here about relationships between and among the parts. This is being a personal scientist.

The conflict between our outside beliefs and our ability and right to exercise individual free choice is gone. We are now exercising mature free choice. We have kept our power, all of it, and are now using *inside beliefs* in our thinking. We can now at any moment confirm *in direct experience* (no illusory separate part is present) they are accurate truths, in the same way we can in any moment turn our attention to our direct experience to confirm rocks are hard and fire is hot.

Whenever we are being self-conscious, words are always between us and whatever we are thinking or observing. This is so important, allow me to state it again. Because it is words that allow us to be self-conscious, whenever we are being self-conscious words are always between us and whatever we are thinking or observing. Therefore, *it is essential that the words we are using as beliefs are inside beliefs* as a result of using our sixth sense to identify them.

In relationship to these truths, now also inside beliefs, we experience natural confidence, the same confidence we experience about the truths and inside beliefs rocks are hard and fire is hot.

By giving priority to your direct experience while studying it to answer the above 7 questions, you were being a personal scientist. You were using your skill of human self-consciousness in the mature way possible, as a sixth sense.

You were giving priority to experience instead of words to find the truths you will use to guide your thinking.

The result was an inside belief. Our inner experience is natural confidence this inside belief is accurate. And if at any time we have a doubt we can again turn our primary attention to our direct experience to confirm it is accurate.

This is the exercise of mature individual free choice. It is the only activity that is the exercise of our ability and right of individual free choice that allows us to continue exercising it in the future. This is the exercise of mature free choice. This is mature individual free choice. Nothing else is it.

Next, you will never be able to fool yourself into thinking you do not know this truth. Once we know a truth in direct, present, and repeatable by choice experience, we can't ever fool ourselves into thinking we do not know it. Maturation, as we will discuss below, is the fundamental process in nature and within us it is permanent. As stated earlier, once we know how to walk, we do not go back to primarily crawling to get around. Once we know how to use chopsticks with one hand, we do not go back to using them with two hands. Once we know each of the more mature ways of doing something, the rest of our lives we will not be able to fool ourselves into thinking we do not know these more mature ways of doing these things.

Allow me to emphasize this also: these changes are permanent. Maturation is the fundamental process in nature, and it cannot be escaped or stopped.

You now know the universe operates as an indivisible whole. You know it from keeping your power, all of it, and a study of your direct, present, and repeatable by choice experience, by using your skill of human self-consciousness as a sixth sense to identify truths as inside beliefs. Like your discovery rocks are hard and fire is hot, this truth is now *knowledge* in your thinking you know is true. It will naturally, effortlessly, freely, and permanently become a *skill* to continue to honor it as true. It will then become a *habit* to consistently honor it without having to have your primary attention on it. In the same way you are walking, talking, and breathing truth rocks are hard and fire is hot, you are now the walking, talking, and breathing truth the universe operates as an indivisible whole. Because it was discovered to be true in direct experience, it is now naturally, effortlessly, freely, and permanently part of who you are.

In your relationship with it, you can now experience the same natural confidence you experience in your relationship with knowing rocks are hard and fire is hot.

Let's stop focusing on understanding this in words for a few moments. Allow me to invite you to again turn your attention to your direct experience to again study this there.

Wherever you are, take a few moments to close your eyes and turn your attention to your breathing. Don't in any way change it. Just observe it. I repeat, just observe it.

While doing so, notice the **sensations** of these two experiences, in this order and spending a good amount of time with the first one before focusing on the second one:

1) **the *sensation* you are naturally and effortlessly breathing,** and
2) without concern for how large or small the universe is but only of your relationship with it, **be aware of the *sensation* it is the indivisible universe that is doing your breathing.**

Take as much time as you want; then turn to the next page.

While choosing to allow yourself to be aware of the sensations of the indivisible universe doing your breathing, you may have noticed a gentle release of some tightness. When we identify ourselves as only our physical bodies, whether doing so by choice or unconsciously (without choice), there can be some tightness, a preparation for conflict. When we become aware it is the indivisible universe that is doing our breathing and, therefore, the absence of a second thing with which we could be in conflict, any tightness in preparation for conflict dissipates. As I am sure you can easily imagine, this can also be good for the health of your physical body. You are moving as one with the universe rather than against it or any part of it.

This does not mean we cannot deal with conflict when it comes at us. However, dealing with it is now our second priority. We know it is the result of immature behavior, behavior based on the assumption there are separate parts. Therefore, competition for self-interest, rather than participation in maturation, is what is believed to be occurring by the person or people bringing conflict into our lives. Our natural response is compassion and an extension of assistance toward honoring what is primarily occurring. As will be described in more detail later in this chapter, we now know the natural primary intentions of all the parts of the universe, including all the people involved in the conflict, is to be participating in maturation. About this priority in nature none of us have choice.

Now, when responding to conflict, we never lose awareness of the *experience* the universe is operating as an indivisible whole. Inside, rather than pulled into the conflict and reacting in kind, our natural confidence continues to be experienced as contented joy, the most enjoyable joy there is, in the midst of others believing the primary thing occurring is conflict. Our actions help add an awareness to the situation of the value of honoring the primary good intention of all.

I will now describe the *skill* of human self-consciousness, the full mastery of which makes this inner skill possible.

As mentioned earlier, it is not a simple skill like learning to suck water through a straw or use a fork to eat food. It is a complex skill, like learning to ride a bicycle or play basketball. There are seven smaller skills that need to be learned in the natural progression. Each time the knowledge of the next one is learned it needs to become a skill, and then integrated into one skill with the previous learned smaller skills. In the model I use there are seven smaller skills of the skill of human self-consciousness. Herein they are labeled Baby, Toddler, Child, Teen, Adult, Elder, and Mature Elder.

All reading this have learned the first three smaller skills, or you would not be capable of reading this. Briefly, they are being *aware of sensations* (Baby layer), being *aware of differences and therefore feelings* (Toddler layer) and *having learned a human language and the skill of human self-consciousness it allows* (Child layer).

At the Child layer our priority, because we are still unconsciously (without choice) operating on the assumption there are separate parts and we are each one of them, is *getting what our physical bodies wants*. We are experiencing choice but not individual free choice or mature free choice. Someone else is always providing the options, such as do you want vanilla, strawberry, or Ben & Jerry's Chocolate Fudge Brownie ice cream (still the best!)

Next, if you are a teenager or older, you have probably matured into knowing you have the *ability and right to exercise individual free choice*. This is when we discover we can invent the options of choice (Teen layer).

If you have *chosen an outside belief to guide your thinking*, you are operating at the Adult layer.

If you gave priority to your direct experience when answering the above 7 questions, you are entering the Elder layer. As a result of being a personal scientist and exercising mature free choice, it is *giving priority in our thinking to the inside belief the universe operates as an indivisible whole.*

After understanding what is in this chapter and doing the exercise in *Chapter 8: Mutual Mature Love Experience*, you will discover it is possible to know in a relationship with another person the *mutual self-conscious experience of the oneness of nature* (Mature Elder layer). It is easiest to discover the experience of it in a relationship with another person. The mutually agreed upon illusion tool of human language has to be present for the experience to be a self-conscious experience, and there has to be a simultaneous and mutual choice to give priority in the relationship to experience (the oneness of nature) and second priority words.

The Seven Layers of Human Maturation

Maturation of the Universe Continues After Our Deaths

ELDERING
Priority *in behavior each moment is our judgment of our best action of self-conscious participation in maturation;* only this sustains the inner feeling of contented joy

MATURE ELDER
Priority is *the self-conscious experience of the oneness of the universe (nature),* that results in the inner feeling of contented joy

ELDER
Priority is *the accurate fundamental belief on how the universe operates* as an indivisible whole (inside belief using personal science) that results in the experience of natural confidence

ADULT
Priority is *freely chosen fundamental belief* on how the universe operates (outside belief)

TEEN
Priority is *exercising individual free choice* and participating in our shared responsibility of cooperation for maturation

CHILD
Priority is getting what our physical body *wants* from learning a human language and becoming self-conscious

TODDLER
Priority is reacting to *differences,* eventually labeled "feelings"

BABY
Priority is reacting to *sensations*

Maturation of the Universe Was Happening Before Births

Each of these seven layers is a smaller skill that can be learned in the natural progression and integrated together into the one fully mature skill of human self-consciousness. There is not an eighth layer: what could be large than experiencing ourselves as all that exists?

This next part may surprise you.

When we have each achieved full maturity in the skill of human self-consciousness, this is just the beginning of our lives, not our ultimate goal. With wise and artful parenting, this skill can be learned by the time we are twenty years old. One day, I trust, nearly every child will be eldered into full maturity in this skill by then, just as nearly all children on Earth now know the smaller skills of the first three layers.

What we discover when we have mastered the full skill of human self-consciousness is this: we are only able to *sustain* the inner experience of it by each moment giving priority to the maturation of the rest of who we *primarily* are, the indivisible universe. Our personal achievement of full maturity in this skill allows us to now learn how to sustain the inner feeling of contented joy it provides. It is only sustained by giving priority to the maturation of the rest of who we *primarily* are, the indivisible universe.

If the universe is an indivisible whole, our accurate self-definition is not what it naturally is as a child when learning a human language and the skill of self-consciousness: "I am my physical body." When we know the universe is an indivisible whole, we realize we have a new self-definition. Our mature self-definition is "I am first the indivisible universe that will not die and secondly my physical body that will die."

Therefore, at full maturity in the skill of human self-consciousness it is obvious our natural highest priority is not our physical body. It is only a part of the indivisible universe. Once we have achieved full maturity in the skill of human self-consciousness, we discover the only way to sustain the inner feeling of contented joy is to give priority each moment to the maturation of the rest of who we are, the indivisible universe. We discover this activity is best labeled what it has usually been labeled throughout most of history, "Eldering."

The only priority in our behavior each moment that sustains the contented joy of having achieved full maturity in this skill is Eldering. It is each moment, wherever we are each sitting or standing, giving priority to what we each judge is our best unique act of participation in the maturation of the universe.

Our maturation into full maturity in this skill was just the beginning of our lives. *Each moment,* self-conscious participation in the maturation of the rest of who we are is now our natural, effortless, freely chosen, and permanent priority the rest of our lives.

As mentioned earlier, most of us have been raised on the belief competition, with the priority being the self-interest of each illusory separate part, is the fundamental process in nature. If the universe is an indivisible whole, there is not a second thing with which we could be in competition. Therefore, competition cannot be the fundamental process in nature.

A few years ago, at the World Economic Forum at Davos that is a gathering each year in the mountains of Switzerland of the leading CEOs, economists, and government economic officials from around the world, I had the following conversation with Jamie Diamond, the CEO of J P Morgan, one of the largest banks in the world, and Lee Scott, at the time the CEO of Walmart, and other CEOs.

I first asked each of them, "If there is an apple on the table, and neither you or I want the apple, someone could take it and we would both be as happy afterwards as we were before, correct?"

They all responded with the obvious answer, "Yes."

Secondly, I continued, "As another option, if we both want the apple, we could compete to see who gets it. However, without the agreement, the cooperative context, that who gets the apple is important to both of us, there would be no reason to compete, correct?" They all also said that was correct. "Therefore," I continued, "competition cannot exist outside of a cooperative context. We both have to be giving priority to the fact the apple is important to both of us, the cooperative agreement, and second priority to competition." They all agreed.

"If this is the case," I then argued, "what would make sense is for the competitors in each product market to get together, like the teams of a sports league, and voluntarily agree on the common good rules of play as the teams in a sports league do. They could be to have the minimum wage be a livable wage and particular agreements to sustain a healthy environment. They could then *secondly* compete. The auditors could be the referees, indicating in the annual audit, posted for all to read on the Internet in easy to read English, whether or not, and to what degree, each company was keeping the freely chosen agreements. Then, *as their second priority*, they could compete as ferociously as before, as the Boston Celtics and Golden State Warriors do in the National Basketball Association.

"Relative to one another," I continued, "it would not cost the companies a penny. They would both make any changes they agree to on the same future day. This would not be collusion for their mutual self-interest, which is illegal. This would be giving priority to cooperation for the common good, the stated priority of all nations of people and not only legal but encouraged by all nations. It would be their *second priority* to compete as ferociously as before. These companies would then be a very strong force for the common good and cherished by all. With the public able to be fully informed of the decisions, there would be a forever ongoing public conversation of what was appropriate for each of the stakeholders relative to the others. What do you think? Could this be the future of capitalism?"

They all gave me the exact same answer, "That will never happen."

Not only do I think it will happen. I think it is inevitable. It is my hope that by the time you have finished reading this book you will also agree it is inevitable. Maturation is the fundamental process in nature and cannot be escaped or stopped.

As described above, competition cannot exist outside of a cooperative context. Indeed, competition is the lowest form of cooperation, a way to cooperate to determine who gets the apple, a piece of land, or more money. For human beings, *compromise* is the next more mature way of relating, *agreement* is the next more mature way, and *love* is the most mature way of relating. Let's take a closer look at all three of these.

Compromise is when we both do not get what we want but we give priority to giving up some of what we want, as does the other, to be capable of giving priority to moving forward together. *Agreement* is when we arrange the terms so we both experience we are getting all or nearly all of what we want. *Love* is when, as a habit, we both, or all involved, give priority to moving as one with all that is, not just the two of us or group of us but with all of nature. This behavior has usually been labeled, from one angle, "moral behavior" or, from another angle, "love."

When we are doing this with the person with whom we have our most intimate relationship, it is usually labeled "romantic love." It is not something between our two noses as if separate parts exist. It is the two of us always giving priority to moving as one with all that exists and knowing together we are doing it while we are doing it. It is the mutually known experience of giving priority to the self-conscious experience of oneness, the most fundamental fact in physics, that we now know is always present just not able to be seen with our eyes.

This is the unmatchable joy of keeping our power, all of it, and using it to be a continuously fully free, and fully mature, human being and in a relationship with another who also knows this is possible and is doing it with us. This is mature romantic love; this is mutual mature love, mutual with all that exists.

This, as we will discover later, can be our base camp. After the craziness of our days, this is the place we can daily return to and get refueled in the mutual mature love experience of self-consciously and mutually moving as one with all there is. Like a shower after a hot and muggy day, we feel refreshed and ready for the next day.

As mentioned earlier, we are also going somewhere. It is not in the illusion of separate parts being real. We are going somewhere in the reality of the oneness of nature.

We, the universe, is maturing.

The universe is in a constant state of maturing, something that only occurs in oneness and can only secondly be perceived as happening in times and places. It is now primarily maturing through us, its self-conscious parts. Each of its parts are also primarily participating in maturation. We are also each maturing, and our societies (our agreements) are maturing.

All the parts of the universe are in a constant state of cooperating for maturation.

You can notice that we are each continually maturing. Are you more mature now than when seven years old, fifteen years old, twenty-five years old, a few years ago? We can even be maturing on our deathbed. (In my next book, *Your and My Maturation Stories,* I tell the story of how this occurred for my mother on her deathbed.)

You can study history and witness that human agreements have been consistently maturing, sometimes with two steps back and three steps forward, but always fundamentally maturing. For instance, today more than half of the nations on Earth are at least technically democracies. Psychology, as a scientific discipline, did not exist before 1870. Today we have a much better understanding of the how we relate with ourselves and others.

Maturation is the fundamental process, priority, and activity in nature. That is why there is always a reason for doing one thing rather than another. Whether or not we are aware of it our priority is always to be a self-conscious participant in maturation: of ourselves, our children, our friends, our societies, our Earth community, and the universe.

As will be described in more detail later, all maturation occurs in the reality of the oneness of nature. When we learn to ride a bicycle, that knowledge and skill is at all times and in all places (in the reality of oneness) inside us.

The Mature Elder layer, the highest layer, is the discovery of the importance of giving priority to the *self-conscious experience of the oneness of nature* and second priority to the accurate words we use to describe it in our thinking (the Elder layer). Our third priority is the behavior of Eldering. As mentioned earlier, in *Chapter 8: Mutual Mature Love Experience* you will be invited to choose a friend and have the two of you guided into knowing it for some minutes as the priority in your relationship.

It is mutually knowing and experiencing the self-conscious experience of the oneness of nature.

Once known as possible you will not be satisfied until you master the skill of giving it priority at all times and in all places (in the reality of oneness), particularly in your most intimate relationship, your romantic relationship. In parenting, and as they are ready, you will then give priority to Eldering your children into each next layer of maturity in the skill of human self-consciousness and to full maturity in this skill before they leave home and marry.

You will also graduate into the next layer of maturity in your democratic relationships with others, building a community of friends, and by extension into an association with other like-thinking communities, to become a nation by agreement. While continuing to be a fully responsible member of your geographic defined nation, you will give priority to your freely chosen *nation defined by agreement.* With others, this is taking full responsibility for creating the lives you want rather than primarily looking to the state or anywhere else to do it for us.

What is the possibility that everyone living in a town, or any geographic area, would have the same worldview? Obviously extremely remote. Therefore, as stated above, what makes sense is for those who share a worldview to gather into communities of friends, and those into agreement nations, to accept full responsibility for their lives together as they choose. This is easily possible today.

Most democratic geographic nations operate by war of the ballot box, one group trying to get control of the geographic nation to have all live according to its worldview and, therefore, not having to live by another group's worldview. A member of an agreement nation does not need to change one's place of residence to change from being a member of one agreement nation to another. Agreement nations will be of people who share a worldview and take responsibility for creating their lives together based on it. Also, without a deadline and primarily in their freely chosen local community of friends, they can over time build a set of agreements by consensus, or near consensus, rather than make choices *via* ballot box wars on a certain date.

I believe the emergence of agreement nations being the priority in people's lives is the next layer of maturity of democracy.

Examples could be Bernie Sanders Socialist Nation, Tea Party Nation, Environment Care Nation, each religion, and many others. All geographic nations will eventually give priority to supporting the thriving of agreement nations. This will result in the more mature and best run agreement nations having a consistently growing membership. This is described later and fully described, along with the consensus building over time operating procedures, in my book *Common Good Nation.*

As described in my conversations with the corporate CEOs at Davos, the competitors in each product market, and eventually as the free association of all businesses, can, *in the private sector,* voluntarily operate as sports leagues operate. They can agree on the common good rules of play (such as having the minimum wage be a livable wage), keep those agreements with each other, and have the auditors serve as the referees to be sure the public knows who is and is not, and to what degree, keeping the agreements. They secondly compete as ferociously as before, now for the fun, creativity, and innovation of it rather than at the expense of the employees, community, environment, or any other stakeholders. This is also described later and fully described in my book *Common Good Capitalism Is Inevitable.*

The most important agreement to have among all the people on Earth is to resolve all conflicts with agreements rather than any form of war or violent activity. The United Nations was founded on the honoring of the sovereignty of nations, each geographic nation being free to operate as it pleases. Therefore, the next layer of maturity on Earth is the creation of a new global organization of nations, we can call it "United Nations Two," that *by agreement all conflicts both within and between member nations are resolved by agreement rather than violence or war. Think of it as a NATO for all.*

These changes in our social agreements will be described in more detail in *Chapter 6: Maturation Movement and 10 Recommended Priorities of the 2020 US Presidential Candidates.*

As mentioned above, the relationship between the oneness of nature and human language has only recently been discovered by many. Up until recently the dominant linguistic scientists have believed our skill of human self-consciousness was the result of a mutation a few hundred thousand years ago. We now know, as will be described in more detail in *Chapter 5: Three More Personal Science Studies,* it is primarily a skill. It is a complex skill as a result of learning a progression of smaller skills as described earlier.

We also now know something else: without the oneness of nature it would not have been possible to invent words that allows us to be self-conscious.

Without the existence of a human language, it was only possible to agree upon a word for something, such as "wacko wacko" for a coconut, *by looking each other in the eyes and having the experience of self-conscious oneness instead of conflict: moving self-consciously as one rather than moving against each other.* Oneness is experienced as enjoyable. Conflict is experienced as not enjoyable. Given a choice, we prefer oneness.

When, while looking another in the eyes while doing it, we used the sound "wacko wacko" for a coconut, if we had the self-conscious experience of oneness instead of conflict, we experienced it as a self-conscious agreement, *as self-consciously moving as one to use the words "wacko wacko" for a coconut.*

We still do this today. When we have reached an agreement with another, we usually look each other in the eyes and have the experience of local oneness, the *experience of agreement.* The local self-conscious experience of moving as one rather than moving against each other is experienced as agreement. A more detailed description of this process is in *Chapter 5: Three More Personal Science Studies.*

Here is the key recent insight. Without the oneness of nature, we would not have been able to unconsciously (without choice) invented the assumption of separate parts. Without unconsciously (without choice) inventing the illusion of separate parts, we would not have been able to invent the words of a human language. Without inventing words, we would not have been able to be self-conscious. Without being self-conscious, we would not have been able to make agreements. Without making agreements, we would not be able to enjoy a committed romantic relationship, build a skyscraper, or form a society.

What has made this difficult to understand until now is that, as mentioned earlier, by observation, and now from neuroscience, we know biologically children's brains are not able to exercise individual free choice until the early teenage years. Until then they are operating on the assumption the universe is separate parts to learn a human language and be self-conscious at the level of exercising choice, not individual free choice or mature free choice. They choose from among the options chosen by others. Only at the early teenage years do they realize they could invent the options and understand the difference between not inventing them and inventing them.

Up until then, they do not have their power. Their parents have it. Their only option is to obey them. When they discover they have the ability and right to exercise individual free choice, they easily and unconsciously (without choice) sustain the pattern of childhood of giving their power to a parent-substitute and obeying it, an outside belief in words. Without being eldered into understanding they are freely choosing to give their power to a parent-substitute and, therefore, the only relationship option is obedience, they will unconsciously (without choice) do this. From the teenage years on, from when they have discovered they have the ability and right to exercise individual free choice, they will, as described earlier, experience inner conflict and not understand why.

Their priority to obey where they have given their power and their ability to exercise individual free choice will be in conflict.

The only solution is for them to understand, first, they have given their power away and do not have it any more. Secondly, they need to take it back and keep it, all of it. And, thirdly, they need to use it as their sixth sense to study their direct, present, and repeatable by choice experience to identify the inside beliefs they will use to guide their thinking. Only by doing this do they keep their power, all of it, know the truths about life in direct experience so they experience natural confidence, and sustain having the ability in the future to exercise individual free choice.

This is now exercising mature free choice and being a personal scientist.

We now know the universe operates as an indivisible whole. Therefore, we also know the assumption the universe is separate parts is a *mutually agreed upon illusion tool* we invented to invent words and be self-conscious parts of the indivisible universe.

We were not aware we were inventing the assumption the universe is separate parts when we were inventing words. This is our mutual blind spot.

We now know we were. We now know the invention of different words would not have been possible without inventing the assumption the universe is separate parts. We also now know it was the reality of the oneness of nature that made it possible to reach agreement to invent the words of a human language. We now know without inventing words we would not be able to be self-conscious parts of the indivisible universe. Finally, we now know the mutual self-conscious experience of the oneness of nature with another is only possible when we simultaneously give priority to the experience of it and second priority to words.

This knowledge allows us to now study it. We can now find the accurate relationship between the assumption of separate parts and the assumption of oneness.

They are both equally valuable assumptions!

The assumption of oneness accurately represents reality in our thinking. The assumption of separate parts allows us to be aware of this as a self-conscious experience. Therefore, they are both equally valuable. We want to always be simultaneously using both!

There is just one problem. They are opposites. When leaving my driveway to drive toward Boston, we can't turn right and left at the same time. We also can't assume the universe is one thing and separate parts at the same time. They are opposites.

However, there is a way we can *use* both at the same time.

We can do it if we know one represents reality and the other is an illusion, a valuable illusion, but an illusion. Then, like playing Hamlet on a stage, I can at the same time be fully and simultaneously Terry Mollner and Hamlet. But I can only do it as long as I accurately know which one is real and which one is an illusion. Then I can give priority to being what is real, Terry Mollner, and second priority to being what is not real, Hamlet, and do both fully, comfortably, and without experiencing conflict. The key was accurately knowing Terry Mollner is real and Hamlet is an illusion. Now, even though they are opposites, one real and one an illusion, I can comfortably, and without any experience of conflict, simultaneously be both.

This is the mature relationship between the assumption of oneness and the assumption of separate parts that has not been widely known until now. Therefore, we also were unable to discover the next piece that is essential to do both simultaneously: the oneness pattern of thinking.

Human languages are based on the invention of opposites and degrees of differences between them so we can invent words for each, such as boiling-hot-warm-room temperature-cool-cold-freezing. Thus, we easily also unconsciously use polarization of opposites in our thinking: up-down, left-right, good-bad, right-wrong. Then, rather than seeing the value of both of the above opposites and finding the mature relationship between them, we tend to identify one as good and the other as bad. As a result, sometimes spiritual education is focused on being in the experience of oneness *as opposed to* being in the experience of separate parts rather than learning how to do both fully and simultaneously. Also, political positions get structured as liberal *verses* conservative.

This leads us into discovering another maturation in our thinking that occurs when we discover the universe operates as an indivisible whole: *there are two possible fundamental patterns of thinking.* One assumes separate parts are real and the other assumes oneness is real.

Think of our patterns of thinking as coatracks upon which, like coats, we hang all of our words. These unique coatracks project whatever is their assumption about reality, oneness or separate parts, into all we think in words when using each coatrack.

Up until the teenage years we are only aware of using the separate parts pattern of thinking coatrack: this-or-that-in-times-and-places. We are over here, the popcorn is on the table over there, and we want some. We are operating on the assumption there are separate parts and we are each one of them.

We now know there is a oneness pattern of thinking coatrack we could use. It is giving priority to priorities. It is the opposite of this-or-that-in-times-and-places coatrack.

Here is an easy way to witness the difference.

For a moment, place your hands in front of you about a foot apart. Imagine the living room is your left hand and the kitchen is your right hand. Assume you are in the living room. You want an apple that is in the kitchen. It will take time to go from the living room to the kitchen to get the apple, to go from your left hand to your right hand. Here our thinking is assuming two places and time to move from one to the other. We are using the assumption of separate parts pattern of thinking coatrack.

Now move your hands to be separate but on top of one another. This represents the pattern of thinking of oneness, giving priority to priorities. Notice that I used this pattern of thinking earlier when I stated our accurate self-definition is "I am first the indivisible universe that will not die and secondly my physical body that will die."

There are no factors of times and places when using the pattern of thinking of oneness, giving priority to priorities coatrack. The priorities can be in all times and all places (in the reality of oneness).

Now that we know the universe operates as an indivisible whole, we want to primarily use the pattern of thinking of oneness coatrack because it represents the accurate inside belief of oneness. However, we want to also use the pattern of thinking of separate parts coatrack because it allows us to use the skill of a human language, and the self-consciousness it allows, to know the experience of the oneness of nature as a self-conscious experience.

When we know the pattern of thinking of assuming oneness represents reality and the pattern of thinking of assuming separate parts is a valuable mutually agreed upon illusion tool, we can easily do both fully and simultaneously in the same way I can simultaneously be both Terry Mollner and Hamlet.

We can know the universe operates as an indivisible whole as the container in our thinking when leaving the living room to go to the kitchen to get an apple. The illusion of separate parts, the words of a human language, and the skill of self-consciousness they allow are *skills* that allow us to do it as a self-conscious experience.

A Mature Elder not only chooses to give priority to the oneness pattern of thinking while using both, he or she also knows we have all been using both since we learned a human language. We were just not aware of it. Oneness is real. It cannot be escaped. Therefore, we have to have been using the oneness pattern of thinking coatrack all along and not been aware of it. Indeed, that was the case.

We are not able to do anything with the parts of the universe without first deciding where to focus our attention. Doing the latter is a priority activity: we are choosing to focus our attention in one place rather than all the other possibilities.

We can only *secondly* do something with the parts of the universe where we are focusing our attention. The latter is using the assumption of separates parts pattern of thinking. However, we gave *priority* to the use of the oneness pattern of thinking coatrack when we chose where to focus our attention.

Not only can oneness not be escaped, but also the oneness pattern of thinking cannot be escaped. Becoming aware of this mature understanding of the relationship between the two patterns of thinking is part of the mastery of the sixth layer of maturity of this skill, the Elder layer. Learning to give priority to the *experience of doing this* is the mastery of the seventh and highest layer of this skill, the Mature Elder layer.

Notice something else important here, described in the *Introduction*. Skills are the same for everyone. There is only one way to remain balanced on a bicycle. We either do it the right way or we fall off of it. There is only one way to stop an automobile at a red light. We either stop it from going forward or we do not. Beliefs are different. There is no limit to what can be packaged in an outside belief and it could be accurate or inaccurate.

Outside beliefs are the opposite of skills. There is only one way to do each skill. There is no limit to what accurate or inaccurate information can be in an outside belief.

The smaller skills of the seven layers of maturity of the skill of human self-consciousness are skills, and the words representing them are inside beliefs, not outside beliefs. There is only one accurate way to do each of them and they are the same for everyone. This is what will make it easy for people who know them to work together as Mature Elders. All will have mastered the smaller skills of all seven layers, be using the same or similar words to describe each, their behaviors will give priority to cooperation for maturation, and they will continuously be getting more skillful at Eldering and Eldering with others. Of course, this will include learning many human relationship skills, such as relating consensually with others, facilitating groups, and providing servant leadership where appropriate.

You may have noticed that people operating at the same layer of maturity tend to gravitate toward each other. Children tend to play with other children who know what they know, for instance knowing how to ride tricycles or knowing how to ride bicycles. People at each layer of maturity of the skill of human self-consciousness also are attracted to being with each other. Married couples are often operating at the same layer of maturity and their relationship can sometimes become difficult and end if one of them matures into a higher layer. This is one among the many things that can be a challenge for a couple.

A major problem for people living according to outside beliefs, at the Adult layer of maturity or lower, as if it is the highest layer is they are very vulnerable to skillful marketing. As described now a couple of times earlier, outside beliefs are two steps removed from reality. They are all *equally illusions*, and unlike inside beliefs there is no way to double check in direct experience to be sure they represent reality. Skillful marketing can now easily convince people to do as the marketing requests.

To have our children not be vulnerable to this, we want to succeed at Eldering them into full maturity before they leave home and marry. Then they will also know the importance of having their children aware there are layers of maturity of the skill of human self-consciousness, and each one they are currently operating on as they are able to understand it. From early childhood on, this will have us give priority to assisting them to master this most important skill for them to learn. They will then only easily marry another who also has mastered this skill. If they do, the two of them will know they will each moment not only enjoy the self-conscious experience of the oneness of nature as the container of their relationship, but they will also know they will be able to joyfully remain together the rest of their lives. They will also know the smaller skill of each of the layers of maturity and the importance of Co-Eldering their children up them when they are ready for each.

Nothing is more enjoyable than Eldering.

It is the only behavior in our actions that sustains within each of us the self-conscious experience of the oneness of nature, the most enjoyable joy: contented joy.

The most fundamental crisis on Earth today, the fundamental cause of all of our trials, tribulations, and violence, is we are not Eldering our children to full maturity in this skill before they leave home and marry.

There is nothing more important in a society than the Eldering of our children to full maturity in this skill before they leave home and marry. To do this we each, as parents, must Elder ourselves up the layers of maturity our parents were not wise enough to Elder us into before we left home.

Next, from the Teen layer on, Self-Eldering is an inside job. Each layer builds on and does not negate the skills of the lower layers. Therefore, the mastery of the last three layers have to primarily be the result of the exercise of *mature free choice*, the mature skill at the Teen layer. This is why they are seen as inside jobs. Whereas as parents we are able to Elder our children into the mastery of the layers up to the Teen layer, no one can make another master the smaller skills of the last three layers and the skill of Eldering.

As Elders, we can be very helpful, but from the Teen layer on it is an inside job.

Also, much of the Adult layer, the choosing from among outside beliefs, can be skipped if one in the early teenage years is Eldered into giving priority to experience when answering the 7 questions to discover it is obvious and self-evident the universe operates as an indivisible whole. That is the beginning of the mastery of the Elder layer.

At the Teen layer, we initially give priority to exercising individual free choice. This results in us creating rules for relating with everyone and they are often different. We have rules for relating with mom, with dad, with our coach, with our lover, with each of our friends. At some point we experience too many rules in our lives, and we realize we made them all up. This has us decide to identify one fundamental rule we can use at all times and in all places (in the reality of oneness but we are usually not aware of this at that time) to make our lives easier, more enjoyable, and us not having to remember all the particular rules for particular people. If we choose an outside belief, we have moved into the Adult layer. However, if we have wise parents who are artful at Eldering us into each layer of maturity as we are able, they can Elder us from the

Teen layer directly into the Elder layer by having us keep our power and use it to study our direct experience by answering the 7 questions to discover the universe operates as an indivisible whole. To learn to be a personal scientist exercising mature free choice.

Think of the layers of maturity as those wooden Russian dolls where there are seven of them and each smaller one fits inside the next bigger one so, when they are all together, it looks as if there is only one large doll. However, using our sixth sense, we know the *relationship among them* is they are inside each other even though we can't see the other six dolls. It is the same with the seven layers of maturity of the skill of human self-consciousness.

When they become knowledge, skills, and habits, we are experienced as one person. However, all seven of them are operating as one skill called "full maturity in the skill of human self-consciousness." Like the wooden Russian dolls, each lower layer is experienced as inside the more mature layer, not separate from or in opposition to it. This is the result of primarily using the oneness pattern of thinking. Then, when fully mature in this skill, we give highest priority to the self-conscious experience of the oneness of nature that results in the feeling of contented joy (Mature Elder layer), second priority to have what we are doing being accurately represented in words as an inside belief that results in us experiencing natural confidence (Elder layer), and third priority to the behavior of Eldering that sustains our primary inner feeling being the feeling of contented joy. We give fourth priority to our exercise of mature free choice (mature Teen layer). We give fifth priority to our use of the skills of human language and self-consciousness to get what we want, as the universe first and our physical body second (Child layer). We give sixth priority to being aware of differences and the relative feelings they generate (Toddler layer). And we give last priority to sensations (Baby layer).

Again, notice we are experiencing them as all equally valuable but no longer jumping from attention on one to attention on another. We have added and given priority to the pattern of thinking of oneness, prioritization. Now we do not experience anything in conflict with another but all playing a role within a set of priorities for maturation.

Of course, if our finger gets pricked by a pin, we will suddenly give priority to sensations. Or if we are being inappropriately ordered what to do, we will give priority to exercising mature free choice. However, any turning of our attention for a moment to the priority of the operations of one of the lower layers is now *always habitually known* to be occurring within the reality of the oneness of nature. A Baby, Toddler, or Child will cry loudly. We will not. Operating at the Teen layer or higher, we can choose how to respond.

Another piece of evidence the universe operates as an indivisible whole is the contradiction we are assuming when we think it is not operating as an indivisible whole.

For many of us, inside our skins we experience all the parts within us, our heart, liver, stomach, lungs, muscles, bones, and blood, in a constant state of *cooperation for the continued health and maturation of our physical body*, even when we are dying it is doing its best to continue doing so. Yet outside us, when we are operating on the assumption separate parts exist, competition is assumed to be the fundamental process in nature. Therefore, it is assumed the priority of each part is its self-interest. This is the opposite of what is obviously going on inside our skins.

Therefore, we are living as if reality is a contradiction. We are assuming cooperation for maturation is the fundamental process in nature *some places, inside our skins*, and competition for self-interest is the fundamental process in nature *other places, everyplace outside our skins.* The one thing all religious, philosophical, and scientific thinkers agree on is life is not a contradiction. It is obvious each moment there is a reason for doing one thing rather than another and those reasons are always the same everywhere. It is always accurate to turn right when leaving our driveway to drive to Boston. Granted, their fundamental beliefs about reality are different, but they all operate on the more fundamental belief life is meaningful and, therefore, there is always a reason for doing one thing rather than another. They all agree reality is not a contradiction.

Therefore, either what is obvious inside our skins is the fundamental process in nature, cooperation for maturation, or what we are assuming is occurring outside our skins, competition with the priority being the self-interest of each separate part, is the fundamental process in nature.

If there are no separate parts, as we now know, it is obvious that the assumption we assume is the fundamental process in nature inside our skins is the fundamental process everywhere. Everywhere the parts of the universe, like we think of the parts inside our skins, operate as parts of an indivisible whole.

Here is an obvious example that cooperation for maturation is the fundamental process in nature. When we get a cut on our finger, we can't stop it from healing. That natural process of healing is maturation in motion. Here is another example. When two lovers have a misunderstanding occur, such as the belief by one that the other did not put the trash out on the road Tuesday night when it was done, they naturally initiate actions to clear up the confusion. That natural process of relationship healing in close relationships is also maturation in motion. Here is another example. When two nations discover operating within agreements rather than fighting each other is more enjoyable and forge agreements to do so, that is maturation in motion. Agreement, as we will see below, is more enjoyable than conflict. That natural process of relationship maturation is maturation in motion.

Maturation cannot be escaped or stopped. It is oneness in motion. In our skill of using human language to be self-conscious, it is the fundamental process, priority, and activity of oneness.

Maturation, not evolution, is the fundamental process in nature everywhere. Evolution only explains why something occurred, such as a monkey changing into being a human being. It does not answer the question, "Why did it do that?" Maturation does answer that question. Maturation is cooperation among all the perceived parts of the indivisible universe for continuous maturation as an indivisible universe.

The theory of evolution was a step in the right direction. It just did not go far enough. It did not affirm the universe operates as an indivisible whole and, thereby, answer the question, "Why is evolution the fundamental process in nature?" The answer to that question is "for continuous maturation" that is also obvious in plain sight as the examples above reveal. This will be fully embraced by scientists when they fully embrace the obvious fact in plain sight the universe operates as an indivisible whole.

Next, when we have achieved the Teen layer, and relate with others which we all do, we discover we have only two options: war or agreements. There is not a third option. We are stuck together as parts of one indivisible whole. Therefore, the only two choices are to move as one with all the other parts (loving behavior) or not do so which puts us in conflict with all the other parts (painful behavior).

When a child matures into the teenager years, initially the priority becomes exercising individual free choice. This is why we often see teenagers wearing different clothes and haircuts. They also use language in a new way and like new kinds of music. They are making a public statement they are now giving priority to exercising individual free choice, the youngest mastery of the smaller skill of the Teen layer. People still operating at the Child layer are giving priority to getting what their physical bodies wants. They will then use their skill at the Teen layer to also get what their physical bodies want. This easily puts them in conflict with others.

When I was a teenager, I was so drunk on my new opportunity to exercise individual freedom of choice I had a hard time following any rules, for example the rules for driving an automobile. I often got speeding tickets. Also, if we ever have a contest to determine who was the first hippie in Omaha, Nebraska, I think I would win. In my twenties, my hair became long, I grew a beard, I became a vegetarian, I left the Catholic Church, and each Sunday for a summer I visited every different religious denomination church to find another community that was a fit for me—never did. I attended every personal growth workshop I could find and afford, and I loved folk music. I was one of the earliest members of the baby-boom generation and was a full member of the freedom frenzy of the 1960s before I knew I was a member of it—it took a while for it to get to Omaha! In hindsight, I can see that I was clearly using my new found skill of being able to exercise individual free choice to get what my physical body wanted (Child layer). I was still assuming I was a separate part and did not know that was my unconscious (without choice) assumption. This consistently put me in unintended conflict with others.

The only way to begin working our way out of the pain of the conflicts that are the result of our drunkenness on exercising individual free choice is to switch to giving priority to some agreements with others, everything from forming a romantic relationship and raising a family, to organizing a band, joining a sports team, or building a business with some friends. For me, it was forming a community of friends to see if we could discover how to re-village our lives in a modern context. Each time I did it I tried to do it in the more mature way I had learned from the shortcomings of the last efforts. (I tell the stories of some of these efforts later.)

Also, frustration and conflicts set in when some people in any group mature and are no longer willing to have the priority be making money in a hierarchical power system. For instance, this love of freedom at the Teen layer has fueled the United States into being the greatest entrepreneurial nation in history. People seek to leave the paternalistic companies where they are working so they can have the freedom of running a company of their own, even if they initially receive much less income.

We are a nation fixated on exercising individual free choice and this fixation is rapidly spreading around the world. Everyone wants to at least achieve full maturity at the Teen layer. Nearly everyone now has a smart phone and every commercial is screaming at us, "Think only of yourself!" However, in this new era into which I believe we are entering, people around the world will, instead, become fixated on Eldering.

When companies discover it does not cost them a penny to join with their competitors to mature into being common good capitalist because, for instance, on the same future date they will all raise their minimum wage, there will be a rapid maturation of capitalism into common good capitalism, both locally and globally. Climate change will be one of the things that will demand it of us all. We can either use wisdom to get out in front of it by maturing into common good capitalism or we will do it in response to crisis. One way or the other, we will do it. We have to. To most, this is now obvious.

Nature has this pattern: we either mature or we mature. Maturation is the fundamental process, priority, and activity in nature, and it cannot be escaped or stopped.

I was one of the people in the 1970s who saw the wisdom of socially responsible investing, as it was labeled then: companies caring more for their employees, communities, and the environment. The same activity has gone through many names since then, from "ethical investing," to "ESG (environment, social, and governance) investing," and now often labeled "impact investing." Fundamentally, it is consistently moving toward giving priority to the common good and second priority to profit and it will eventually fully get there through maturation into common good capitalism. Today, socially responsible investing is rapidly moving into the mainstream. It is both increasingly clear environment factors in particular can affect profits. Also, as all on our team in the 1970s believed would eventually be the case, recently it has been financially outperforming conventional investing. Common good companies have fewer problems with their employees, local communities, and government laws. In addition, employees are happier and more productive. Increasingly boards and executives are discovering there is nothing to not like about moving toward common good capitalism and it will happen. I am confident it is inevitable.

In summary, using personal science we can learn the following skills:

Using Personal Science
We Can Learn the Following Skills

1. We know the mature way to use the skill of human self-consciousness is as our sixth sense. Like the other five senses, it is a way to know through a study of our direct experience the truths about the relationships between and among the parts of the universe.

2. We now know, by doing the above, the universe operates as an indivisible whole,

3. We can know the experience of natural confidence by giving priority in our thinking to inside beliefs, that is, using the exercise of mature free choice to be a personal scientist.

4. We know our accurate self-definition is "I am first the indivisible universe that will not die and secondly my physical body that will die."

5. We know the skill of human self-consciousness is a complex skill with seven smaller skills that build on one another in a natural progression that can result in us giving priority in our behavior to Eldering to sustain the contented joy feeling of full maturity in this skill, our most important skill to learn.

6. We know there are two patterns of thinking, one based on the assumption there are separate parts and one based on the assumption the universe operates as an indivisible whole. They are both equally valuable. The latter because it accurately represents reality, and the former because it allows us to be self-conscious parts of the universe. When we know the first represents reality and the latter is a mutually agreed upon illusion tool, something we invented so we can be self-conscious, even though they are opposites we can do both fully and simultaneously with no experience of conflict. This is so as long as we prioritize them by giving priority to the assumption of oneness, thinking that accurately represents reality, and second priority to the assumption of separate parts. We now know the latter is a mutually agreed upon illusion tool we invented that allows us to know the experience of the oneness of nature as a self-conscious experience.

7. We know competition of each part with its priority being the self-interest of its part is not the fundamental process in nature. Cooperation of all the parts for maturation of the indivisible universe is the fundamental process in nature.

The important thing to point out at the beginning of this book is there is no authority standing behind anything you will read. Everything you read has been solely discovered by me keeping my power, all of it, and using it as a personal scientist to study my direct experience. I want to emphasize this because I want to encourage you to also keep your power, all of it, and primarily be a personal scientist to discover the most fundamental truths you will use to guide your thinking. This is essential to master the Elder layer. Therefore, be sure you do not give your power to me or the words in this book! They can be helpful, but for you to become a fully mature human being you need to keep your power, all of it, and give priority to your direct, present, and repeatable by choice experience to identify the truths you will use to guide your thinking.

You must primarily exercise mature free choice by being a personal scientist.

We do need a common language to talk about these things. I have endeavored to create that for us in this chapter. At the same time that we use it, be sure to *primarily* keep your power, all of it, and use it to *primarily* study your direct, present, and repeatable by choice experience to observe the truths you will use to guide your thinking. Be open to the possibility they may be different from what I have just reported to you I have discovered. And along with using this or any common language, definitely choose the words for this knowledge and these skills that work best for you, your private language, or your community's private language.

As described earlier, there is a very important reason it is wise to give priority to personal science: you will then be fully confident the truths about relationships you have identified using your sixth sense are indeed true. You can at any time again turn your attention to your direct, present, and repeatable by choice experience to confirm the words in your thinking, your inside beliefs, accurately represent truths.

You will then consistently know the experience of natural confidence and feeling of contented joy the only way they can be known, by being a personal scientist and, as a result, primarily Eldering in your behavior.

When I was in my late twenties, I spent a year reading everything I wanted to read to assist me in my quest to discover the meaning of life. The person I concluded was one of the wisest people of the last century was Mahatma Gandhi, the man who led India into independence from Great Britain. Fortunately, I was asked to serve as a consultant to a very successful US company that had been started by an Indian man. He wanted it to be re-organized into a structure based on Gandhi's economic theory of trusteeship. It is based on the assumption we are each primarily the trustees of our wealth, knowledge, and power and our priority is to use it for the common good while freely deciding how much of it we should keep for ourselves. He didn't want to create a paternalist system (as Mao Zedong had done) but trust as people matured they would voluntarily live frugally so they could use more of their wealth and talents to perpetuate the common good. In 1979, I accompanied him and some of his top employees on a trip to India to learn more about it.

After our two weeks of study, I remained in India for three months. Through him and his wealthy family, which is one of the ruling families of India and were supporters of Gandhi, I had access to all those still alive who had worked closely with Gandhi, including Morarji Desai, the Prime Minister at the time, and Jayaprakash Narayan, the second father of India known as JP. Some of these stories are in my next book, *Your and My Maturation Stories.* (My favorite quote from my adventures there was from Grandfather Tata, the head of one of the most powerful families in India: "It cost me a fortune to keep Gandhi in poverty!"))

I read many of Gandhi's writings, as well as his autobiography, as I rode the trains to visit, live with, and learn from those still alive who had worked closely with him. I learned something profound that helped me on my journey toward discovering the meaning of life. In my words, not Gandhi's words, this is what I concluded was the way Gandhi related with others.

He concluded that at any one moment there are four things occurring within each of us:

Four Things Occurring
Within Each of Us Each Moment

Our Primary Intention
Our Beliefs
Our Secondary Intention
Our Behavior

We now know, whether or not we are aware of it, our *primary intention* at all times and in all places (in the reality of oneness) is cooperation for maturation. About this we do not have choice. This is the natural process, priority, and activity of the oneness of nature in each of us and all of nature. It cannot be escaped or stopped and is always what is primarily occurring everywhere. This is most often labeled "giving priority to the common good." For instance, it is why we do not bump into each other when walking down a sidewalk full of people. We could walk in a straight line to where we are going and knock everyone down in our way. Instead we naturally give priority to the common good by making sure we do not bump into others.

Our *beliefs* can be anything accurate or inaccurate. From the teenage years on about this we have free choice. In the absence of wise eldering, many people are still unconsciously (without choice) living according to the beliefs of their parents. Or they are living according to the ones that were stimulated in response to major events in their lives. Or they have chosen them from the smorgasbord of outside beliefs they have come upon and may have often changed their choice. If discovered in direct, present, and repeatable by choice experience as obvious and self-evident, they are accurate inside beliefs. Otherwise, they are outside beliefs.

Our *secondary intention* and *behavior* will flow from our beliefs. When being self-conscious, beliefs in words are always present and between us and whatever we are thinking, observing, or doing. It is words that allow us to be self-conscious.

If outside beliefs, it will be in obedience to the one's we have given our power, often unaware this is what we are doing. If inside beliefs, we would probably be giving priority to the common good. However, Gandhi did not make a distinction between inside and outside beliefs.

The wisdom of Mahatma Gandhi was that in his own way he understood this. Therefore, he mastered the skill of always *primarily speaking* to another's primary good intention. He knew that was *who the person primarily is,* whether or not he or she is aware of it: someone giving priority to what he or she thinks is best for the common good. Fundamentally, this is the activity of what became known as "personal non-violent action."

The method he developed for bringing about changes in our social agreements he tied to the term "satyagraha," defined by Gandhi as "the natural force of truth." His process for changing immature social agreements became inaccurately translated into English as "non-violence." It was not the choice of non-violent behavior rather than violent behavior.

His goal was to mature the way we all think, not just the way those who disagreed with him were thinking. This he knew would result in a more mature agreement based on a more mature truth that would have all easily and genuinely keep the agreement.

The behavior of non-cooperation with an operating immature agreement (belief), for instance that the Indian people needed England to continue operating as a parent, was for the purpose of having all, *both the English and the Indian people*, agree the latter were ready and able to manage their affairs themselves.

Giving it the name "non-violence" was giving priority to behavior, the above fourth priority. Gandhi's intention in using the word "satyagraha" was to give priority to the *primary intention to honor the natural force of truth inside all of us*, in my words "to self-consciously participate in cooperation for maturation by choosing more mature agreements." This is giving priority to the highest of the four priorities naturally inside each of us: our natural primary intention to act for the common good by honoring the natural force of truth.

Socially, this is forever reaching agreements based on more mature self-evident truths.

When unable through conversation to reach a more mature agreement, Gandhi's social maturation process was non-cooperation with the immature agreement. This disruption caused more conversations that he trusted, because he knew the primary intention of all involved was to mature into more mature agreements, would result in agreement on a more mature policy. England and all the Indian people eventually agreed the Indian people were ready to govern their nation themselves and they gained their independence from England.

In my judgment, knowing the importance of giving priority to "the natural force of truth," to the priority of cooperation for maturation moving inside all, was the genius of Mahatma Gandhi.

By the way, Gandhi accurately discovered the most accurate fundamental fact that the universe operates as an indivisible whole and built his life and actions on it. However, like nearly all up until now, he did not understand the relationship between human languages and the oneness of nature. Therefore, he also was not aware there are two fundamental patterns of thinking, one that assumes there are separate parts—the one we only use up to the teenage years, and the one that assumes oneness we can then learn. We can then simultaneously use both and give the latter priority. These two pieces of knowledge are necessary to master the last two layers of maturity of the skill of human self-consciousness, the Elder and Mature Elder layers. What attracted me to Gandhi was he did not take his wisdom into a monastery. He took it into the marketplace, into the middle of what was going on in his Indian society.

He was *accepting shared responsibility* for what was most important for the Indian people, shedding the paternalistic relationship with England and taking full responsibility for themselves. By the way, this is the other side of the coin of, at the Teen layer, having the ability and right to exercise individual free choice that appears to be seldom noticed today. Making sure this was also fully embraced was the reason villagers and tribes in the past had a major ritual to make their teenagers aware of this other side of the coin of having the ability and right to exercise individual free choice.

At this time on Earth, the Gandhi in each of us needs to accept shared responsibility for Eldering ourselves, each other, and our children into full maturity in the skill of human self-consciousness as early in our lives as possible. It is the fundamental source of the solution to all of our problems. Large or small, personal or social, the source of all of them is immature behavior.

I woke up at 2:30am this morning and was wide awake. I got up, came downstairs, went out onto the deck, and again sunk myself down into the warmth of the hot tub. When I looked up, the sky was clearer than I had seen it at any time my entire life. I could see thousands of stars.

I instantly became aware of not only how small a part of it I am but of how small the Earth is in relationship to all of it.

Then something happened that had never happened before when I have looked straight up at the stars on a clear night. I became aware I was experiencing it as a three-dimensional experience. I could tell some stars were closer to me than others and all of them were at a particular distance from me and each other. I, of course, had always intellectually known this, but I became aware that I had never before *self-consciously and directly experienced* its three-dimensionality.

I was not only directly experiencing different stars being at different distances from me but also the three-dimensionality experience of the entire scene. It made me become aware I had never before given priority in my thinking to the *three-dimensionality experience* of being on a very small planet in the midst of other planets and stars, not only above me where I was looking but of the many stars and planets if I was at night looking out from Earth from all locations on it.

I became aware I had always unconsciously (without choice) been projecting my two-dimensionality pattern of thinking, the separate parts pattern, into how I experienced looking into space: only being aware of up and down and right and left.

Experiencing the stars in the night sky three-dimensionally, with the third dimension being the oneness of nature, is obviously a more accurate way to be experiencing them. Therefore, as a result of noticing the inaccuracy of my previously unconscious (without choice) immature way of looking at the night sky and of the more mature way of doing it, I am sure I will always experience it in that more mature way in the future. All maturation in our thinking is permanent.

What was stunning to my thinking was I was fully unaware I was unconsciously (without choice) projecting two-dimensionality onto my experience of the night sky, thinking of it only in terms of looking up and down and then right and left.

This is what this book is about. It is about uncovering the many unconscious (without choice) ways you are still thinking two-dimensionally instead of three-dimensionally. It was the only way we were thinking at least until the teenage years. In addition, much of the surrounding society is still only using the two-dimensional pattern of thinking and unaware of the existence of the three-dimensional pattern of thinking, the oneness pattern of thinking, much more using it and giving it priority.

If from a study of your direct experience, you come to agree with what you have read in this chapter and want to integrate it into your thinking, I would suggest you do six things:

Six Things to Do If You Come to Agree With What You Have Read

1. **Primarily Be a Personal Scientist.** You do this by taking your power back from any fundamental outside belief you have been operating on. Then use it as your sixth sense to study your direct, present, and repeatable by choice experience to

identify the fundamental truth you will use to guide your thinking, whether or not it agrees with what I have concluded is the most fundamental one from answering the 7 questions.

2. **Have Your Words Accurately Represent Reality.** When being self-conscious, words are always between us and wherever we are focusing our attention, whether in thinking, observing, or doing something. Do the work to get into inside beliefs in your thinking all you need to know to operate at full maturity at the Elder layer. Much of that knowledge is in this chapter.

3. **With a Friend, Do the Mutual Mature Love Skill Experience in Chapter 8.** This is essential. While reading most of this chapter you have been giving priority to words. To achieve full maturity in the skill of human self-consciousness, you need to learn to give priority to the self-conscious experience of oneness (Mature Elder layer), second priority to inside beliefs in words (Elder layer), and third priority to Eldering to sustain the contented joy feeling of it. Knowing, for those few minutes, the skill of giving priority to the oneness of nature and second priority to words will have the two of you know it can be *a mutual self-consciously known experience.* You will then know it as a *skill* you can choose. You will then also know how to choose this mutual experience with another who knows it. Or alone with others who do not know it. It will be a wavelength you know is always present, where it is, and how to choose to participate in it as the context of everything else, and to have your third priority always be Eldering to sustain the feeling of contented joy.

4. **Primarily Relate with Another's Primary Good Intention.** When relating with another, as Gandhi did, see his or her pri-

mary good intention as who he or she primarily is. This is also who the person self-consciously or unconsciously (without choice) understands himself or herself to primarily be. About this the person does not have choice. This is honoring the oneness of nature in others.

5. **As Much as Possible Choose Consensual Agreements.** When relating with others, be aware you have only two options: war or agreements (moving against or with the indivisible whole). As much as possible, choose to operate with your friends, lover, teenage or older children, and everyone else based on consensual agreements that give priority to the common good, cooperation for maturation. This is both honoring they also have the ability and right to exercise mature free choice and moving as a part of the indivisible whole for the maturation of us all.

6. **Identify the Particular Roles You Are Playing in the Maturation of Us All and Know That Is What You Are Primarily Doing: Eldering.** At any one moment we are playing a role in maturation, and we may also be playing a particular role over time. No matter how large or small is our immediate role, or role over time, of participation in the maturation of the universe, we always want to know that is primarily what we are doing. It could be raising our children to full maturity before they leave home. It could be running, or participating in, a for-profit or non-profit organization that is giving priority to the Eldering of all involved to full maturity in the skill of human self-consciousness. It could be both. It could be a particular mission you have chosen for our maturation. Whatever is the priority of your attention, and particular missions you have chosen for your life, you want to be sure it is the

best unique thing you in particular can be doing for the maturation of us all. Nothing is more enjoyable than being on the cutting edge of improving in our skill of Eldering.

Since the invention of human languages most of us have been unconsciously (without choice) using our skill of human self-consciousness it allows in an immature way. We have been using it to choose the outside beliefs we will use to guide our thinking. The mature way to use it, as I hope you did when you answered the 7 questions, is as our sixth sense. This is using it as a sixth way to discover and know truths about the relationships among the parts of the universe by giving priority to direct experience, the way we learned rocks are hard and fire is hot. This results in natural confidence in what we determine to be true. Like the use of our other five senses, we can at any time confirm our observations are accurate by again keeping our power, all of it, and giving priority to studying our direct, present, and repeatable by choice experience to observe they are accurate. As a personal scientist, this is exercising mature free choice and living our lives based on inside beliefs.

In the *Introduction*, I pointed out that even though since human beings were first on Earth it was obvious in plain sight the Earth is round, it was not until 1492 that it began to become a widespread truth known by all. Until then it was assumed to be flat.

There are three things that are noteworthy about this discovery.

First, it was not a reversal into knowing the Earth is round. It was a maturation. It was not wrong to behave as if the Earth is flat when chopping vegetables on a cutting board or building a house. It is just such a big round that even to this day it makes sense to assume it is flat when chopping vegetables or building a house.

The knowledge it is round is a more mature knowledge about the Earth.

Secondly, once this maturation in our knowledge about the Earth occurred as a result of keeping our power, all of it, and using it to study our direct, present, and repeatable by choice experience, this knowledge was permanent. We can at any time confirm it is accurate by again watching a boat disappear when sailing out to sea or witnessing the full 180-degree horizon meeting the ocean is in a perfect half circle. This means we will never be able to fool ourselves into thinking we do not know this more mature knowledge.

Inside us, this maturation is permanent. And socially, this maturation is permanent.

Thirdly, our relationship with this more mature knowledge is now natural confidence, again because we can at any time confirm it is accurate by watching a boat disappear when sailing out to sea. Thus, this knowledge is now naturally, effortlessly, freely chosen, and permanent knowledge in our thinking we label as "true." No effort, force, or discipline is necessary to continue to skillfully and habitually act on the assumption this knowledge, this inside belief, is true. As a result, our relationship with it is natural confidence. Like knowing in direct experience rocks are hard and fire is hot, we now know in direct experience the Earth is round.

Natural confidence is the value of knowing something to be true by keeping our power, all of it, and studying our direct, present, and repeatable by choice experience to discover it is true.

Allow me to ask you this question, "Are you going to die?" If your answer is "yes," then it is obvious there is something more important than your life. If you have matured to where you know the universe operates as an indivisible whole and is always maturing, then you know it is Eldering. It is giving priority in action to being a self-conscious participant in that maturation process. It is this that sustains in you, as the container feeling of all other feelings, the feeling of contented joy.

CHAPTER 2

Eldering Teenagers into the Teen Layer

Recently I was asked to meet with a family by a mother, Nancy, who was desperate because she thought her fourteen-year-old son, Sam, and husband, John, were in danger of seriously hurting each other in their consistent and very angry arguments. When I arrived at their home, Nancy was waiting for me on the front porch, her entire face and eyes red from obviously crying for a long time.

I hugged and comforted her for a few minutes and assured her that I thought I could be helpful.

When she was ready, we went into the very upscale home with a large receiving area with a beautiful circular staircase going up to the second floor. The windows provided a majestic view of the entire valley.

After meeting the father, John, whom I had never met before, and learned that Sam was in his bedroom and would not come out, I assured them I could get him to come out. They were doubtful, but they told me to go up the circular stairway and to the end of the hall. The door to his room was the last door on the right. I knew Sam because he was friends with my grand stepson and had often been to our home.

I knocked on his bedroom door and said in a calm and friendly voice, with which we had always spoken to each other, it was me and I would like to talk to him. He said in a normal voice that his room was a total mess. I said, "Fine, why don't you come down so we can sit at the kitchen table and I can talk to you and your dad and mom?"

He said in his normal voice, "Ok, I will be right out."

"I will see you down there," I said.

I returned downstairs and sat at the kitchen table with his mother and father. Within only a few minutes he joined us and sat at the end of the table opposite his dad, his chair a bit back from it in an unconscious statement (without choice) he wasn't sure it was safe to be there. However, and clearly for my sake, he was being friendly.

As we began to talk, it became clear that John thought love was teaching his son things and was fully unaware his demeanor was assuming dominance each time he turned to say something to Sam. Sam thought love was exercising his new-found ability and right of exercising individual free choice. Therefore, he was no longer willing to put up with his father's dominating behavior. The result was consistent war energy between the two of them, even with me present and them both trying to behave respectfully.

John was clearly still treating Sam as a child who should at all times follow his directions. He was fully unaware Sam had matured into knowing he had the ability and right to exercise individual free choice and would no longer allow himself to be ordered to obey by his father or anyone.

I gently walked all three into understanding that Sam was now a teenager and had discovered the ability and right to exercise individual free choice. When relating with others, this leaves him with only two options: war or agreements. I then asked John if he had prepared his son for this maturation in his abilities and rights. He had no idea what I was talking about.

When I asked him what his childhood was like, he responded, "I did not have one."

Startled, I asked him to tell us more. He told us his father was in prison and his mother was an alcoholic. He said he does not remember anything about his childhood. As he talked further, appreciative that I wanted to know about his life, he said he valued being married, loves his two children—he also has a daughter a few years younger than Sam, and is proud of having achieved financial success.

He emphasized that along the way he has learned much. His priority now is to teach Sam what he has learned. He fought back tears when he said he sure wishes he had known the things he is trying to teach Sam when he was Sam's age. This clearly revealed his primary intention was to be a participant in maturation.

Teaching Sam these things was what he judged to be loving. The result, only when talking to Sam, was the tone of someone teaching from someplace higher up some ladder of authority. He was operating on the assumption if Sam is not following his directions, he is being an irresponsible young man. He is also being disrespectful toward his father. John was also clear that he is not being a responsible father if he allows that behavior toward him.

Sam found this to be oppressive, offensive, violent and aggressively violating his ability and right to exercise individual free choice. Therefore, he was no longer willing to put up with that tone or demeaner and follow any of his father's orders.

Over three hours, often with stories from my life to have all experience some edifying, I hoped, and entertaining experiences to allow all to more easily relax, I gently helped them each freely choose agreements that would work for everyone in the family. I explained this was honoring both sides of the coin of the Teen layer of respecting each person's ability and right to exercise individual free choice and accepting shared ownership of operating for the common good. Sam freely chose to vacuum the living room once a week, only smoke marijuana once a week and tell his parents if he smokes it more than once a week, to not do opiates, and to not use vulgar language around the house. John voluntarily agreed to end all teaching ways of relating with his son to honor his now ability and right to exercise individual free choice. He also agreed to stop when he unconsciously does it whenever Sam asks him to stop.

John came to understand this was how he could regain the trust and love of his son by demonstrating he is able to consistently do this out of love and respect for his son's new ability and right to exercise free choice.

Nancy agreed to get her face out of her computer when the kids are around, relate with them more, and get back to the joyful person she was two years ago, making the family meals and being fun. She said she would do this out of confidence John and Sam would succeed in keeping their agreements.

All three also agreed each time there was a problem or conflict, they would have a meeting around the kitchen table and solve the conflict with consensual agreements they would all keep or re-negotiate at another kitchen table meeting solely for that purpose.

I also explained that this will be a new activity for everyone, making and living by consensual decisions. "Do not think you will be good at it right away," I cautioned. "Be comfortable forgiving each other for failing often.

"To keep it simple," I continued, "there are two skills you need to learn. First, when making a decision about anything, first issues are discussed one at a time. Secondly, space needs to be created for each person to share what he or she thinks, feels, judges, and wants about the issue being discussed. Thirdly, someone has to facilitate the meeting, which can rotate so all learn to do it well.

On each issue, the facilitator breaks the meeting into two parts. The first part is everyone having the space to share his or her thoughts, feelings, judgments, and wants. Only when all feel fully heard so all the relevant information is on the table for all to consider do they move into the second part of the meeting: creating together an agreement that as much as possible speaks to the concerns of everyone and, therefore, will be genuinely agreed to and fully kept by all.

"These are two of the most important skills for us to learn for the rest of our lives—facilitating and making consensual decisions," I shared. "Therefore, having issues to resolve are a golden opportunity to learn these important meeting skills."

I then had the four of us sit in chairs in a close circle with John and Sam facing each other, with less than two feet between their knees. I then had each, while looking the other in the eyes, state the agreements each had voluntarily chosen. The other then reflected it back until the speaker judged he or she was fully and accurately heard by the other. I then had Nancy, while going back and forth from looking each of them in the eyes, share with both the agreements she had made. They then repeated back to her what she said to her satisfaction.

I then explained that these are the kinds of healing experiences we need to create when conflicts emerge. They need to be based on honoring each person's ability and right to exercise individual free choice and resolved by the making and keeping, and renegotiating when necessary, agreements. Life with others is either war or agreements. There is not a third option.

"Whenever necessary," I further and gently coached them, "this needs to be done, and in a formal meeting solely for the purpose of doing so. It can't be done as something unilaterally stated by someone while making breakfast. It also needs to be ceased as an opportunity for all to get good at something they will be doing with other people the rest of their lives: executing the skills of facilitation of meetings and achieving consensus agreements all will keep."

This completed my time with them. I am not a psychotherapist and do not have an on-going relationship with them. I was asked to help in a crisis. What I can report is that the mother, Nancy, called and asked me to have coffee with her a couple of weeks later and reported it had made a significant difference in the life of their family. Months later I checked in with her and she sent this as part of her report in an email to me: "Each of us has some slippage in our commitments, but there is more awareness about it and attempts at re "righting" are common." Therefore, it appears to have had some lasting effect.

For emphasis, allow me to now state something again. From the teenage years on there are only two choices of relating between and among people: war or agreements. The universe operates as an indivisible whole. All of its parts are all stuck together. Our only two options are moving against each other and, therefore the whole, or moving as one with each other and with the whole. There is not a third choice. In our thinking, this moving as one with each other can have borders, such as primarily for our family, our team, our company, or our nation. This is a continuation of thinking as if separate parts are real. It is giving priority to some parts verses some other parts. At full maturity in the skill of human self-consciousness we know there are not only no separate parts but there are also no borders. Then our natural, effortless, and freely chosen priority at all times and in all places (in the reality of oneness) is the common good of us all, cooperation for the maturation of the universe.

In my community of friends, we often make a very big deal out of the transition of a child into the teenage years. Let me describe it for you in the hopes you may choose to do something similar to make a big deal out of this transition that results in him or her realizing there are two sides to the coin of having his or her new ability and right to exercise individual free choice. The other side is knowing the universe operates as an indivisible whole and, therefore, it is accepting full shared responsibility for being part of the indivisible whole. This is giving priority in each moment to what he or she judges to be the best action of self-conscious participation in the fundamental process in nature, cooperation for maturation. If done well, it can allow the teenager to skip getting stuck at the Adult layer, of giving his or her power to an outside belief and obeying where it has been given. Instead, he or she can mature directly into mastering the Elder layer.

We have the boy (the women do something similar) choose the men he knows and respects to spend a Friday night and Saturday day meeting in the woods with his father and him. On Friday night, we sit around a campfire and share many things with each other. In particular, the men each share what their lives were like when they were the age of the teenager and their first bumbling actions in discovering how to relate with women and homosexuality if that happened. This allows the boy to discover that these men all had experiences when they were his age that are both similar and very different. It takes him out of thinking about his life as the only way a teenage life can be lived and legitimizes many different ways of being in the world. All are encouraged to share not only their discoveries around having the ability and right to exercise individual free choice but also their challenges in understanding how to share with all a responsibility for the common good.

Before it is dark and this sharing around the campfire, the boy and his father pitch a tent a distance into the forest, preferably by a running stream. After the time around the campfire, the boy is invited to sleep alone in the tent for the night with one question in his thinking as he is falling asleep and waking up: "What is the meaning of life?" The men have brought tents and sleeping bags and sleep by the fire.

On Saturday morning, and before eating anything, we do a sweat lodge. This is an ancient as well as Native-American tradition of using saplings to bend them over, tie them to each other, and create the skeleton supports of an "igloo looking" structure no higher than five feet. Many blankets are thrown over it so no light can enter, leaving a flap for a door. In the ground in the center of it, a 6-inch-deep-by-2-feet-in-diameter hole is dug. In a nearby campfire, rocks are cooked to be glowing red.

When they are ready, we all get naked (not necessary) and crawl into the structure to sit on the ground in a circle around the hole. Before the door flap is closed, the person playing the role of facilitator invites some men with pitch forks to bring, one by one, the glowing hot rocks into the sweat lodge and the facilitator gently places them in a pile in the hole. When there are eight to ten glowing rocks in it, the door flap is closed. That leaves the inside of the sweat lodge pitch black. The facilitator has a couple of buckets of water and uses a ladle to periodically spill water on the rocks in between prayers, such as honoring the seven directions, leading us in songs, and inviting all to share what is being stimulated inside them. The sweat lodge becomes very hot, like a sauna.

At the right peak time, the facilitator asks the boy what he learned about the meaning of life while going to sleep, dreaming, and waking up. Afterward this, and in the darkness and heat, a few men usually share some of what they have learned about the meaning of life, particularly things that resonate with what the boy discovered.

After the sweat lodge and breakfast, and again sitting in a circle in the grass but without a fire, each man shares what he has learned about the meaning of life and some of the dramatic stories of his bungling and backing into some of his discoveries. Sometimes the stories are of profound eldering by an older man. There are other activities, often different each time based on what is appropriate for that boy. Often it is done with some good laughs orchestrated into them, and he comes to enjoy camaraderie with men. It is hoped that he will realize there is something called "male energy" and he gets to know it as a positive, fun, and eldering energy, different and no better or worse than female energy, but an energy that is distinct and valuable to know as distinct from "female energy." This is usually not talked about, but it is hoped it will be at least recognized as existing.

The climax comes when the boy is asked to give priority to direct and present experience when asked the seven questions in *Chapter 1: The 7 Questions* that reveal to him it is obvious in plain sight the universe operates as an indivisible whole. It is then explained to him that up to now he has been allowed to operate on the assumption it is separate parts to master using a human language and being self-conscious. Also, his brain was not sufficiently developed to be able to easily understand he was doing it and that the universe actually operates as an indivisible whole. He was also not able to understand well until now the difference between choice, exercising individual free choice, and mature free choice. These things are explained to him by the men until he fully understands them.

The seven layers of maturity of the skill of human self-consciousness are then described to him: Baby, Toddler, Child, Teen, Adult, Elder, and Mature Elder layers. It is pointed out that he is now able to enter the Teen layer. This is where he is able to move beyond only exercising choice when others present options to being capable of creating the options himself. In our and his mother's relationship with him, we now want to honor that he has that ability and right. We, of course, also point out the other side of the coin of this right is the responsibility he shares with all of us now to operate for the common good, in cooperation for the maturation of the universe.

We also point out that when relating with others who also have this ability and right there are only two options: war or agreements. It is also pointed out that, since he now knows the universe operates as an indivisible whole, the correct priority for those agreements is the common good, not the common good of our family, our team, our company, or our nation. There are no borders to the common good.

Therefore, from this point on decisions on the rules he will follow within the family will be made by consensus agreements with his parents. This is to both honor his now ability and right to exercise individual free choice and the choice to live by agreements rather than war. We will also now directly reach agreements that share accepting responsibility for the common good of the family living in a house as part of learning the importance of this other side of the coin of the Teen layer, sharing ownership with us all for the self-conscious maturation of the universe.

The remaining layers of maturity for him to learn are also described and we can help in his self-eldering process, but it is emphasized that they can only be learned by exercising his ability and right of individual free choice, now hopefully mature free choice as a result of how he answered the 7 questions. The smaller skill of each layer builds on the smaller skills of the previous layers and does not negate any of them but eventually integrates all of them into the one mature skill. Therefore, from this point forward he can only self-elder himself into the Adult, Elder, and Mature Elder layers of this skill. We can all be helpful, and we emphasize that we are all available at any time he wants us to be helpful, just ask. However, it is now an inside job. From this point forward, he is responsible for self-eldering himself into full maturity in this skill.

It is also emphasized that the purpose of this initiation is to assist him in understanding these things. This will keep him from getting stuck at giving priority to the smaller skills at the Child, Teen, or Adult layers. If he well understands what has been shared with him, he is not only mastering the Teen layer but also in the process of mastering the smaller skills of both the Adult and Elder layers. They are, as a personal scientist, choosing his fundamental belief (Adult layer) and using the skill of personal science by giving priority to keeping his power, all of it, and studying his direct experience to name in words, words that work best for him, the most fundamental fact of how the universe operates: it operates as an indivisible whole (beginning of the Elder layer). It is also emphasized this is the only way they will naturally, effortlessly, freely, permanently, confidently, and primarily become skills rather than beliefs in words. They will also be the latter, the words that work for him. What is important is that they *primarily become skills* and secondly words as a result of learning them by being a personal scientist.

It is also emphasized the other side of the coin of now having the ability and right to exercise indivisible free choice is sharing responsibility with the rest of us of cooperating for maturation, the fundamental process, priority, and activity of oneness. How he organizes his life and does it each moment is fully up to him. However, he also now knows we are all in this together and share the responsibility of giving *priority* to this common good without borders. A thousand years ago the common good was of all we knew, our village and nature. Today, Earth behaves as one village. Therefore, it is now the common good of our Earth village and all of nature, the indivisible universe.

As mentioned in the *Chapter 1: The 7 Questions*, a Russian wooden doll with the six smaller dolls inside it can be used as a demonstration how we each, as our physical bodies being the smallest doll, have from the inside sole and complete control of what we do. However, we are inside and inseparable from the full set of dolls where each is within the next bigger doll. We are each first the universe that will not die, the biggest doll with all the other dolls inside and inseparable from it, and secondly our physical bodies that will die, the smallest doll. From the inside, we each only have sole and complete responsibility for the behavior of the smallest doll and from the inside none anywhere else; yet we are not only the smallest doll. We are all seven dolls as he just discovered by using his sixth sense of self-conscious knowing when answering the 7 questions. He is only able to naturally, effortlessly, freely, and consistently enjoy the contented joy of this when he has mastered as skills and turned into habits the smaller skills of all seven layers of maturity of human self-consciousness.

It is emphasized that whether or not he is aware of it he is now on the course of mastering the smaller skills of all seven layers and Eldering. Maturation is the fundamental process in nature and cannot be stopped. Therefore, he would be wise to give highest priority to mastering this skill.

Finally, the boy and the father are seated facing each other, knees to knees, and at eye level with each other. The facilitator, usually the man most respected by the boy, guides the boy and the father into knowing, eyes-to-eyes, the direct self-conscious experience of the oneness of nature with each other.

(As mentioned above, for some minutes you will be invited to choose a friend with whom to know this experience in your relationship with each other in *Chapter 8: Mutual Mature Love Experience.*)

Once the two of them have fully settled into enjoying together, eyes-to-eyes, the self-conscious experience of the oneness of nature, the father informs the boy that from this point forward decisions about how he lives his life while living with his parents will be made by consensus agreements rather than him following their rules. If consensus cannot be reached, the parents will maintain the right to determine the decision. However, he strongly emphasizes, they will try to never exercise that right to determine the decision but instead have all succeed in finding an agreement that will work for all.

This is important! The teenager, although often not able to admit it, wants to know the parents have his back. At the same time, he wants to now primarily be honored as having the ability and right to exercise individual free choice. By the agreements now being determined by consensus, that ability and right is being honored. By the parents having the right of veto power while clearly and boldly committing to try to never use it, the boy feels supported inside a context of still being protected by his parents if necessary.

Parents realize this means the teenager will need to continue to talk to them to make these consensus decisions, create new ones, and renegotiate some. The teenager will also learn to either keep the agreements or re-negotiate them, an extremely valuable skill for him to learn. This is responsible relating with others. Their relationship will continue to be full of mutual respect; they will live together using agreements rather than war; and, most important, their relationship will continue to be close and full of easy talking to each other about all things.

If the above does not happen, the teenager will easily float into giving priority to people, groups, beliefs, and activities outside the family and cease talking about important things with his parents.

As a result of the above guided experience with his father, and with his mother guided into it with him by the father when they return home, he now knows that the direct self-conscious experience of the oneness of nature can be known as a direct experience by choice. If the parents have self-eldered themselves into full maturity in this skill, when with their teenager they will be watchful to give that *experience* priority at all times. Like discovering riding a bicycle is possible by seeing other people riding them, we want our teenagers to know the joy of watching their parents always operating as Mature Elders. Or getting back to doing so as soon as possible when they fall out of doing so. Instead of lamenting their drop out of it, they will see it as a gift. They will share with their teenager what happened, how it happened, and how they got themselves up and back to mature behavior.

As we have all heard and is ancient wisdom, our children become who we are.

These skills, by the way, will be essential for the teenager to be capable of later knowing if the person he or she chooses to marry also has achieved full maturity in the skill of human self-consciousness, the skill of being able to enjoy mutual mature love. That is, mutual one with all love, true romantic love. Not something between their two noses.

The initiation activity to do the above does not need to be as elaborate as we sometimes do it in our community of friends. It could be as simple as, when the teenager is ready, having a special dinner at the house or taking him or her out to dinner at a fancier restaurant than he has been taken to before. During dinner or after it, the most important parts of the above can be executed: the answering of the seven questions, describing and understanding the seven layers of maturity of the skill of human self-consciousness, guided into the mutual mature love skill experience with each parent, and reaching agreement that the rules he or she will live by within the family will now be determined by consensus agreements. (A valuable addition can be putting the information shared in this meeting on a piece of paper that can be given to him or her afterwards to keep and refer to if memory is weak.)

What is essential is that it is done.

The more elaborate the better, but what is most important is that our relationship with our teenage daughter or son is changed to living in the family by consensus agreements with the one above caveat. Also, that the new teenager understands the universe operates as an indivisible whole by studying direct and present experience when answering the 7 questions. And, finally, having the experience with both parents of the direct self-conscious experience of the oneness of nature as a skill able-to-be-chosen and sustained with others as a mutual skill experience.

This is just the beginning of the teenager learning these skills within the safety and Eldering skills of the parents. As our children are growing up, we want to be sure we keep them consistently aware there are layers of maturity of the skill of human self-consciousness. They will then be fully ready for this initiation when they are teenagers. They will also know they have not only mastered the smaller skills of the Baby, Toddler, and Child layers but also that they want to master the smaller skills of the remaining layers to become a fully mature human being. We want to be valued Mature Elders in their lives who artfully assist them in achieving full maturity in this skill before they leave home and marry.

Maturation is the fundamental process in nature, and it cannot be escaped or stopped. Keeping them aware the entire time they are growing up there are layers of maturity of the skill of human self-consciousness is one of the ways we have them know in their teenage years it is wise for them to have their priority be the mastery of the remaining smaller skills.

It is important to note if they are not Eldered into knowing there are layers of maturity of this skill, they could unconsciously (without choice) remain stuck at the Child layer the rest of their lives and not know it. When living in a society where this is the case for many people, it is all the more important to be sure we attend to self-eldering ourselves to full maturity in this skill so we can also set our children on the path of self-eldering themselves. Now that you know there are layers of maturity of this complex skill, and that by nature our highest priority at all times and in all places (in the oneness of nature) is self-eldering ourselves to full maturity in it so we can enjoy Eldering the rest of our lives, we can self-consciously attend to it. We will discover it is quite easy to do. It is only learning two or three additional smaller skills we do not know.

Nothing is more enjoyable than primarily Eldering each and every moment of our lives, whether it is Self-Eldering, Eldering our children, or Eldering each moment wherever we are.

One moment it could be Eldering a teenager to both love the newfound ability and right to exercise individual free choice and also the shared responsibility that is the other side of that coin, the next moment it could be taking the organic scraps out to the compost pile, the next moment it could be negotiating an agreement on a business deal, the next moment it could be leaving a public bathroom cleaner than we found it.

Nothing is a more enjoyable behavior than Eldering. It is the only priority that sustains the inner feeling of contented joy. It is this that allows us to discover the next layer of challenge of Eldering of which we are capable and joyfully accepting that responsibility.

CHAPTER 3

Experience Is Oneness

There are two ways we can relate with experience: with a particular experience or with experience that is the container of all particular experiences.

Typing on a computer or going to a movie are particular experiences. That which is always present and within which typing on a computer and going to a movie exist is "unbroken-up-into-parts experience," the container within which all particular experiences exist.

Unbroken-up-into-parts experience is oneness.

To directly experience the oneness of nature, we can't use our seeing knowing, tasting knowing, smelling knowing, hearing knowing, or touching knowing. Our first five senses are only able to directly experience a quality of a part of the universe relative to other parts. We can only directly experience the oneness of nature by keeping our power, all of it, and using *our sixth sense, self-conscious knowing.* It is answering the 7 questions by giving priority to a study of our direct, present, and repeatable by choice experience that allows us to *know the relationships among the parts of the universe,* that for us to be breathing it has to be operating as an indivisible whole.

Only our sixth sense of self-conscious knowing allows us to know the relationships between and among the parts of the universe as an indivisible whole.

The second most important place we use this sixth sense is in discovering maturation, not competition, is the fundamental process in nature. We know a baby will mature into using a human language and thereby learn the skill of self-consciousness. We know, given the right conditions of soil, water, and sunlight, a tulip bulb will mature into a tulip plant and tulip flower. We know an oak tree, given similar conditions, will grow into a large tree.

Where is this maturation process? Can you point a finger at it? I think you will discover that is not possible. The *process of maturation* does not exist in what we call "times and places," in the mutually agreed-upon illusion tool of separate parts. We can witness it occurring in terms of times and places, *but we cannot point at the process of it occurring*. Yet, we *know* these maturations are occurring. Maturation is predictable. In the same way we know oneness exists and we can't point a finger at it, we are aware, using self-conscious knowing, maturation exists, and we also can't point a finger at it. Maturation, like oneness, is everywhere and always present and occurring. Therefore, like oneness, it can't be pointed at with our finger. Anywhere we point our finger is pointing at it. It only exists in the reality of the oneness of nature. When I have matured into knowing how to ride a bicycle, we know that knowledge and skill exists, but we can't point at either one of them. They both only exist in the all times and all places of the oneness of nature.

"Experience," *unbroken-up-into-parts-experience*, is the word we use to identify what is fundamental in nature and within which everything else exists.

Experience is oneness.

It is always present and can't be escaped. We can directly know it is present, not just imagine it is present.

Look up from reading for a few moments and look around wherever you are. Is there any place you witness something not inside experience? A lamp, a chair, a picture, another person as not a part of experience?

Look at each part of the universe you see. Is each one in experience?

Take as much time as you like to do this; then turn to the next page.

Witnessing everything *inside and a part of experience* is the direct, present, and repeatable by choice experience of the oneness of nature. It is always present and can't be escaped. Experience *is* the oneness of nature. You can directly know it exists and have a relationship with it.

It is nothing more or less than unbroken-up-into-parts-experience.

Wherever you are, it is present and can't be escaped. Everything exists inside it and is secondary in importance.

It is the oneness of nature not sitting still. It is always going somewhere. It is always maturing.

It is only by using our sixth sense of self-conscious knowing that we can *directly know and experience* this relationship among all the parts.

Cooperation for maturation is the process among all the parts. It is the fundamental process, priority, and activity within the oneness of nature.

To live with it, and have a relationship with it, we have to give it a name. Since we enter this conversation already having broken up experience into parts to be self-conscious, the fully accurate name for it is "unbroken-up-into-parts-experience." Since that is a mouthful, we will use the term "experience" knowing it is referring to unbroken-up-into-parts-experience.

Using our sixth sense of self-conscious knowing, we now know oneness, and its process of cooperation for maturation, exist. We now also have names for them and can choose our relationship with them.

At the highest layer of human maturity, the Mature Elder layer, oneness is reality. Within it everything else exists as second in importance. Therefore, in our thinking we freely choose to give priority to the experience of the oneness of the universe, including its process of maturation, and second priority to everything else, any part of the universe.

This is why it is important to know self-conscious knowing is our sixth sense. It allows us to know the self-conscious experience of oneness as *knowledge* in our thinking and as a *skill* to consistently honor it. We can now execute this skill any time we choose. We now know in direct experience oneness exists. It is real. We can at all times and in all places (in the reality of oneness) be aware of it. We can at all times and in all places choose to give priority to direct, self-conscious participation in its fundamental process of cooperation for maturation: Eldering. In doing so we are honoring, and in direct relationship with, this most fundamental fact about the operation of the universe.

It operates as an indivisible whole that is at all times and in all places maturing.

Unbroken-up-into-parts-experience can be known. It is real. It is here right now. It is always here. It is that within which everything else occurs as secondary in importance. We can know it and have a direct relationship with it.

Thus, in summary, the five changes we naturally begin to make in our thinking when we discover the universe operates as an indivisible whole are, first, to keep our power, all of it, and use it as our sixth sense to study our direct, present, and repeatable by choice experience to identify the inside beliefs as the truths we will use to guide our thinking. Secondly, to give priority in the words in our thinking to the accurate fundamental inside belief about how the universe operates: it operates as an indivisible whole. The third one is to define "self" as "I am first the indivisible universe that will not die and secondly my physical body that will die." Fourthly, there are two patterns of thinking and to always give priority to the oneness pattern—giving priority to priorities, and second priority to the separate parts pattern—choosing between this or that part. This includes knowing the separate parts pattern of thinking represents the mutually agreed-upon illusion tools we invented of the assumption of separate parts and words. This allows us to simultaneously give priority to the priorities pattern because it accurately represents reality and second priority to the illusory separate parts pattern that allows us to know the experience of the oneness of nature as a self-conscious experience. And the fifth is to know cooperation for the health and maturation of the universe is the fundamental process in nature, not competition between and among the illusory separate parts.

Maturation into the last two layers will take some attention to this maturation process. Most of us live in societies where most are still operating on the assumption separate parts exist. Each person is giving priority to the self-interest of his or her physical body, the smallest wooden doll, perhaps the next bigger wooden doll, their romantic relationship and children, and maybe even one of the bigger wooden dolls but not consistently executing the skill of giving priority to the biggest wooden doll. And, therefore, competition is assumed to be the fundamental process in nature between and among separate parts that do not exist.

When we discover, as I hope you did by giving priority to experience when answer the 7 questions, the universe operates as an indivisible whole, we begin the process of mastering the skill of the Elder layer. As summarized above, it is changing all the words and processes of our thinking to accurately represent this most fundamental fact. This is the mastery of the Elder layer

This, I believe, is the next layer of maturity for humanity we are now ready and able to master. It is the new, more mature course of humanity.

Increasingly, there will be widespread understanding of the relationship between the oneness of nature and human languages. This has not been widely understood until now, both in spiritual and scientific communities. People will increasingly be aware their skill of human self-consciousness is a sixth sense, a sixth way we can know reality in direct experience, as a personal scientist. We can then also know we are not born with the skills of using a human language and the self-consciousness it allows. We can notice it is a complex skill with layers of maturity, and biologically we can only begin to master the smaller skills of the highest layers when in the teenage years. We can also notice that the best thing, simultaneously for our children and us all, is Eldering them into mastery of the smaller skills of all seven layers before they leave home and marry. To do this, we must first elder ourselves into full maturity in this skill, into being Mature Elders, and thereby consistently enjoying the most enjoyable joy there is, consistently maturing in the skill of Eldering.

Now that we understand what has not been widely understood until now, we can rapidly Self-Elder ourselves, and Elder our children, to full maturity in this skill. It is a skill. Skills are the same for everyone. We can all learn it. At this time, nothing is more important to resolve all our challenges on Earth than to rapidly Self-Elder ourselves, each other, and our children to full maturity in the use of this skill.

Humanity, in our now global village, is being confronted with the largest challenge it has ever had. *Fundamentally,* the only solution is the rapid eldering of ourselves and our children to full maturity in this skill. Let me describe two more challenges that necessitate this..

Most of us know we are damaging our Earthly environment, and continuing to do so, at such a rapid rate that we could destroy the ability for life to continue on it. This is not a wild idea. It is a fact.

Secondly, few of us are aware of what will happen if the United States continues economic growth at the desired pace of 3%. If it is now a $20 trillion economy, in 100 years it will be a $385 trillion economy. My friend, Chris Martenson, wrote the following about this in his *Peak Prosperity* (peakprosperity.com) blog on May 21, 2019 entitled *Gone: They Have Stolen our Future*:

> That would make the US economy *alone* nearly 5 times larger than the entire world economy right now. Need we point out again that even 1x current world GDP is killing the planet? Is it not self-evident that it's not possible for the US alone to be 5x larger than the entire current world economy without destroying everything that even makes having an economy possible (or worth it) in the first place?
>
> Or what if we magically held world population steady from here, but then delivered the equivalent of an Australian standard of living to everybody? Well, then we'd increase consumption by the planet's citizens by a factor of more than 20. Oops. Another unworkable idea.
>
> These are very simple thoughts to entertain. However, let me first list every single question of this sort posed by the journalists covering the Federal Reserve's recent hearings and press announcement: 0
>
> None. Nada. Zilch.
>
> How is this even possible? How can the most powerful entity in the world, charged with steering the economy to ever larger levels never, not once, be asked a question along the lines of *"tell us please, if you are as successful over the next 100 years as you have been over the past 100, what sort of world do your models indicate for us?"*
>
> How is this not a legitimate question to ask? Every one of us has an interest in the answer, including every single journalist, but the question is never asked.
>
> Why?

Clearly, there is a major waking up of us all to what needs to be done. This situation will surely necessitate major changes to the way of life of us all. Waking up and dealing with these challenges is now a matter of life or death for us all.

It is not one person who needs to be eldered into full maturity in the complex skill of human self-consciousness. It is everyone, particularly those in greatest need of it whose immaturity poses the greatest danger as the access to the tools to cause horrific damage to others becomes even more widespread.

In my judgment, humanity will only make the necessary maturations of our lives together to meet these challenges to the degree we all master the highest layers of maturity in the skill of human self-consciousness, the Elder and Mature Elder layers. Only then will the natural, effortless, and freely chosen priority by all of us at all times and in all places (in the reality of oneness) be the common good of us all, cooperation for maturation, natural morality. We will then also know we are all using the exact same skills, the skills that are the same for everyone. We will also know we are all enjoying working together to consistently get better at giving priority to self-conscious participation in the maturation of us all, Eldering.

This can happen. It can happen rapidly. It is not confronting anyone's religious, philosophical, or scientific beliefs. It is mastering a skill. A skill everyone would like to learn because it is the only skill that can lead to true personal happiness that is knowing the joy of participating in universal happiness. It is a skill everyone can learn before leaving home and getting married. Or, if that does not occur, we can each begin to achieve full maturity in it quickly once we take back our power from wherever we have given it and give priority to our direct, present, and repeatable by choice experience when answering the 7 questions at the beginning of *Chapter 1: The 7 Questions*.

Today, one person is capable of tremendous damage to our lives together on Earth. It is time to respond appropriately. It is time for all of us—parents, teachers, religious leaders, business leaders, politicians, and activist of all kinds, to give priority to Eldering every person on Earth into full maturity in the skill of human self-consciousness.

In 1800, fewer than 10% of the people on Earth were literate. Today, 86% are literate. In 1776, the first modern nation based on honoring the Teen layer was created, the USA. Today, a majority of nations are democracies. Our future on Earth will primarily be the result of more people each day Self-Eldering themselves into full maturity in the skill of human self-consciousness, and then Eldering their children into it by the time they are 20 years old and all of our organizations into it as well.

This can begin to happen rapidly.

The solution to all of our challenges—from the management of Earth's environment, to the ending of war and violence to resolve differences, to the maturation of democracies into giving priority to Self-Eldering and encouraging the emergence of agreement nations, to an economy that voluntarily gives priority to the common good, to ending poverty for the good of us all—is dependent upon each of us Eldering ourselves to full maturity in the skill of human self-consciousness. This is the future of life on Earth. How rapidly it happens is determined by how rapidly we Self-Elder ourselves and each other into full maturity in this skill.

Fortunately, maturation is the fundamental process in nature and cannot be stopped.

If you have not been eldered by your parents or others into full maturity in this skill, you can use this book, other books, support groups, the formation of communities of friends, and other activities to Self-Elder yourself into full maturity in this skill, the skill of mutual mature love. The agreement nation I will be forming if there is enough support for it, Chrysalis Nations, will also be an opportunity for you to be with others who share the worldview in this book (www.chrysalisnation.org).

Allow me to repeat this again.

Once, when as a teenager, we discover we have the ability and right to exercise individual free choice, using the answering of the 7 questions we can Elder ourselves into knowing the more mature choice of mature free choice. Also, we can then discover that when relating with other human beings we have only two choices: war or agreements—moving with others in cooperation for maturation or against others for some form of separate self-interest. As we each learn to keep our power, all of it, and become personal scientists, the course of humanity will forever be the making, keeping, and re-negotiation of agreements. Wars or violence to resolve differences will be abandoned and any emergence of it will be handled by police forces and courts, not armies or terrorism. The natural priority of each of us will be known to be moral behavior and about this we each do not have choice. It is the nature of oneness moving inside each of us. Any action of a person not honoring this will be seen as behavior at one of the lower layers of maturity. The primary response will be compassion, not judgment. And then assistance in helping the other mature up the remaining layers of maturity of the skill of human self-consciousness. We know if he or she knew of the next higher layer he or she would be operating on it. Maturation cannot be stopped.

I now love words. They allow me to know what I am doing while I am doing it and to exercise mature free choice. I love experience even more. It heals, matures, and sustains the only part of the indivisible universe where from the inside I have sole and complete control, my physical body. It also allows me to know the joy that is the result of giving priority to Eldering.

Nothing is a more enjoyable behavior than Eldering.

When we have achieved full maturity in the skill of human self-consciousness, especially when supported with the skill of mutual mature romantic love as our base camp, in our actions Eldering is our priority each moment.

In the next chapter, I will tell the stories of the significant events that, without Mature Elders to guide me, I backed into the discovery of the smaller skills after the Child layer. It took me seventy-two years to complete the process and I am still making big mistakes (I recently made a huge one) and, as a result, continuing to get better at Eldering.

Experience is oneness. It is always here, right now. It is always maturing. And without it we would not be able to breathe.

Being a self-conscious participant in maturation is the only priority in our actions that sustains the experience of natural confidence and the feeling of contented joy.

CHAPTER 4

How I Backed into the Discovery of Mutual Mature Love

In this chapter, I tell the stories of how I, in the absence of a Mature Elder to guide me, backed into the discovery of the last four layers of maturity of the skill of human self-consciousness.

When I was a sophomore at Creighton Preparatory High School in Omaha, Nebraska, USA, two of my fellow football teammates, Jim and Larry, and I were given permission during lunch period to go to our lockers to get our *American History* books to study for a test. While walking down the long, empty shiny green and gray hallway to our lockers, Jim said he had read that milk causes pimples. We all had pimples. I extremely enthusiastically, very extremely enthusiastically, responded with the word "Really?!!" In hindsight, I can now witness that the way I said it was fully and easily giving my power to that piece of information. They laughed so ferociously at me giving my power away so fully and easily that they physically fell all over themselves and the hallway. Their loud laughter echoed vibrantly down the long empty space.

I was devastated, demoralized, humiliated, and fully deflated of energy. My body became a walking puddle anyone could stomp through.

After getting my *American History* book, I closed my locker that was blocking my view of them at their lockers. All I saw was their backsides rushing through the nearby swinging doors to get back to the lunch room without me.

Across from our lockers was a small chapel. To escape from returning to the lunch room, I went inside and sat in the last pew of the empty chapel. It was a cloudy day. The chapel was very dark except for the one red vigil light to the left of the alter.

I grew up in the Austrian-Hungarian, working class Catholic community on the other side of town. I began working in my father's small meat market, Mollner Meat Market, from the age of five and was working there every day after school and all day on Saturdays, every weekday after football practice rushing to get there to help clean up. I was one of the first boys from our many ethnic neighborhoods to attend this all boys preparatory school far into the wealthy part of town. I had a strong feeling of being from a lower class and less worthy of being there than the other boys. I had clearly evidenced this in the way I had said, "Really?!!" But, of course, then I did not know that was the reason I had behaved the way I had behaved, and they had behaved the way they had behaved.

I just knew I was feeling like I shouldn't exist.

I found myself in a pile of flesh, bones and clothes on a pew and eventually asking myself this question, "Who can I say loves me, behaves lovingly toward me?" When I couldn't think of a single person who behaved lovingly toward me, I began to cry. Tears I couldn't stop kept flowing out of my hunched-over linebacker's body and onto my pants.

Eventually I looked up and through the darkness at the crucifix above the alter. I suddenly realized there was one person who loved me!

God loves me!

I crawled up onto the kneeler. A smile came to my face. Through the darkness I looked at the crucifix above the alter and realized there was one person who loved me. God loves me!

Then I became deflated again and again slid back into a pile of flesh, bones and clothes on the pew. I realized I already knew God loved me and that had not made any difference when those two boys were so cruel toward me.

After a bit of time I realized I was ignorant. In any moment, I had no idea why to do one thing rather than another. I became clear I didn't want this ignorance inside me any longer.

After some minutes of sitting there and thinking about this I slid back up onto the kneeler with my arms leaning on the pew in front of me and decided to take my first vow with myself. It was to discover "the meaning of life." Those were the words I used. I wanted to understand why I should do one thing rather than another and I realized I currently had no idea how to make that choice.

I wanted to make sure I stayed focused on this new priority. Therefore, I made it a commitment with myself at the deepest level I knew, as a vow. I also agreed with myself that I would attend Mass every lunch hour from that day forward and use that time mainly to think. To think for the purpose of figuring out the meaning of life.

Once this plan was firmly in place at the deepest level of commitment inside me, I stood up, smiled with enthusiasm for my new priority, wiped away the tears, brushed my hair back into place, did not genuflect as I had always done in the past when leaving a church, and walked out of the chapel and back down to the lunch room with no concern about what Jim or Larry thought of me. I now had a more important reason for living than being concerned about what they or anyone else thought of me.

What at the time I did not know I was doing was instead of continuing to give my power to my parents, my coaches, Jim and Larry, or anyone else, I was ceasing my new biological ability as a teenager to keep my power, all of it, and use it to primarily live my life according to my choices, *from among the options I identified*, rather than from the one's others identified. I was not aware that by making this vow with myself I was maturing into the Teen layer of giving priority to exercising individual free choice in this way, *choosing from among the options I invented in my thinking rather than from among those chosen and presented to me by others.*

I was also unaware I was to some degree moving toward mature free choice. I was purely going to do a study of my direct experiences to find the answers to this question. Of course, I was fully unaware I was to some degree doing this and, therefore, not at all aware of the unconscious ways I was not doing it. For instance, I was fully unaware that by doing my thinking while attending Mass I was accepting Catholicism as the container of my thinking.

I now know this ability I have of human self-consciousness, self-conscious knowing, is a skill, not a belief.

No one in my life was behaving toward me as a Mature Elder and guiding me into understanding this teenage change was now possible. That having this ability, I had a responsibility to begin using it. I accidently backed into doing so. It was both in response to the hurt caused by Jim and Larry laughing so profusely at me and my time thinking in the chapel to the point of making a vow with myself to discover "the meaning of life." And choosing the actions that would sustain having it be my priority. In hindsight, I am very thankful to Jim and Larry for laughing at me.

From that day forward, I attended Mass during the lunch period every school day, not only during my remaining three years of high school but also during my years at Creighton University.

I also was not aware I was giving priority to the oneness pattern of thinking, giving priority to priorities. I was also not aware I was giving priority to responding to experience instead of words, the experience of judging I was ignorant of why to do one thing rather than another.

I remember well the day I returned from the noon Mass to the Theater Department at Creighton University and announced to my then dear friend Father Tony Weber, chairman of the department, that I had discovered the most important fundamental belief for one to have: accept every person and thing just the way he, she, or it is. Being unhappy and complaining about the way things are was not only a waste of time, but it was also going the wrong direction. I can't do anything about the way things are. The only sensible thing to do is as a starting point to accept everything just the way it is and then the direction to go is to identify what I can do to make things better and focus on that. This was a good insight and one of many I had identified as wise.

At this point, what I was not aware I was doing was choosing my *fundamental beliefs in words*. In doing so I was maturing into exercising my ability and right at the Adult layer.

As a teenager I had freely chosen many rules. There were rules for relating with my parents, my friends, my girlfriends, my coaches, my theatrical directors, my boss, and others. Now I was focused on identifying a fundamental rule, a *fundamental belief*, I could use at all times, in all places, and in all relationships. I had reached the point we all reach where there are just too many rules, we made them all up, and we can't always remember which one goes with which person. I wanted to find fundamental beliefs I could use at all times, in all places, and in all relationships. This, I now know, is graduating into the Adult layer.

What we are usually not aware of at the time, as I wasn't, is this is moving toward honoring the oneness of the universe: we are choosing a fundamental belief we will honor at all times and in all places (in the reality of oneness).

In the Teen and Adult layers, most of us make the mistake, at least for a period of time, of giving our power to the outside belief to which our parents and community want us to give priority. Parents in the future, who have mastered the skill of mutual mature love, will be sure they do not do this. Instead, they will assist us to primarily study our direct, present, and repeatable by choice experience to identify self-evident truths to guide our lives, to identify inside beliefs that will allow us to master the skill of human self-consciousness. To be a personal scientist. It is fine to remain in the community, religion, philosophical, scientific, or any other community of people as long as they do not prevent us from focusing on mastering this *skill*, of continually maturing in the skills of human self-consciousness and Eldering, the most important *skills* for us to learn.

Was my belief that I should accept everyone and everything as he, she, or it is as a fundamental belief an outside or inside belief? Of course, and without using those words, at the time I thought it was what was earlier defined as an inside belief. I was able to confirm in my direct, present, and repeatable by choice experience that it was an accurate belief. I consistently witnessed that my relationships with others and situations always went better when I began with accepting them or it without judgment or demand for change. This meant it was not only an inside belief but also a skill I had learned. Not the most fundamental inside belief or skill, but it was an inside belief. I was able to consistently confirm it was wise in direct experience.

At the time I was still unaware of the first blind spot of which much of humanity is still not aware. Unconsciously (without choice) I was operating on the assumption the universe operates as separate parts. I now know it is necessary to operate on this assumption in childhood to learn the words of a human language and thereby be self-conscious. Instead of reacting, operating on this inside belief was executing my ability and right to exercise individual free choice. I had fully matured into the Teen and Adult layers but was fully unaware of this context for understanding what was occurring, that I was still unconsciously (without choice) assuming the universe is structured as separate parts.

The above story and the following stories are more fully told in my next book, *Your and My Maturation Stories.* This next story is how I unconsciously (without choice) also backed into discovering the skill of the next layer of maturity, the Elder layer.

The purpose of the stories in my next book, *Your and My Maturation Stories* is to have you take a look at similar experiences like I had to identify the times you probably also backed into the discovery of each layer. This will allow you to understand your life in what may be for you a new way: as primarily the discovery of layers of maturity in the skill of human self-consciousness. It is the mastery of the smaller skills of each layer in the natural sequence that can result in knowing the full skill of human self-consciousness, the skill of mutual mature love.

After my junior year at Creighton University, I entered the Jesuit seminary to become a Catholic priest. When I met with the Admission Officer, Father Haley, I emphasized that my priority was to discover the meaning of life. He assured me that was the priority of the Jesuits as well and I would have the ability to fully apply myself to that task, even able to get a doctorate in philosophy or psychology. That was what I wanted to hear. I was still fully loyal to my priority to discover "the meaning of life."

While in the library at the seminary I discovered a book of prayers by Father Pierre Teilhard de Chardin, a Jesuit priest who had spent much time in the Far East. I loved them. In the back of the book was a bibliography of some of his other books. When I asked the librarian if he had them, he said no and that they would not get them. They did not think they were good for me to read.

When in a meeting about this with the head of the seminary, I was told the same thing.

Suddenly, I realized I was being trained to be a salesperson of their ideas, and the Jesuit priesthood was not a safe place to give priority to discovering the meaning of life.

I returned to Creighton University and, once I was settled back into a dorm room, one night I took a long walk on the circular path in the garden behind the Administration Building. The Jesuits used it while saying the rosary or reading prayers. The transition back to the university was over, and I wanted to think through things to determine what I was to do next to continue my quest.

I first realized not only the Jesuits but nearly everyone I knew was trying to sell me something. The one group I thought I could trust was the Jesuits and I was wrong. This mistake had cost me years of my life. I didn't want that to happen again.

Therefore, I decided I didn't want to again put my trust in anyone else. I saw only one other option. I had to solely go to my direct experience to find the truths I could trust were accurate. In hindsight I can see that I was influenced by science—find truths in experience; but since I could not trust anyone, I also could not trust scientists.

It became crystal clear in my thinking that my only choice to find truths I could know were accurate was to solely study my direct, present, and repeatable by choice experience. I could then always again turn my attention toward my direct experience to confirm they were accurate. I decided to throw out from my thinking all my beliefs, every one of the ones I knew were there and did not know were there, and solely study my direct experience to find the self-evident truths I would choose to use in my thinking to guide my life.

I concluded that this was so important that I made it my second vow with myself.

I also concluded that I would leave the garden with the only two truths I knew from direct experience were accurate: 1) there is always a reason for doing one thing rather than another and 2) I will only study direct experience to find more self-evident truths.

Then, as I was beginning to leave, I had a question emerge: "Am I going to also throw out the believe there is a God?" That stopped me. I decided I needed a few more walks around the garden's circular path to find the answer to that question.

I concluded that I had to also throw out any belief in the existence of a God. This was a hard one to throw out. However, I knew if I held on to even one fundamental belief from the past, I could not consistently confirm is true in direct experience, I was not *solely* going to direct experience to find self-evident truths. I concluded I had to throw it out the window as well. This was hard, I realized, but I knew I had to do it.

I then comfortably left the garden agreeing on only the above two facts I knew from direct experience were accurate. If there was a God, I was confident he, she, or it would at some point show up in direct experience.

What I was not aware was happening in the Jesuit garden was that I was leaving the Adult layer, living according to the beliefs of the Catholic Church in how I should live my life—my parent-substitute, and entering the beginning phase of the Elder layer of maturity in the skill of human self-consciousness. This is when we keep our power, all of it, and give priority to studying our direct, present, and repeatable by choice experience to identify the self-evident truths we will use as inside beliefs in words to guide our thinking.

I would eventually realize, only decades later, the most important one to discover is the fundamental operating process of the universe (nature), that it operates an indivisible whole. This is the discovery that defines the Elder layer. However, I did not know this then.

I was twenty-one years old when I made this second vow with myself. In my judgment now, this is the luckiest thing I backed into doing: keeping my power, all of it, and giving priority to a study of my direct, present, and repeatable by choice experience to discover the fundamental facts, inside beliefs, I would use to guide my thinking.

Years later, after graduating from Creighton University and teaching and directing musicals for two years at Deerfield High School in the suburbs of Chicago—a fun time, I spent a year training the priests, ministers, rabbis, and leaders of their churches and synagogues in the Deerfield and Highland Park communities in positive self-concept skills. This led to a job teaching those skills to students and adults at Saint Leo College north of Tampa, Florida. Teaching these skills was one of the skills I had learned attending many personal growth workshops with my Chicago friend Jack Canfield, later one of the co-authors of the *Chicken Soup for the Soul* series of books.

It was 1969, a year after the Democratic Convention in Chicago that was surrounded by demonstrations and confrontations with police. The demonstrations were mainly against the Vietnam War but also against racism and for women's rights.

In September, just a couple weeks after I arrived, Saint Leo College was the first campus in the US to have demonstrations that school year. It was by students demanding the right for boys to visit girls in the girls' dorms, not anywhere near as significance as the other issues but, given ours were the first demonstrations on a college campus that year, all the major media showed up for a gathering of all the students, faculty, administrators, and town leaders in the gymnasium, nearly 3,000 people, to decide a course of action.

I tell this full amazing story in my next book, *Your and My Maturation Stories.* The conclusion is that I stepped up in the middle of the chaos that resulted when the student body president invited those who wanted to go into the dorms that night to go to one side of the gym and those who wanted to not go into them to go to the other side of the gym. The numbers were evenly divided. Chaos and screaming at each other broke out as the huge bright lights for the television cameras went on, from all three major TV networks at the time—ABC, NBC, and CBS. This encouraged the screaming and chaos even more.

By this time, I had already met a couple of times with my five classes and I had done something dramatic that had them all immediately respect me—I used a skill I had learned to remember all of their names. I stepped into the middle of the chaos, offered to facilitate a process, my students got all the other students to trust me to do it, I did it, and it brought the conflict to a peaceful solution.

This was essential. If there was not a peaceful solution that day, the chairman of the board, who was running for governor of Florida in an election that was only a few weeks in the future and on a law and order platform, had told the Acting President he was going to close down the college. Sister Lucy, the Acting President of the College because the President was in the hospital, had confided this in me just before the gathering in the gym when I sought her out to report on my meeting with the radical professors and students behind the demonstrations. At that moment, she and I were the only people who knew this. She could not act. Therefore, I had to act.

That is why in the chaos I found the courage to offer to facilitate a process to resolve the conflict and make sure I guided it to a peaceful conclusion.

Afterwards, the conservative faculty thought I was irresponsible for only allowing students to speak without adult input and wanted to basically have a faculty court to decide my fate. The President, having returned from the hospital, asked me to take my $12,000 annual salary and leave to put a permanent end to the conflict that would definitely continue if that happened. After much inner conflict that also led me to an important insight, that was rather than stand on a principle I needed to do what was obviously best for all, I ultimately agreed to do leave. For me, this was another indication of the importance of giving priority to direct and present experience instead of what I now label "outside beliefs." Personally, I had a right to defend my actions (an outside belief). However, what was best for the college was for me to leave.

I was soon driving north through the Great Smokey Mountains in Georgia with the goal of rendezvousing with my friend Jack Canfield, who was attending the University of Massachusetts School of Education, to also get a doctorate in humanistic psychology. That was his goal and now my goal also.

I was once again alone. I was also deep in thought about the drama I had just experienced and left. It now felt far behind me, and the feeling of being alone was strong.

In a pervasive rainstorm, I ended up parking my car, walking to be out of sight of the highway, and sitting naked and cross-legged on a rock overlooking rivers flowing in two valleys that seemed to be a mile below me. I had taken my clothes off and hid them under a rock so they would not get wet. This entire story in also in my next book, *Your and My Maturation Stories.*

Ultimately, I decided to say the word "God" as if he, she, or it was real just to see how I would feel if I did it. It was to be another one of my experiments of going to my direct and present experience to find self-evident truths.

I wanted to see what feelings and experiences would arise inside me when I said that word as if there actually is a God. It was now more than four years since I had thrown the belief in God out the window and I hadn't had a thought about it since.

Would it feel real to act like there is a God when I said the word "God"? I wanted to know in direct experience if it would.

I was also clear that "I" was not going to say the word. I was going to wait until my "physical body" wanted to say the word and it spoke it. That, I believed, would result in an experience that would help me know whether or not God is real. Without being aware of its importance as I am now, I was giving priority to experience to find the facts, inside beliefs, I would use in words in my thinking to guide my thinking.

I waited a number of minutes watching the welling up inside my body for it to say the word God. I was aware of actually witnessing the building up inside my physical body occurring.

I did nothing. I just watched.

When my physical body finally spoke the word "God," at that exact instant there was thunder and lightning like I had never seen or heard before! It pounded, cracked, and screamed not just for seconds but for a couple minutes! It was extremely and continuously loud. It filled the entire sky of low clouds and fog with its thundering and flashes of lightening.

I realize it was just a coincidence and nothing to get excited about. I had a hardy laugh at the coincidence.

When my delight in what happened came to an end, I went back to doing my experiment. I did not think I should build a church or anything like that. I knew it was just an amazing coincidence. I went back to doing my experiment.

Again, "I" was not going to say the word God. I was only going to let my "physical body" say it when it was ready to do so. I could again feel the energy to do it welling up inside me. I again did nothing but watch the building occurring. After a few minutes of this, my physical body spoke the word God.

Again, in that instant, the world blew up in the exact same way with continuous roaring, screaming, crackling, and pounding of thunder and lightning like I had never seen and heard before filling the sky with its extremely loud thunders again for a long time, not just moments but again for a couple minutes.

I suddenly realized that the welling up inside me to say the word God and the welling up of nature to pop into thunder and lightning were the same welling up!

I instantly realized I had just had the direct experience the universe operates as one thing! It is not just an idea in words! It is a fact. It is a truth.

At the time, I had no idea what to do with this knowledge. None. I had no awareness of the relationship between a human language and the indivisibility of the universe (nature). I had no knowledge of what I now know are my blind spots as a result of learning a human language. And I had no awareness of the existence of layers of maturity of the skill of human self-consciousness that, once mastered, result in the skill of mutual mature love. All I knew was I had just had a direct, immediate, and full *experience* that the universe is an indivisible whole and that is a fact, a self-evident truth. I simply added it to my pile of self-evident truths that I was accumulating.

Most important, it was not just an idea in words. It was a self-evident truth. I couldn't repeat that experience at will, but I was certain that experience had convinced me that the universe was one thing, an indivisible whole.

In hindsight, I can now see that I wasn't even including me in that one thing. My Catholic upbringing that had conditioned me to live for others instead of for myself had me also unconsciously (without choice) assume I was not a part of the oneness of nature. My job was to be in service to it. I would only discover this very personal and unconscious blind spot within me much later.

This instantly became the most important self-evident truth I had discovered in direct and present experience, what I now know was using personal science. From this point on I would know this is accurate knowledge, an inside belief, although I did not have in my thinking an understanding of the difference between inside and outside beliefs.

By this time, I had read many books on Buddhism, Daoism, Zen, and many other Eastern religions, but this felt very different. I greatly valued what I had learned from them and meditating, but as hard as they all tried to escape whatever they were trying to escape and into what they called "enlightenment," none of it had had as profound an effect on me and my thinking as much as this experience in the Great Smokey Mountains of Georgia.

I knew I had just had the direct experience of the oneness of nature. It was a direct self-conscious experience of it: I knew I was experiencing it while I was experiencing it. This, I did not know at the time, is the beginning of mastering the smaller skill of the Elder layer. I now assist others to know it by inviting them to give priority to their direct experience when answering the 7 questions.

From that point forward, everything else I had read or listened to about oneness could not approach being equal to my direct experience of it In my words in my thinking I represented it as " The universe is an indivisible whole." Only much later would I change it to be: "The universe operates as an indivisible whole."

From that day forward, it became my most important inside belief. It is what led me, over the next forty-eight years, into the discovery of all the other inside beliefs I am sharing with you in these books.

My third and final vow with myself, thus far, did not occur until I was fifty-five years old. Here is how it came about.

When in January 2000 I read Ben & Jerry's ice cream company, the most well-known of our socially responsible companies of the last decades of the twentieth century, was about to be bought by a multinational corporation I did not respect, I called Ben Cohen. He is the Ben of Ben & Jerry's who I knew enough to be comfortable giving him a call. I had been a founder of the Calvert Social Funds, one of our other well-known socially responsible businesses at that time. I had an idea. I wanted to see if Ben thought my suggestion would be helpful. This led to the two of us teaming up in a way that ultimately resulted in us orchestrating a purchase by Unilever, a far more responsible multinational, that allowed Ben & Jerry's to remain the only independent company owned by it. Our board, now with me now on it, would choose its own future board members. And most important, we signed a legal contract that, using specific measurements, allowed us to continue primarily being a socially responsible company forever. Of the many socially responsible companies that got so big they needed to be bought by a multinational, we were the only one to accomplish this. (This very dramatic and edifying story is also fully told in my next book, *Your and My Maturation Stories*.)

A couple months afterwards, the CEO of Unilever journeyed from London to Burlington, Vermont, spoke to our 500 employees, met with the board, and then the board and he went to dinner. I sat next to him and during the couple hours of dinner we got to know each other quite well.

At the end of the evening, drinking decaf coffee, I decided that our relationship had become so comfortable and mutually respectful that I judged it would be acceptable to ask him the question that I had the greatest desire to ask. So, I asked it.

"I would like to ask you a question," I began, "and I would understand if you choose to not answer it. It is a very difficult question. But I do not often get to be in a conversation with the CEO of a $60 billion-dollar multinational corporation. Therefore, I would like to ask it."

"Sure," he replied with great confidence, "What is it?"

"I believe that when a person achieves full maturity in the skill of human self-consciousness, he or she freely chooses to give priority to the common good. Throughout history this has been labeled 'moral behavior.' Do you agree with this?"

"Yes, of course!" he replied.

"Well the highest priority of Unilever is the financial interests of a few people called the 'shareholders.' I see this as an immoral contract with the state. What do you think we should do about this?"

The following are his exact words in reply.

"That is not my business. I am here for four or five years. My job is to increase the value to the shareholders. What you are talking about is not my business."

I had become so comfortable with him that I looked him directly and calmly in the eyes and said, "Are you telling me there is no human being running Unilever? That you too work for the immoral contract?"

He gave me the exact same answer.

"That is not my business. I am here for four or five years. My job is to increase the value to the shareholders. What you are talking about is not my business."

I went into a state of shock.

Fortunately, sensing discomfort, Pierre Ferrari, a fellow board member, asked him something about soccer in England.

I suddenly realized there is no way a person could consistently graduate up the hierarchy of a multinational corporation if he or she is not devoted, like one is devoted to a religion, to the belief that the highest priority of a corporation is the financial interests of its shareholders. I also realized that some of the most powerful organizations on Earth, multinational corporations, are full of people committed to this immoral priority. I also realized that this places

Earth in great danger, not just environmentally but in every way including using their financial power to advocate within governments to support this priority of corporations and even, for some, going to war to make money selling more weapons or providing drugs they know are not best for people.

The rest of the evening I was in shock at his answer. Everything else that happened until I was in my hotel room was within a blur. Yes, there were governments that are very powerful where the highest priority is self-interest, not building and sustaining a moral order; but I had just heard one of the most powerful people in our Democratic West saying the same thing. I was permanently agitated, discombobulated, flummoxed, and add whatever disruptive word you want to add to that list, and unable to sleep.

The next day, I was thinking deeply about this while driving the three hours from Burlington, Vermont to my home in Western Massachusetts. It resulted in me making my third and last, thus far, vow with myself. This, I judged, was another insight that necessitated action at the level of a vow.

My priority the next years of my life would be to figure out "how to mature capitalism into moral capitalism," what I came to label "common good capitalism" and eventually wrote a book with that name.

Over the years of overseeing our Calvert Social Funds, I had become aware the foundation of capitalism was *free markets*, which is an honoring of the Teen layer of maturity: the ability and right to exercise individual free choice. The priority is not capital making more money for the owners of capital. That is secondary to honoring individual freedom in free markets and is why communist countries have allowed for the emergence of free market capitalism under state control, "state capitalism." I recognized that for them it was maturing their societies into honoring to some degree the Teen layer of maturity while also maintaining strong parental control as the container to make sure it did not go in an immature direction as we know teenage behavior can often easily go. (I am not suggesting this is the way they think about it. In my judgment, it is what is either self-consciously or unconsciously—without choice—used to justify the continuation of the paternalistic system as the container of free market economic activities in their nations.)

In my judgment, our Earth society is in transition into the Elder layer. While still operating at the Teen layer, China is leaning toward maintaining paternal control, and the US is leaning toward allowing as little restriction as possible on the exercise of individual freedom.

Neither has matured into giving priority to maturation instead of competition, cooperation for maturation being the priority at the highest two layers. However, I judge they are both now ready to mature into mastering the full skill of human self-consciousness.

Also, now that we live in a global village, they will have to do it together. Neither has discovered the relationship between human languages and the indivisibility of the universe. Neither has discovered that self-consciousness can be used as our sixth sense of self-conscious knowing. Neither has discovered this skill is a complex skill with layers of smaller skills, and those skills, unlike beliefs, are the same for everyone. However, now that Earth is one village, eventually they are going to be discovering and embracing this wisdom together. They are the next layer of maturity in this skill for both of them, and skills are the same for everyone.

I knew I had been a deep student of spirituality, psychology, philosophy, science, economics, business, finance, politics, and social activism. I knew none of those disciplines had unraveled this riddle. I knew there had to be something we were all missing. I did not know what it was, but I concluded I was one of the people on Earth capable of attending to the task of finding what we still did not understand about life that has us stuck in these immature ways of being with each other. What is it that has our leaders, and many of us, comfortably operate in such an immoral way? Some even think it is moral to give priority to the self-interest of our physical bodies at the expense of others. For instance, nearly all of us who invest are comfortable with most companies still giving priority to the financial returns to shareholders.

I had done many different kinds of spiritual retreats and read nearly every major book on the different religions. I had studied the history of philosophy. I had been trained to be a psychotherapist and for years in Western Massachusetts I ran an adult psychological growth center like Esalen in Big Sur, CA. In the 1970s, I had been one of the pioneers of socially responsible business and investing, leading a group of leaders from around the country in meetings once a month for over a year to write one of the first set of social screens for business and investing. In 1982, this led me to teaming up with Wayne Silby and John Guffey to create the Calvert Family of Socially Responsible Mutual Funds, the first family of such funds now with $17 billion under management in over forty mutual funds. I had also taken the lead to create our Calvert Foundation, recently re-named Calvert Impact Capital, that has lent over $2.5 billion around the world at low interest rates to reduce poverty. I had been the founder and Chairman of my town's Democratic Committee and represented us at annual state conventions. I had taken the lead to orchestrate the $342-million-dollar purchase of Ben & Jerry's by Unilever, working closely with the firms that were part of the process: Goldman Sachs, the largest investment banking firm on Wall Street, and Skadden Arps, and largest merger and acquisition law firm in the world.

I realized I was familiar with the thinking of all of these communities and none of them had solved this problem. I also realized I was financially able to turn my major attention to solving this fundamental crisis within humanity. Therefore, I judged I had a moral imperative to do so.

I also realized that I had to isolate myself from the thinking of all of these other schools of thought.

Their thoughts would distract me from solely going to my direct, present, and repeatable by choice experience to find the still unknown solution. Driving home it was abundantly clear to me that there had to be something none of us had discovered that was the answer, a mutual blind spot. Therefore, I had to isolate myself so when I discovered one piece of it, I could remain with it while I found another piece of it without the disruption to my thinking of having to dialogue with others about it. Conventional wisdom would surely not honor it when I had not yet found all the pieces to the puzzle. I had to be free to find the new pieces, their relationship with one another, and put them together into a more mature form of free markets before I could reveal it to others.

When I got home, I resigned from some of the boards I was on and only remained on the boards of Calvert Funds, Calvert Impact Capital, Ben & Jerry's, and my local United Way. Over the next eighteen years my priority was thinking and writing as the linear discipline to find the answer to this question. I also knew I needed to find my way to represent it in words that would be ease for people to understand and use.

I soon discovered, as I had already been discovering, that without a more mature understanding of how we mature as human beings, I would just be selling another theory. To have the solution be irresistible, I had to ground it in a deeper understanding of how we each mature. Once we know it, we can't resist embracing the smaller skill of each next layer of maturity in the skill of human self-consciousness. Maturation is the fundamental process in nature and can't be escaped.

I eventually wrote three books, *The Love Skill: We Are Each Mastering the 7 Layers of Human Maturity*, *Common Good Capitalism Is Inevitable: It is the only economic model that both builds on free markets and represents our next layer of maturity in the skill of self-consciousness*, and *Eldering: What We Do Between Enlightenment and Death*. Yet inside I knew I had still not found the deepest answer to the question. Therefore, I didn't promote the sale of those books.

I now know I have found the deepest answer, the mutually agreed upon illusion we are still unconsciously (without choice) assuming is real. The correction is understanding the relationship between human languages and the indivisibility of the universe. It is knowing as a result of not understanding this relationship, nearly all of us have been giving priority to outside beliefs in words ignorant of the fact we have created an inner conflict: we think we have exercised individual free choice by choosing and give priority to obeying our outside belief and unaware this is in conflict with the continuation of our ability and right to exercise individual free choice. We no longer have our power. It is where we think we have freely given it: in an outside belief in words. This unknown inner conflict is the result of unconsciously (without choice) operating on the illusion the universe is separate parts when it is an indivisible whole. As a result of now fully unraveling this riddle, I will promote the sale of this book and later re-write the above books to include what I didn't know when I wrote them.

Finally, at the age of seventy-two, I found the final piece that gave me the full answer. Of course, where I found it was not at all where I thought I would find it. I again backed into it.

When lacking the assistance of Mature Elders, this backing into it is the way we usually discover the smaller skill of each next layer of maturity. It is always very different from the smaller skill of the last layer or it wouldn't be the next layer. We are also still thinking it is important to give priority to the smaller skill of the current highest layer we know. It was the last choice that brought us greater happiness in our lives. Without a Mature Elder to guide us, we are not aware there are layers of maturity of the skill of human self-consciousness and, therefore, what is the next layer. We are unconsciously (without choice) operating on the self-consciously known and chosen assumption that the skill of our currently highest known layer is the skill of the highest layer.

I had been in a men's group that met at my home every Tuesday evening for the previous twenty-two years. It was the result of all of us having gone through the New Warrior Training Adventure Weekend of The ManKind Project community of men. (This is a wonderful organization, and this is a weekend training every man would be wise to attend, www.mkp.org). My ex-wife and I had ended our twenty-year marriage in 2001 in a way that had us remain the best of friends. It was now 2016, I had over the previous fifteen years tried to create another relationship with three women, and all had ended without becoming the joyful committed relationship I was seeking. The men in the group laughed at me when I declared that I was not going to hunt for a woman, but I would be open to exploring a relationship if one that was a possibility showed up. They thought I should get on Match.com and be aggressive about seeking a committed relationship with a woman. My priority was to unravel the capitalism riddle, not to find a woman. Secondly, and more important, I knew I would *experientially* know it when I saw it and it was best to not have any distractions from that potentiality. I would then be fully free and undistracted from recognizing it when it showed up as a possibility with a woman. I had at times tried Match.com and such and found them not a fit for me. Their priority for the possibility of romantic love was primarily using words and pictures. I wanted the priority for the possibility to be experience.

One night I arrived early at our local grade school gym to play basketball, which, since 1980, for 38 years, I have usually played Monday and Wednesday nights each week. There is a women's exercise class before our game and two women were still standing by the stage end of the court talking. My attention immediately went to the shorter woman. As I walked toward them looking into her eyes, I was aware of the experience of love, of oneness, happening within, around, and through both of us. I recognized it as such immediately.

Then the following words came into my thinking: "she had a loving mother and she loves loving." This experience and those words emerged in my thinking as the two of us, comfortably and fully receptively, continued looking into each other's eyes as I walked toward her.

As I talked with her and the other woman, this mutually-self-consciously-known-experience-of-oneness continued to be present. I made sure to privately give it priority, *what we were mutually experiencing,* while I talked with the two of them. It easily remained present the entire time as the "experience container" of what was occurring while we talked and as they left the gym.

So much so that I had to ask for her name a second time.

While playing basketball that night I realized we had mutually had the experience of oneness, of love, and that was what was most important, a love at first sight experience. I had found a woman with whom *that experience* could be naturally, effortlessly, and consistently present. I committed to giving her a call. More important, I committed to doing something I had never done before.

I would consistently give priority to the experience of love, which I now knew as the self-consciously known experience of oneness, we mutually experienced in our first moments together.

Her name is Lucy. I met her in my seventy-second year. By then I believed I had mastered all the layers up to and including the Elder layer. It is where through personal science I had identified the important self-evident truths and had them accurately represented in the words I was using in my thinking. I thought I had also mastered the last layer, the Mature Elder layer; but, as you will discover, I actually hadn't.

As an exercise, I had long ago mastered the skill of guiding another person into the self-conscious experience of the oneness of nature with me, what you will be guided into knowing with a person you choose in *Chapter 8: Mutual Mature Love Experience*. However, I wasn't able to have it be my priority at all times. I was meditating and training myself to unilaterally do it, but it wasn't easy and becoming a habit.

I now know that the Mutual Mature Love Experience you will be guided into in *Chapter 8* is an exercise. It is something we are doing at a particular time and in a particular place.

It is not doing it at all times and in all places (in the reality of oneness) as a skill with at least one other person. This, I now know, is the primary attraction of romantic love.

We are each seeking to know the self-conscious experience of oneness at all times and in all places (in the reality of oneness) beginning with one other person. Then we can expand it into knowing it with others in community. Then we can expand it into knowing it with others by associating our community with like-thinking communities into an agreement nation. We accept the responsibility of doing this because we know we are all in this together as parts of an indivisible whole and need to begin to all self-consciously, by choice, relate that way with each other.

We cannot easily experience it as real alone. That was what I was trying to do. What I did not know was, *initially,* it can only be easily discovered in a relationship with another person and *easily sustained* in a relationship with another person. As stated above, this is the real, and today not widely known, fundamental attraction of romantic love.

Human language is a *mutually agreed-upon illusion tool.* It allows us to be self-conscious. Therefore, language has to be present to know the experience of oneness as a self-conscious experience. At the same time, since its assumption of separate parts is not real, we need to be giving priority to the experience of oneness and *simultaneously giving second priority to the words* that allow it to be a self-conscious experience. Human language is a relationship experience, the use of a mutually known and agreed-upon illusion tool.

Therefore, at least initially to learn it is possible, this experience necessitates relating with another person!

The search for consistently moving as one with one other person, usually romantic love, is part of the process of mastering the last layer of maturity of the skill of human self-consciousness. Initially we can only know it as continuously executing a skill in a relationship with another person! This is why Lucy coming into my life was essential. I was finally willing to take the risk to give priority to experience instead of words.

The mutually agreed-upon illusion tool of human language needs to be fully present, and second in priority, for us to experience self-conscious oneness as real.

We learn each layer in a natural progression, one at a time. We can only learn the next one when we have mastered the last one and turned it into a habit. Only then will it be habitually sustained as part of who we are when we turn our attention to the discovery and mastery of the next smaller skill.

It is the fundamental process of maturation in nature that motivates us to continue this maturation process. That is why I took the logical risk to give priority to experience when Lucy and I had the love at first sight experience.

What allowed me to comfortably and consistently give priority to the experience of love with Lucy was my understanding of all of this *in words* at the Elder layer. I had mastered the smaller skill of that layer, understanding all of this and representing it in words that work for me. And, I had turned it into a habit. Therefore, I was fully ready to have my attention on the discovery of the next layer, the Mature Elder layer: consistently giving priority to experience instead of words. I intellectually, in words, knew it was giving priority to experience over words while fully allowing the latter to be present, *but I had not had an opportunity to do this consistently with another person.*

When Lucy came into my life, I had the opportunity. I immediately jumped to give it a try. (I now want every teenager and older person to know this skill before he or she has the experience of love at first sight that is what Lucy and I were experiencing.)

It was the mastery of all of this in words at the Elder layer that allowed me to fully, comfortably, and consistently give priority to the experience of love when it showed up as a possibility with Lucy. Privately, I chose to consistently give the experience we were experiencing priority to see what would happen.

I made sure all the words spoken were second in priority to sustaining the giving of priority to that experience. That was why I had to ask for her name a second time!

I later learned that when they got to the parking lot, the other woman, Kathy Carey, told Lucy, "He is very attracted to you. He is going to give you a call." Kathy saw what was happening. Lucy responded, "I don't think he will," but admitted to Kathy she was aware of the attraction between the two of us, two people in their early seventies.

With the other three women with whom I explored a committed relationship since my marriage I had always waited for the right time to share with them my ideas about love in words.

My priority was words. Ideas in words. And I did not know my priority was always words. (Sorry, Amber, Jan, and Bec, now all friends.)

This time, I resolved, I would give priority to the *experience of oneness* we had naturally and effortlessly experienced in our first meeting and see where it went. I trusted that if I did this the *mutually chosen words* to understand it would show up in the right way and at the right time. I now know the only mistake I could make would be to accidently slide into giving priority to words.

I resolved to let the *self-consciously known together experience of oneness* lead me. I now know I was letting the fundamental process in nature of cooperation for maturation lead me. Doing so allowed Lucy and I to directly, consistently, and self-consciously experience mutual mature love.

We knew we were mutually experiencing it while we were experiencing it.

While driving the next day to New York City for a board meeting of PCI Media, I telephoned Lucy. We talked for over an hour. The next day, we also talked for over an hour on my drive home. Within two weeks I was sleeping at her home every night. It was down the road from mine.

At all times I made sure to give priority to the self-consciously known and able-to-be-chosen experience of oneness I had with her the first moment we met. I loved that I was able to do it. She also loved it. Whenever I found myself losing it as my priority, I immediately was able to again choose it as my consistent highest priority. I now knew the distinction between giving priority to words or experience. When she would leave it, she also became aware she had and consistently chose to give priority again to the experience of love she knew we were experiencing.

As I write this it is more than two years later. Mutually choosing to give it priority has made it easy for each of us to continue doing it and getting better at it. I have been very self-consciously using the oneness pattern of thinking, giving priority to it. She had been riding inside my ability to do that until about a year and a half into the relationship. You will read the story of how that changed into a mutually known skill below.

There is much more I tell about this beautiful love story in my next book, *Your and My Maturation Stories*. However, here is the important point to make here.

Using my sixth sense of self-conscious knowing, with Lucy I discovered how to consistently give priority to unbroken-up-into-parts-experience that is always present and is oneness. I could experience its presence, especially when relating with Lucy.

I now know experience is oneness. It is always present, can't be escaped, and is always not broken up into parts except in our thinking, called "words." Everything is always occurring within experience. It is only in the mutually agreed upon illusion of separate parts that we perceive particular experiences as different and separate parts of the universe. I now know separate experiences do not exist accept in the mutually agreed upon illusion tool of human languages. Only oneness is real. This is hard to grasp until we have mastered all seven layers and experienced the consistent joy of Eldering, but what I have discovered when known and given priority is it is what results in the consistent experience of natural confidence and the feeling of contented joy.

By this time, I knew it was possible and how it was possible, but I didn't know how to consistently do it with another person. This was primarily because I did not have another person who was ready and able to consistently do it with me.

Then Lucy showed up!

The desire for romantic love is the desire to achieve full maturity in this skill. It is the desire to know the joy of consistently giving priority to the self-conscious experience of oneness with at least one other person. All the time giving second priority to words so we can know we are doing it *self-consciously together.*

Only this affirms for each of us oneness is real, and it can be consistently experienced (at all times and in all places—in the reality of oneness) as a mutual self-conscious choice experience, the mutual mature love skill.

Initially, it can only be a mutually known skill in a relationship with another person. Cooperation for maturation inside each of us is primarily using the attraction of romantic love for this purpose.

If we are able to operate at the Mature Elder layer because we have mastered the lower layers and turned them into habits, we can then, and only then, recognize we can not only directly know this with another person or group of people; but we can also know it in the world at all times and in all places (in the reality of oneness) when with people who do not know it, regardless of their layers of maturity.

I think of mutual mature love as a "wavelength" I now know. I now always choose to give priority to participating in this wavelength by choice, as a skill.

However, without first discovering its existence with another person, we do not know where it is. Once we do discover it with another person, we know where it is and can learn as a skill to give it priority at all times and in all places (in the reality of oneness) from that point forward. It is always present and able to be participated in. It is the wavelength of cooperation for maturation, the fundamental process, priority, and activity of nature.

Our personal maturation was only the beginning of our lives. From full maturity in this skill forward our priority is the maturation of the rest of who we are, the universe. It is now our mature self-interest.

It is giving priority to unbroken-up-into-parts-experience, the oneness of nature. Now that we know where it is, we can unilaterally and privately choose to participate in it at all times and in all places (in the reality of oneness). Privately and without a need to talk about it, we can also do it with all other people regardless of the level of maturity they have mastered. This skill is particularly essential for raising children.

However, without mastering the smaller skills of the six lower layers, we cannot discover and sustain with one other person the smaller skill of the Mature Elder layer. Also, without mastering it with one other person, we cannot learn to unilaterally and privately give priority to participating in the mutual mature love wavelength that is everywhere at all times. It is only when we have mastered the smaller skills of all six lower layers that we are not easily distracted into giving priority to the priority of one of them, the only mistake we can make. We now know each of them, their relationship of priorities with each other, and unhappiness of giving priority to any one of them: sensations, differences and feelings, wants, exercising free choice, or giving priority to an outside or inside belief in words.

Mastering the smaller skill of giving priority to experience, to unbroken-up-into-parts-experience, is mastering the last layer of maturity of the skill of human self-consciousness, the Mature Elder layer. Until I met Lucy, it was only words in my thinking; but I thought it was a skill. Only by actually doing it as a skill and by choice with Lucy did I discover the Mature Elder layer as a skill instead of words in my thinking.

Initially, it is only possible to know it *as a consistent experience* with another person. It is the mutually, consistently, and self-consciously known experience of oneness, mutual mature love, and knowingly giving it priority over words while fully comfortable with words being present. Only then can we extend it into our relationships with others.

When I met Lucy, I was comfortable with my self-definition being "I am first the indivisible universe that will not die and secondly my physical body that will die." (Notice again I am giving priority to using the oneness pattern of thinking, giving priority to priorities, and second priority to the separate parts pattern of thinking.)

As Lucy and I began spending more time together each day, and I sustained giving priority to unbroken up into parts experience, I noticed six things I had not anticipated:

Six Things I Discovered
When Lucy and I Sustained Mutual Mature Love

1. Everything else was experienced as trivial.

2. I discovered what I now call "the eternal now" in contrast to the "material now."

3. The *experience* of local oneness and universal oneness is the same.

4. My highest priority is now Eldering: each moment wherever I am sitting or standing giving priority to my judgment of the best thing for me to do for the maturation of the rest of me, the universe (nature).

5. I discovered natural morality.

6. I have access to information directly from unbroken-up-in-to-parts-experience, the oneness of nature, that has access to all the information that exists. It is downloaded into words. It is not information that begins, processes in, and ends using words.

First, everything else was experienced as trivial. Wow! Was this experienced wonderful!

In my romantic relationships in the past, particularly with my previous wife, we were always giving priority to issues, issues always expressed in words, and didn't know we were giving priority to words. We were not only trapped in the illusion of words, but we were also trapped in processing our issues in words. We got so sick of this there were long periods of time when we simply lived parallel lives, with some emotional distance between us, so we could more easily ignore the discomfort. We had gone to therapy and had so often processed our issues with our friends they were no longer willing to do it with us.

We were lost in the illusion that giving priority to words was wise.

In my first moments with Lucy I was so thrilled to be in the self-conscious *experience of oneness with her* I realized later I had given almost no attention to her physical appearance. In fact, I had given little attention to anything else those first weeks. I eventually discovered something even more interesting: whatever behaviors of hers I eventually identified and did not like were experienced as trivial.

They were not "issues" I put into words and privately thought about as issues!

As I watched this experience further, it was so beautiful I didn't want to ever leave it to talk to her about anything that came into my thinking I judge would be wise for her to change. I didn't want to risk doing something that would end the beauty I was experiencing. What made this easy to do was everything else seemed so trivial in comparison to the joy of giving priority to the consistently and self-consciously known experience of mutual mature love.

Of course, I eventually sought appropriate times to share something with her I would like her to take a look at, but they were few and I did not have a need for her to change in the way I suggested but to only hear me.

To the great surprise of some of the men in my Men's Group, this experience of mutual mature love is more important than anything else, including having sex. We enjoy our sexual times with each other, but it is not a need. Nothing is a need! Everything seems to come and go as we mutually let it happen enjoying *every moment* rather than having it have to be expressed sexually or any other way in some particular future moments.

This was my first new discovery: knowing together the mutual self-conscious experience of oneness has everything else experienced as trivial. I did not expect this to occur, but I loved it when it happened.

The second unexpected discovery was what I now call "the eternal now" in contrast to the "material now." The latter is something between the past and the future. The eternal now is all past, all present, and all future as one experience. I began thinking of my time with Lucy as in the eternal now. Therefore, with the eternal now as my priority I had no need to deal with anything in the past or seek anything in the future.

This freed me to be fully present each moment by giving priority to the self-conscious experience of oneness, to that wavelength. I now knew there is nothing more important to do with my thinking. All else became handled as secondary, always secondary.

This had me fully present with no agenda and free to enjoy mutual mature love as the container of whatever was going on. The fact Lucy loved it made it easy to continue choosing this set of priorities. I also found myself fully comfortable doing all the things that were important to her. For instance, our homes are deep in the woods and I had not locked the doors to my home for nearly thirty years. She had grown up in Colombia and needed every door locked at all times. I had no difficulty switching to keeping them locked.

Thus, my second unexpected discovery was giving priority to the eternal now and second priority to the material now also made it easier to experience everything other than our mutual mature love as trivial.

The third unexpected discovery was the *experience* of local oneness and universal oneness is the same experience. Let me explain.

Lucy did not understand any of this in words, but I knew she would be able to learn the words and skills as we all can. What was important was that she was a person who loved loving and did intuitively know the experience of loving from having had a loving mother and being a mother herself. She has two children, both now in their forties. I quickly discovered that what had been downloaded directly from unbroken up experience the moment I met her, what we usually label "intuition," was accurate. Her mother lived to be ninety-five and was so loved by everyone in the large family that they created a cookbook not only with her favorite recipes but also with a different picture of her on the opposite page and a piece of writing by each family member describing why they loved her.

For Lucy, her "biggest whole" was her family: her children, her grandchildren, her sisters, and their children. And for her, initially our love was only surrounding the two of us, a two-person "whole."

It was observing this that had me discover with Lucy something else very important I had never imagined.

Regardless of where our attention is focused, the experience of oneness is the same if the priority there is the assumption of oneness.

Each morning Lucy and I make breakfast together, eggs topped with chopped stir-fried vegetables. Once seated at the kitchen table, and before eating it, we hold hands and look into each other's eyes. For a few minutes, we do this consistently, comfortably, and receptively. Eyes-to-eyes, we directly enjoy the self-conscious experience of mutual mature love we know with each other. We rest our eyes in the eyes of the other, self-consciously together enjoying the experience of mutual mature love. (If you have a lover and do not at times enjoy this experience with each other, I am sure you would like to know this experience with him or her. My hope is this book will assist the two of you to do this, or something like it, each morning as well.)

For the first year, while we were doing this, I would sometimes state what I understood to be occurring: "We are being totally receptive because there is nothing to fear, we know we are doing it while we are doing it, and we are defining ourselves as all that exists, the universe." Lucy was fully comfortable with the first two statements, but not with the third. When I would say the third phrase, her eyes would become glassy and leave me. Those words did not compute in her way of thinking.

I quickly learned that I needed to change the third phrase to be, "and we know local oneness." While saying it I would move my hand around the two of us to indicate I was defining only the two of us as one thing. That she fully understood and was then fully comfortable experiencing self-consciously chosen oneness with me.

What I discovered was this. Since she was still unconsciously (without choice) assuming separate parts exist, she could understand the two of us being in a self-consciously chosen oneness experience ("a whole") but did not know the option was available of the direct mutual self-conscious experience of universal oneness, the real oneness.

However, what I discovered was the *actual experience of oneness* is the same wherever we are focusing our attention and choosing to give priority to oneness. When with her in local oneness the *experience* was the same as being in mutual self-conscious universal oneness.

The *experience of oneness*, I discovered with Lucy, is the same experience regardless of where our attention is focused *as long as we are giving priority to oneness, to unity, to team where it is focused*. It is what is real and can be experienced anywhere at any time. It can be a *mutually known self-conscious experience* anywhere and at any time wherever two or more people choose to give priority to being aware of it *where their mutual attention is focused*.

When assuming separate parts are real, and whether or not we are aware of it each moment, what is always most important is where our attention is focused. Oneness is always present; it can't be escaped. It also has us always giving priority to priorities in our thinking. Therefore, oneness can be fully self-consciously experienced wherever each of us is, or a group of us are, *mutually focusing our attention*.

When with Lucy in these moments before eating our breakfast, this made it easy for me to be in universal oneness while she was in local oneness: *the experience was the same!*

This also made it easy for me to discover again the beauty and joy of Eldering.

I knew Lucy would eventually know universal oneness the way a father knows his one-year-old child will learn to walk and later learn a human language. I was not *primarily* with Lucy's ignorance of the higher layers because it had no effect upon me. I was also able to enjoy Eldering without any experience of superiority. (As described in *Chapter 1: The 7 Questions*, Mahatma Gandhi discovered this is always giving priority to the primary good intention of each person because about that they do not have choice. It is also who they know themselves to primarily be. Therefore, they feel seen by us. There is also no experience of superiority because we are coming from and speaking to who we know we both are, the oneness of nature.)

What made it easy was that I knew she was primarily giving priority to the oneness pattern of thinking and just did not know it. Whether or not we are aware of it we are always doing this. Oneness is real and can't be escaped. That is why we are consistently pulled toward cooperation for maturation and being moral.

She was only applying it to where she was focusing her attention.

Therefore, the experience we were able to mutually experience was the same experience, the mutual experience of the oneness of nature happening where our attention was focused, on our relationship.

We can eventually discover that being at one only with where our attention is focused is one of the last unconscious (without choice) sustaining of the illusion of separate parts.

The experience is, indeed, the same; but we now know the universe operates as an indivisible whole. Therefore, discovering that experience is the experience of oneness everywhere and not only where our attention is focused is the final step in mastering the Mature Elder layer.

Immature love is thinking it is between two or more noses; mutual mature love is knowing the love we are experiencing is the mutual awareness and experience of the oneness of nature that is everywhere.

With Lucy I had my third wonderful discovery. The local experience of oneness, where we are focusing our attention, and the universal experience of oneness *is the same experience.*

The fourth thing I discovered with Lucy I knew intellectually but now it became a moral imperative inside me. I was no longer primarily interested in spending my retirement sitting on the beach, playing golf, or traveling to see different parts of the world I had not seen. My highest priority is now Eldering: each moment, wherever I am sitting or standing, giving priority to my judgment of the best thing for me to do for the maturation of the rest of me, the universe (nature). Not just each moment but to also identify the best thing I can do with my talents and opportunities.

That is why I am writing this book. It is what I judge to be my best contribution to the maturation of us all. Therefore, my greatest joy, that which sustains the inner experience of natural confidence and the feeling of contented joy, is when I am giving it priority in my life. When I am done writing these books I will primarily teach and, if others join me, we will build the Chrysalis Nation, Trusts for All Children, Common Good Capitalism Movement, Maturation Movement, and other organizations described herein. And I will do my best to do it in a way that after my death they easily continue to thrive and serve humanity's maturation process.

Of course, Lucy and I enjoy going to dinner at a restaurant with friends, babysitting the grandchildren, and traveling particularly to learn things we want to learn and visit family. However, I do not think of retirement the way it is often thought of today, as primarily finding personal pleasures.

For me retirement is primarily Eldering. It is being a direct self-conscious participant in what is primarily going on around here: cooperation for maturation.

I am thinking as I write this of all of my fellow baby boomers, many of whom were social activists in the 1960s and 1970s, who are now retiring. They are a huge group of talented people who will live longer and in good health than people in the past. They have the potential to complete the process of Eldering themselves into full maturity in the skill of human self-consciousness which was what we were seeking to accomplish back in the 1960s and 1970s whether or not we were aware of it. We have now spent decades playing the roles of father, mother, and participants in our workplaces and communities.

It is now time to Elder, to enjoy the greatest personal pleasure.

Of course, I am also thinking of the younger generations as well. In the 1960s, the intentions of our generation were so beautifully high, but we did not know how to Elder ourselves into the smaller skills of the layers of maturity in the natural sequence to achieve mature love as a mutually known skill. As a result, our divorce rate has been high. Our current younger generations have the option either to not marry until they both know this skill or mature their marriages to where the two of them mutually know this skill while still young. You are not stuck in the ignorance we had and each day there will be more Mature Elders who can be of assistance.

Fundamentally, what is going on is oneness is being self-conscious through us.

Wherever it gets a chance to do it, that is everywhere every moment, its only concern is greater cooperation of all the parts of the universe for maturation! For human beings, this begins with using our mutually invented skill of human self-consciousness to mature ourselves up the layers to full maturity in that skill, to give priority to our actions of Eldering.

Then each moment the highest priority of our attention is being aware we are first the *self-conscious experience* of the indivisible universe that will not die (the reality of oneness) and secondly our physical body that will die (the illusion it is a separate part). We are each not a whole. We are each a part of the only whole. Yet from the inside we each only have sole and complete control over our physical body. Therefore, we are fully responsible for its actions. At full maturity in this skill, at all times and in all places (in the reality of oneness) our priority in action is what we each determine is our best action of cooperation for the maturation of the universe. From achieving full maturity in the skill of self-consciousness until death, this is our highest priority each moment. It is this Eldering behavior that sustains inside us the feeling of contented joy.

I also discovered something else when reflecting on all of this and the experience of mutual mature love with Lucy. I discovered when I looked to find the beginning of experience, I could not find it. When I looked to find the end of experience, I could not find it. When I looked to find the size of experience, I could not find it. When I looked to find the up or down or right or left of experience, I could not find it. I realized more than at any time in the past that experience is unbroken-up-into-parts. It is oneness.

Unbroken-up-into-parts-experience is always present and is always the container of the mutually agreed-upon illusion tool of separate parts called "words." This is why when we are operating at the Mature Elder layer we always give priority to experience and second priority to words, the mastery of the Elder layer.

Take a moment to look up from reading. You can notice that the *fundamental thing* you are experiencing is unbroken-up-into-parts-experience. Experience is to us as water is to fish. All the different and colorful parts you see are secondary in importance in your thinking to the fact you are alive, have the skill of human self-consciousness, and living self-consciously in unbroken-up-into-parts-experience. This is being aware of the self-conscious experience of oneness as real, present, and the container of everything else. It is always present and can't be escaped. We are either aware or not aware of its presence. Everything you see, including you, is like a different color and shape fish in an ocean called "experience."

Being aware of unbroken-up-into-parts-experience as the ocean everything is in is the direct and present awareness of the oneness of nature.

If you would like another metaphor, think of all the different parts you see, including you, as different pieces of vegetables in a soup. The soup is the unbroken up into parts experience, the oneness of nature that is always present and the container of all of the parts, in this metaphor the pieces of vegetables.

When you do the personal study with the person you choose in *Chapter 8: Mutual Mature Love Experience,* you will easily experience it as a *mutually known and able to be self-consciously chosen experience.* It is easy to experience it in a relationship with another person. You will then know it as an option of choice, as a skill, and can then learn to unilaterally choose it as your priority when alone, with others who do not know it, and mutually with others who do know it.

But in my thinking, how do I give priority to experience? As I hope you just witnessed, experience is at all times and in all places unbroken-up-into-parts. Therefore, in my thinking in words I have to give priority to what is best at all times and in all places, to my true self-interest of being first the indivisible universe that will not die and secondly my physical body that will die. In thinking, this is giving priority to unbroken-up-into-parts-experience, to the reality of the oneness of nature that is unbroken-up-into-parts-experience and consistently maturing.

I then realized I had also discovered natural morality. This was the fifth thing I discovered was natural and effortless once I discovered the mutual experience of oneness with Lucy.

I now always naturally, effortlessly, and freely give priority to the common good, cooperation for maturation. My now mature self-definition is "I am first the universe that will not die and secondly my physical body part of it that will die." Being a consistent participant in maturation is now always my mature primary self-interest.

Next, here is a description of the sixth thing I learned.

When I began to self-consciously give priority to experience, I also discovered there was information coming into my physical body that was valuable and I had previously not given much attention. It wasn't coming into my thinking beginning with words. It also wasn't a feeling. It also wasn't a sensation.

It was a knowing.

For instance, the other day I was about to telephone someone, and I got this *knowing* that I should not call the person. I should wait a couple days. When I then checked the rational reasons for postponing the call, I realized there were some good reasons to delay. When days later I contacted the person, it turned out it was very wise to have waited. With Lucy the words that were downloaded into my thinking the moment I met her were, "She had a loving mother, and she loves loving." This was a knowing. It did not start, process, and end in words. It was from the oneness of nature directly downloaded into words in my thinking.

I now know this as information directly from unbroken-up-into-parts-experience, the oneness of nature that has access to all the information that exists.

It is not information that begins, processes in, and ends using words!

I now watch for it. I know it is at all times downloading into my thinking knowledge that is valuable and I am constantly alert to receive it and rationally consider it before making a choice.

I also know I sometimes have difficulty discerning between an unconscious physical body want and it. I keep my power and make sure I use my rational thinking to confirm anything I think is a knowing is confirmed by other data to be a wise choice. I have consistently gotten better at discerning between the two.

Let me now return to my story of backing into the discovery of the smaller skill of the highest layer of maturity in the skill of human self-consciousness, Mature Elder layer.

For the first year and a half Lucy and I enjoyed local oneness. I was fully comfortable doing it with her because I discovered the *experience* was the same as universal oneness. I waited until she and I had had enough deepening of our trust in each other, and she knew enough about all of this in words without me ever making a demand of her about it. She learned about it from reading some of my writings, attending workshops I led, and being in conversations between others and me about it. Only then, when I judged she would be fully comfortable with accurately naming in words the experience we were enjoying—"the universe operates as an indivisible whole and we are mutually enjoying the self-conscious experience of it"—did I invite her into us very self-consciously and mutually knowing it, choosing it, and naming it.

We were naked in the hot tub on our deck and it was a calm Fall day. I took her hands and guided us into what you will do when you do the Mutual Mature Love Experience in *Chapter 8*. We gently held hands and, while comfortably resting our eyes in each other's eyes, affirmed we were giving priority to the reality the universe operates as an indivisible whole, we affirmed we were being fully receptive because there was not a second thing to fear, and we knew we were choosing this experience while we were choosing it. She immediately realized *experientially* nothing was different other than her *knowing it as universal oneness instead of local oneness*. She directly experienced it as real in relationship with me and the universe. Given that the experience was not different and that she now knew intellectually the universe operates as an indivisible whole (the skill of the Elder layer), when she allowed it to be known as universal oneness, she had the direct, present, and repeatable by choice experience it is real (the personal science experience). She now knew *experientially* it is the only thing that is real.

There were three experiences that revealed to her rational thinking it was real: 1) the absence of fear, 2) it was enjoyable, and 3) no interest in leaving it. These three particular experiences are always the rational evidence that has one recognize it is real.

Oneness does not have places. It does not have times. It only exists in all times and all places. Using self-conscious knowing as our sixth sense, it can be self-consciously known and directly experienced.

Initially, it needs to be with another human being because the mutual illusion of separate parts upon which human language is based needs to be present for it to be a self-consciously known experience. Finally, with the words present, the priority needs to be the mutual choice of the self-conscious experience of oneness. Without mastering the Elder layer smaller skills, particularly knowing how to give priority to the priority pattern of thinking, this choice cannot be consistently chosen. However, you will be able to do it with the friend you choose when you do the exercise in *Chapter 8: Mutual Mature Love Experience* because the two of you will be guided into it by the words in that chapter. This will allow both of you to know it is possible.

However, you will not have mastered the skill of sustaining it. You will just know it can be mastered. That is the value of that exercise. That is the value of knowing it for a few minutes as a direct and mutually self-consciously chosen experience with another person.

Why was it essential that Lucy and I come to know the difference between local oneness and universal oneness if the experience is the same? This is a very important question. Sharing the answer is the main reason I am writing this book.

Many people throughout history have intellectually, in words, discovered the universe operates as an indivisible whole. However, that is only the beginning of the mastery of the skill of the Elder layer.

As stated earlier, to achieve full maturity in the skill of human self-consciousness, mutual mature love, it is necessary to intellectually know in words the difference between the oneness pattern of thinking and the separate parts pattern of thinking. We also need to know the latter is valuable but not real, therefore not a threat to the former even though an opposite. Only then can one have both fully present and choose to give priority to the oneness pattern of thinking and second priority to the separate parts pattern of thinking.

Only then can the experience of oneness be a direct, present, repeatable by choice, and self-consciously chosen continuous experience as the container of everything else we experience. Only then can the experience of mutual mature love be primarily a skill and secondly a belief in words.

Once you know the direct, present, and continuous experience of the oneness of nature with another, you will eventually seek to master it as a skill. And the first place you will probably seek to do it is in your romantic relationship, your most important and most intimate relationship. If you succeed, you will then confidently choose it as the container experience when raising your children and in all other relationships the rest of your life. They will not have to mutually know it with you. As a *skill*, you will now be able to privately sustain it as the container of all you experience.

With Lucy I was doing an experiment. I wanted to see if giving priority to experience—the unbroken-up-into-parts-experience that is always present is oneness and can be self-consciously known—is practical. I discovered it was more than practical. *It was mutual mature love.* Not only in romantic love, but also the most beautiful experience it is possible to know *as a self-conscious choice at all times and in all places (in the reality of oneness) each moment wherever I am and with whomever I am with.*

It was giving priority to unbroken-up-into-parts-experience that can be mutually self-consciously known, chosen, and consistently given priority. Like riding a bicycle, it is a skill we can learn to consistently execute. We can then turn it into a habit. Then, also like riding bicycle, we can be thinking about something else while we are habitually doing it, habitually sustaining it as the container of all we do.

Choosing to give priority to the *universal experience of oneness* in a relationship with another person is the choice of mutual mature love, the only experience of love that exists. When two people have the skill of choosing to do it together, they *mutually know the self-conscious experience* of mutual mature love. When they learn in their relationship it is real, grounded, sane, and enjoyable, they learn they can also unilaterally choose it as their priority at all times and in all places (in the reality of oneness).

These two skills, being able to choose mutual mature love *unilaterally or mutually with another*, are the mastery of the Mature Elder layer, the highest layer of maturity of the skill of human self-consciousness.

I share this story here because it was with Lucy, in a relationship of mutual mature love with one other person, that I discovered I had fully solved this riddle. It was with Lucy that I discovered the skill of consistently choosing to give priority to unbroken-up-into-parts-experience as a possibility in a relationship with another person. It was with Lucy that I discovered *mutually doing it consistently with another person,* not just in an exercise for a few moments as you will later be guided into experiencing in *Chapter 8*, is the at all times and in all places (in the reality of oneness) direct self-conscious experience of universal oneness I knew in my bones had to be possible.

We all need a base camp. A place we can come back to each day where we can affirm the experience of self-conscious oneness as a direct, present, and repeatable by choice experience is confirmed as real.

This is the primary value of a romantic relationship.

I also realized why our Creighton Prep high school football team was so often the state champion football team in Nebraska. Coach Don Leahy was fantastic at having us focus our attention on moving as one as a team. In high school, we all loved the *mutual experience of oneness* when doing it in one of the most important areas of the focus of our attention, playing on the football team. I just wish he and the Jesuits knew what you are learning in this book. Then they could have eldered us into the mastery of the Teen, Adult, Elder, and Mature Elder layers of maturity in this skill before we left high school. That would have been possible and is now possible at every high school throughout the world. Teachers, coaches, religious, and business leaders can all participate in Eldering our children into the mastery of this skill.

Words are always present when I am talking with Lucy. However, they are never the priority, except, of course, when I am tired or inordinately invested in something else. However, I now know mutual mature love as a skill, mutual with all that exists. Once I catch myself not having it present and as my priority, I am able to choose to execute this skill again. Since Lucy and I know *mutual self-conscious oneness*, it is easy to go back into it with her because she also always wants to be giving it priority, particularly with me. It becomes the safe place to fumble my way back into executing it well myself. With Lucy I don't have to worry about not being understood. My relationship with Lucy is a loving home to which I can always return. It is base camp. I very much like knowing there is a base camp to which I can return to feel secure when having to relate with the immature behaviors I come upon during my days, in me and in others.

This is the great value of romantic love. Once known there, we can more confidently do it without a need of this base camp. However, we love having a base camp.

Each year for the month of February, Lucy returns to Cali, Colombia where she was born and raised in an American community of ex-patriots. This year I did not go with her to remain focused on finishing this book. A week after she returned, I discovered I was feeling down and insecure. I eventually discovered in her absence I had unconsciously (without choice) gone back to giving priority to words instead of experience. When I finally discovered I was doing this and again gave priority by choice to experience, I was back to emotional health.

I had been affected by the daily absence of my base camp.

The self-conscious experience of oneness has often been equated with silence, the absence of words (still polarization, words or no words). Or escaping from polarization as if there is a second place that is equally real (duality and non-duality). There is not "enlightenment" and "not enlightenment" as if they are both real. When you know the self-conscious experience of oneness as a *priority by choice, as a skill,* I think you will conclude it is not mysterious, inaccessible, unusable, or nothingness. It is directly knowable and able to be experienced by choice. However, it is only possible when we have used our skill of human self-consciousness as our sixth sense to, as a personal scientist, discover the relationship between human languages and the indivisibility of the universe. We can then use it in our thinking as an inside belief and turn it into a skill and then a habit and then part of who we are.

You will discover it is a skill you can learn, know you have learned it, and use it.

I do enjoy the silence of meditating and do it most mornings. Like falling asleep and waking up, I find those two times, and sitting in silence, as the times I have the most direct relationship with the universe. That has me more easily receive direct information from it, downloaded into words. The absence of words being used by me makes it easier for me to experience its wise downloads into words. For instance, after more than twenty working titles, a few months ago it gave me the title for this book. I have confidently stayed with it ever since.

It was this knowledge that allowed me to fulfill my third vow, to find the next layer of maturity for free markets that gives priority to the common good. I discovered what I now know is the inevitable next layer of maturity of free markets, what I am labeling "common good capitalism."

As briefly mentioned earlier, it is where, in the private-sector and without the need of government involvement (although a public official could attend their meetings to assure cooperation for the common good and not collusion for self-interest), the competitors in each product market behave like the teams in a sports league. They meet, legally reach agreement on the common good rules of play, and the auditors act as the referees making sure the agreements, the mutually and voluntarily chosen rules of play, are the priority at all times, as when sport teams are competing. The competition then continues as ferociously as before only now, as with sports teams, second in priority to keeping the agreements, the agreed-upon rules of play. They are the cooperative context for the competition. The auditors serve as the referees, reporting at least annually if or to what degree each company is keeping the agreements. No company will want to be discovered to be breaking the agreements because of the strong negative response from the public that will now know of it.

As mentioned earlier, the legal agreements could be to have the minimum wage be a livable wage in each location where employees work (we already do this at Ben & Jerry's and would be happy to share the formulas we use). It could include agreements on environmental management, relationships with local communities, and even the percentage of annual profits that will be donated to end poverty around the world (and increase the number of potential customers). This would be companies keeping their power, all of it, and freely choosing to give priority to the common good. Relative to one another, it will not cost them a penny. All will make the agreed-upon changes on the same mutually agreed-upon future date. And it is legal, not collusion for mutual self-interest. It is open cooperation for the common good, the priority of all societies that is encouraged.

This is maturing our economic activity to at least the Elder layer of maturity.

What will make this much easier than one at first might think is that currently the quiet highest priority on the Wall Streets of the world is mergers and acquisitions to create a "duopoly monopoly" in each product market. This is where as few as two companies are dominant. Some with which you are familiar are CVS-Walgreens, Home Depot-Lowe's, Boeing-AirBus, Pepsi-Coca-Cola. The US airlines that control 82% of the domestic seats have shrunk from ten down to four—Delta, United, American, and Southwest—and they now even openly reveal how they are coordinating their activities, such as at the same time raising the price for checking a second bag.

Working toward duopoly monopolies in each product market is the new normal.

We now live in the Information Age where nearly all information is almost instantly available. Therefore, it is no longer necessary for companies to directly talk to each other to co-ordinate their actions. This makes nearly all antitrust legislation concerning the relationships between and among competitors mute.

This is beneficial to the emergence of a common good capitalism movement. The fewer the companies in each product market the easier it is to mature into common good capitalism. And new more creative companies can still emerge and become members of the product association, recent examples are Uber and Lift in the taxi cab business and Amazon in retail business.

When it is recognized that this quiet cooperation for strong profits by duopoly monopolies, or near duopoly monopolies, is the new normal, the citizenry will eventually demand we mature into common good capitalism.

There will be more on this in *Chapter 7: Maturation of Relationships and Organizations in the Relationship Age* and much more my next book, *Your and My Maturation Stories.*

The reason it will be essential that we quickly mature into common good capitalism is it will allow us to invite China's companies in each product market to join in our sports league model on an equal basis with equal access to financial and other resources.

As mentioned earlier, when in the teenager years we have discovered our ability and right to exercise individual free choice, and relate with others, there are only two choices: war or agreements.

All wars begin and end in peace. Peace is agreements.

Wars are lose-lose. Agreements are win-win.

As described earlier, anytime two or more people operating at the Teen layer of maturity or higher are together, the other side of the coin of honoring individual free choice is making and keeping agreements for the common good. Otherwise there is perpetual war. There is not a third choice between moving as one with the indivisible universe or moving against it.

Mature Elders do all they can to skip the war part and find a way to reach agreements that are part of our cooperation for maturation, the common good. They know that any war activity will solely be a lose-lose for all and eventually result in an agreement: peace. Therefore, they always endeavor to skip the war part.

We are currently on a collision course with China for economic dominance on Earth.

By default, we are in agreement to not destroy humanity because we have the weapons that could do it. Therefore, also among all on Earth by default, the conflict is now mainly economic. If it is unresolved, it could easily result in immature people advocating military action or, worse, it begins as the result of human error.

To reduce this possibility, during the Cold War we made sure there was never conflict between two nuclear powers. We only fought what at least some of us thought were proxy wars, such as the war between the North and South Vietnamese. This would be the first potential war between two nuclear powers. A direct conflict between them is extremely dangerous. It is human beings who have their fingers on the buttons that send nuclear missiles flying and it is human beings who have their hands near the red phones that call for those buttons to be pushed.

Immature people can easily do immature things. Therefore, we are in a far more dangerous situation than most of us are willing to admit.

The United States determines our agreements among ourselves one way. China determines their agreements among themselves another way. In the unconscious (without choice) maturation process, the US leans toward emphasizing individual free choice and China leans toward maintaining parental control. Whether or not our leaders are aware of it, they are all seeking to mature to where our agreements are representing the Elder layer, or at least the mature end of the Adult layer where we avoid war by choose agreements instead.

The United States prioritizes individual freedom. Also, and partly as a result, many of our current leaders do not recognize the importance of reaching and keep agreements. They are only aware of one half of the coin of our ability, right, and responsibility at the Teen layer, that of exercising individual free choice. They are ignorant of the other half of that coin *of sharing responsibility for reaching agreements when relating with others* rather than going to war in any form. They are also ignorant of the possibility of mature free choice. Many are also comfortable giving priority to an imagined separate part, such as the financial interests of the shareholders as discussed earlier or the agenda of a particular movement or nation.

A citizenry operating at the Adult layer or lower is choosing from among outside beliefs. This makes it possible for people seeking power to use marketing to get power by creatively telling people what they want to hear. Stuck in the world of outside beliefs, the best marketing wins the day. This is the very dangerous milieu we in the West live in today.

Also, at the Adult layer or lower, citizens are unaware they are unconsciously (without choice) still seeking a good parent; and, therefore, are very vulnerable to authoritarian people using marketing, trickery, fake news, and accusing all information that disagrees with them as fake news, to win their votes, often indirectly arguing they will be a good parent for the country. Without the citizenry maturing into the two higher layers of maturity of the skill of human self-consciousness, they will not easily notice they are choosing from among marketing seductions.

This is the result of not being personal scientists either as a result of being eldered into full maturity in the skill of human self-consciousness before leaving home or self-eldering ourselves into it.

There is no way to prove an outside belief accurately represents reality. It is not tied to direct, present, and repeatable experience by choice that can in any moment be confirmed as accurate. Existing solely in words, smart marketing people can package the words and images to seduce people into believing they will get what they want if they vote for a particular person. Unconsciously (without choice) authoritarian people, not knowing they are seeking to be dictators but in their thinking to be a good parent for the citizenry, will use the skills of marketing to win votes.

This is the hidden danger in a democracy where much of the citizenry is operating at the Adult layer or lower.

Personal scientists will be aware of the many ways they can unconsciously give their power to a second thing and make sure they never make this unconscious choice of being a child in a parent-child pattern of behavior. For democracy to work well, the priority of the citizenry needs to be the Eldering of each other and their children to full maturity in this skill. Otherwise it is very vulnerable to sustaining the above unconscious (without choice) parent-child pattern of behavior of choosing an authoritarian leader. That is someone who does not understand the importance of equally activating the other side of the coin of individual free choice of making and keeping freely chosen agreements that give priority to cooperation for maturation, the common good.

China, on the other hand, prioritizes paternalism. They think everyone should do as the "parents" say. This, they correctly believe, will not make their society vulnerable to the above unconscious (without choice) possibility of authoritarian leaders being chosen in a democracy. However, if they also are not giving priority to the eldering of each other and their children to full maturity in the skill of human self-consciousness as early in their lives as possible, to becoming personal scientists, they run the risk of being authoritarian to an extreme as protection against what they fear about democracy. When they have errored, which has been often, that has been their error.

Fear is always a self-fulfilling prophecy. We become what we fear because our attention is there. China's fear of the form of dictatorship the Communist Revolution overthrew (what they saw as the dictatorial Nationalist regime) has had it become the kind of dictatorship they fear, a dictatorship of control. US's fear of the form of dictatorship it overthrew (the East India Company) has had it become the kind of dictatorship we fear, a dictatorship of corporate capital giving priority to the interests of a few.

Whether a punch is thrown in offense or defense, it is still experienced as a punch. Defense by both is based on the assumption the other threw the first punch. It can take the form of either "imposed dictatorial control" (China) or "seduced and accepted dictatorial control" (United States).

They are both the result of still unconsciously (without choice) operating on the parent-child pattern of behavior of the Adult or lower layers.

I remember being a citizen diplomat visiting the Soviet Union in 1983, long before Mikhail Gorbachev came to power. I realized that President Ronald Reagan's strategy was working. Keep Russia in a military arms race. Without a capitalist economic system able to fund it, it will bankrupt their society. That is, indeed, in my judgment part of what happened. When I returned in 1988 to train people from throughout Russia in how to organize cooperatives that were being allowed by Gorbachev, there were two groups. People who genuinely wanted to organize a cooperative and others who wanted to use the new cooperative laws to allow them to be capitalists, as they simplistically understood the way capitalists behaved in the West: use everything and everybody to make as much money for yourself as possible. When, after Gorbachev, they tried a rapid conversion to Western capitalism, it was a disaster. All but the financial winners did not like it. Still operating at the Adult layer or lower, the citizenry became fully comfortable democratically returning to authoritarian leadership. This is currently also happening in Hungary, Poland, and other former Soviet-controlled nations.

I recently spent time in China. The Chinese now assume the last hundred and fifty years were a blip in history, and they are destined to be the dominant nation on Earth as they were for centuries the dominant nation in Asia. Not only that, but they have also discovered the strategy to accomplish it and it will work. It is providing the best product in each market at the lowest price until all competitors leave that product market. The secret to their plan is to simply think a little bit long-term, to financially fund the survival of this strategy a few years into the future. Western companies are mainly interested in short-term profits and cannot easily suffer losses for a significant period of time. Their stock price will fall. Within a few years Western companies will abandon that product market and China will fully control it. It is working—for instance in the production of solar cells, and it will continue to work unless the United States matures its form of free market economics into a form they will not resist joining.

This is the "agreement" that will prevent an escalation into war as the choice of immature people.

China accurately knows dominance on Earth today is not primarily with military power. As stated earlier, our militaries can now destroy Earth as we know it. Therefore, by default, dominance is having economic power. Today, China's strategy is labeled the "Belt and Road Initiative." It is a trillion-dollar global economic development strategy involving infrastructure development and investments in 152 countries and international organizations in Asia, Europe, Africa, the Middle East, and the Americas. Their goal is to become the dominant economic power on Earth. Many in the US and West will not accept this. Those who are immature will seek war as the response. It is essential that we all rapidly elder ourselves into full maturity in the skill of human self-consciousness and identify the form of free markets that will be better for both them and us, not just one of us.

It is common good capitalism.

Few appear to be aware of the danger of not wisely meeting this challenge. To end it we need to end our idealist fights in words. Instead we need to recognize we are all in this together as parts of an indivisible whole, honor each nation's choice of agreements for how they operate as representing a layer of maturity of a society and its approach to continued maturation, and solve conflicts by agreements.

We also need to have the humility of knowing that neither their social level of maturity nor ours is at this time operating at the highest layer of human maturity possible, mutual mature love.

One piece of this for Americans is recognizing that in less than forty years China has brought nearly a billion people out of poverty. That is a major accomplishment no other nation on Earth has ever accomplished. We need to honor and respect them for their paternalist system having accomplished this.

Secondly, we need to think creatively and with Mature Elder wisdom.

For instance, one of the poorest nations on Earth is North Korea. They now also have nuclear weapons. Americans could invite

China to team up with them to assist North Korea in the implementation of state capitalism there to rapidly bring their people out of poverty the way China accomplished it. This would establish a working relationship with China for the common good and eventually neutralize North Korea's belligerence toward the United States.

We need more creative ideas like this that build on primarily working together for the common good, the opposite of confrontation based on ideologies in words, by wisely speaking to the layer of maturity their nation is operating on and the one we are operating on. This will also make it easier to mature North Korea and China into a common good capitalism economy, a common good capitalism that will work well for all.

The purpose of this chapter has been to share with you some of the stories of my maturation up the layers of maturity of the skill of human self-consciousness. This is not solely a personal activity. It is also a maturation of what I understand to be my social relationships, from my romantic relationship all the way to our relationships with each other on Earth. That is why it was appropriate for me to speak to my maturation in how we can mature our relationships among the nations on Earth and in particular our relationship with China where, because of our immaturity, we are both still seeking economic dominance on Earth (war activity) rather than agreement.

One of the other purposes of me telling my story and writing this book is to provide a way for people around the world to discover the wisdom of choosing to be personal scientists and self-elder themselves into full maturity in the skill of mutual mature love. You can do it alone or join with friends into mutual support groups. You can also become part of the community of people doing this by joining and participating in an agreement nation. There will be many different ones emerging because it is the next layer of maturity of democracy. The one I will begin, when I find enough others willing to join with me to do it, based on what you are reading in this book is labeled the "Chrysalis Nation." You can learn more about our plans by going to our website, www.chrysalisnation.org.

Where are we going? What forms will nature take as we mature? In terms of times and places, we do not exactly know. However, we can use our sixth sense of self-conscious knowing to make good guesses. We know the universe operates in a constant state of maturing (just look at the thousands of years of recorded history); and it is now doing so mainly through its human parts.

Through us, it is now able to do it as a self-conscious process.

Mastering this skill is not only necessary for personal happiness but also for global and universal happiness. In particular, it is meeting the major challenges of our generations. One of which is learning together to manage Earth for sustainability of all of life, including human life. Another, mentioned above, is successfully managing the emerging conflict between the United States and China.

Eventually all of our social, political, and economic activities could represent full maturity in this skill, the skill of mutual mature love.

The purpose of this book is to allow the story of my search for the meaning of life, particularly what I discovered in my relationship with Lucy, to inform your search for it.

I used to live in a house in the woods. It was difficult to see the sky. I now live in a house on a hill with a big yard. Anytime I am in it, nearly half of what I see is sky.

As mentioned earlier, at night I can see some of what I know are billions of stars in our galaxy. I also now know there are billions of other galaxies also with billions of stars in them. It makes me realize how small my physical body is relative to the Earth and the rest of nature (the universe).

I now know that how large or small my physical body may be, or how large or small the universe may be, is not what is most important. I now know what is most important is our *relationship* to all the other parts. We can't do anything about how large or small our physical bodies and the universe are, but we can choose how we relate with the rest of nature *as a skill*.

I also now know there are layers of maturity of the skill of human self-consciousness. Today I am not relating the way I did as a Baby, Toddler, Child, Teen, or Adult. I now know there are only two layers of maturity beyond these five to master the full skill of human self-consciousness and there is not an eighth layer (what could be larger than defining "self" as all that exists?). I am now capable of being a fully mature human being and endeavor to operate at that layer of maturity at all times, not always successfully. I also know I will now never stop maturing in the skill of relating with the rest of nature, in the skill of "Eldering."

I also know that, like riding a bicycle, we do not need to be a professional biker. We only need to know how to ride it well enough to get around town. It is the same with mutual mature love. We only need to master all seven smaller skills enough to get around town. Then the rest of our lives it is getting consistently better at the joy of Eldering, our priority in action that sustains the feeling of contented joy.

This is what this book is about.

Allow me to finish this chapter by emphasizing two important things already stated.

First, the following is what this book is not about.

You and all of us will still have our belief that answers the fundamental question inside us, "Why is the universe structured the way it is structured?" Our answer to this question is usually a religious, philosophical, or scientific belief we each choose. The mastery of the *skill* of human self-consciousness, or any skill, will appropriately always be secondary in importance to our choice of the answer to that question.

This book is solely about mastering the skill of human self-consciousness, relating skillfully with the way the universe (nature) operates using self-evident truths. It is about assisting you to become a personal scientist and mastering the skill of mutual mature love.

Secondly, everything you have read and will read is primarily the result of my study of my direct, present, and repeatable by choice experiences. No authority stands behind anything you will read, and if you make me or these words into an authority you will be unconsciously (without choice) continuing the parent-child pattern of giving your power to a second thing that does not exist except in the illusion of separate parts.

Be sure you do not do that!

We can each only achieve true full freedom when we master the *skill* of not doing that anymore. Instead, our primary focus is on keeping our power, all of it, and studying our direct, present, and repeatable by choice experience to identify the fundamental self-evident facts that build on one another and allow us to become fully mature human beings, to know mutual mature love. This is the mutual experience of knowing we are doing it with all that exists. It is knowing and enjoying the fact nature is at all times conspiring to have us and itself mature.

We must each *primarily* use our sixth sense of self-conscious knowing to be a personal scientist executing mature free choice to have the *inner experience* of natural confidence and the *feeling* of contented joy.

We will also reach agreement to mutually use certain words, such as the ones I am using in this book, to talk about all of this with each other. To have a common language. However, in addition you want to privately develop the words that work best for you and give them priority in your private relationship with yourself. Also, change them from time to time when you find better ones that stimulate the experiences and insights you want. That way you know you are keeping your power, all of it, and Self-Eldering yourself.

It is the time in history when we will assist each other to complete the process of self-eldering ourselves, and eldering our children, into full maturity in the skill of human self-consciousness and all enjoy being Mature Elders from early in our lives. We are entering what was earlier labeled the "Relationship Age," the time when our relationship of oneness with the rest of the universe is more important than anything else

By 2050, why not, nearly every child on Earth could be eldered by his or her parents, teachers, religious leaders, and others into full maturity in the skill of human self-consciousness before the end of their teenage years.

It is the most important skill for each of us to learn, in schools more important than any of the other skills we teach our children.

In summary, allow me to list the seven most important fundamental facts I have discovered:

7 Fundamental Facts I Have Discovered

1. The universe operates as an indivisible whole.

2. I am a part of it, not a whole.

3. I am not born with the skill of human self-consciousness; it is a skill I can learn.

4. I learned it by learning the smaller skills of the seven layers that build on one another and can integrate together into full maturity in executing this skill.

5. When I am learning the skills of a human language and the self-consciousness it allows, I naturally give priority to my physical body. However, from the teenage years on I am capable of maturing out of operating on the illusion there are separate parts and into the reality the universe operates as an indivisible whole. Then my self-definition can become the accurate one: "I am first the indivisible universe that will not die and secondly my physical body part of it that will die."

6. The pattern of thinking that is present in that self-definition is giving priority to priorities. In my thinking at the Mature Elder layer, I give priority to that pattern of thinking. I give second priority to the separate parts pattern of thinking because doing both, prioritizing them in this way, and knowing the separate parts pattern represents a mutually agreed-upon illusion tool we invented allows me to know, choose, and directly experience the oneness of nature as a self-conscious experience. Continually giving this priority is the smaller skill of the seventh and highest layer, the Mature Elder layer.

7. To master full maturity in the skill of human self-consciousness I need to know as an ongoing experience the self-conscious experience of oneness with at least one other person, usually one's romantic relationship. I can then learn to unilaterally give priority to participation in this wavelength at all times—I now know where it is, have it consistently and daily affirmed as real in my romantic relationship, and can choose to participate in its fundamental process of cooperation for

maturation. The latter is the activity of Eldering, the most enjoyable behavior priority because it provides the inner experience of contented joy, the most enjoyable joy.

We now know at full maturity in the skill of human self-consciousness our natural highest priority is not personal happiness but universal happiness, our mature self-interest. We also not only have the mature self-definition but also a new perspective. Everything we have thought up to now was outside us is experienced as inside us. Everything is actually me relating with me. We are all parts of an indivisible whole. We are not wholes. We are all in this together as parts of the only whole, and we are the self-conscious parts. Consistent contented joy is the result of Eldering: each moment each of us giving priority to whatever we each determine is our best cooperative action for the continuous maturation of us all.

From the inside, we each only have sole and complete control of our physical body. From the inside, we have none anywhere else. Yet we also are each first the indivisible universe and secondly our physical body. It is from this position we enjoy Eldering, giving priority to participation in our true self-interest, from wherever we are each sitting or standing each moment. This is giving priority to cooperative action for the continuous maturation of us all.

That is natural morality in action. This is natural loving behavior in action. This results in natural confidence. It is also the only priority each moment that sustains the inner feeling of contented joy, our birthright.

It is my hope everyone reading this finds your base camp, a lover who knows the skill with you of mutual mature love.

CHAPTER 5

Three More Personal Science Studies

Each day more people will choose to primarily be personal scientists.

For them, the result can be full maturity in the skill of human self-consciousness. They will then be giving priority to the unbroken-up-into-parts experience of oneness. Their second priority will be living their lives based on inside beliefs, not outside beliefs.

As described earlier, giving priority to an outside belief is unconsciously (without choice) sustaining the parent-child pattern of our childhood. It is giving our power, all of it, to a second thing—another person, a group, or usually today a belief in words. We are then unconsciously (without choice) acting as if it is something separate from us that can receive our power. It is a parent-substitute we then primarily obey as we obeyed our parents. This is easily done at the Teen layer. Since up to then it is the only relationship we have known, until we discover it is giving our power away and having to give priority to obeying where we have given it and that is in conflict with our ability and right to exercise individual free choice, we will unconsciously (without choice) continue that pattern of relationship.

If we were aware we were ending our ability to exercising individual free choice, we would definitely not do it.

Individual freedom can only be sustained by keeping our power, all of it, and using it as our sixth sense to study our direct, present, and repeatable by choice experience to identify the self-evident facts we will represent in words in our thinking to guide our lives.

These are inside beliefs. They are a result of being a personal scientist by using our skill of human self-consciousness as our sixth sense to execute mature free choice. Only this can result in the experience of natural confidence and the feeling of contented joy.

This builds on and sustains our ability to exercise mature free choice. Nothing else does. Therefore, it is essential we each *primarily* be a personal scientist. It is the mastery of half of the Teen layer of maturity and the most fundamental ability and right to exercise mature, not just individual, free choice. The other half, not given as high a priority today, is accepting shared responsibility for giving priority to the common good, cooperation for maturation.

If we have relationships with Mature Elders in our lives, they can assist us to master full maturity at the Teen layer. Then, we can completely skip the immature Teen layer, only giving priority to individual free choice and the self-interest of our physical body, and Adult layer, giving priority to choosing an outside belief of how the universe operates. Another part of the immature Teen layer will also become second in priority: choosing of different rules we will follow in relationship with the most important people in our lives: our parents, coaches, teachers, and boss.

Both are the result of not knowing the importance of keeping our power, all of it, and using it to be a personal scientist. Both are unconsciously (without choice) sustaining the parent-child pattern of behavior.

It is at the Elder layer that we not only know of the oneness of nature as our most fundamental inside belief but also master the skills of consistently holding it as our fundamental inside belief about how the universe operates, having our self-definition be the accurate one, discovering the two possible patterns of thinking, and the importance of giving priority to the oneness pattern. With wise eldering by Mature Elders, we can, beginning in the teenage years, master the full skill of the Teen layer, to a large degree skip the Adult layer, and begin the mastery of the Elder layer.

In this chapter, you will be guided into acting as a personal scientist to discover three more important self-evident facts. You did a personal science study to discover the first one in *Chapter 1: The 7 Questions*, the study of your breathing to discover the universe operates as an indivisible whole.

All four of these facts are self-evident: in any moment we can keep our power, all of it, and turn our attention to again study our direct, present, and repeatable by choice experience to confirm they are accurate facts. This is the same way we discovered rocks are hard and fire is hot. We did not primarily discover them using words but in direct experience: by touching. We earlier discovered, also in direct experience, the universe operates as an indivisible whole by using our sixth sense of self-conscious knowing to directly experience this relationship among all the parts of the universe. We will now do the same thing to discover three more important personal science facts.

When learning a complex skill, including the skill of human self-consciousness, there are layers of smaller skills that build on one another in a natural sequence, integrate into one skill at each layer, and ultimately result in the mastery of the full skill. Allow me a paragraph to emphasize this pattern.

When learning to ride a bicycle, we need to first learn the smaller skill of holding the bike up so it does not fall down, next to put our outside foot on the closest pedal with it close to the ground, next to remained balanced on it when we push off into a glide, next to maintain balance while it glides, next while it is gliding to throw our body up onto the seat without losing balance, next to pedal without losing balance, and finally to turn it without losing balance.

There is only one way to do each smaller skill. Like all skills, these skills are the same for everyone. And we learn them in a natural progression with each smaller skill building on, and integrating into moving as one with, the smaller skills we have previously mastered.

To master the skill of mutual mature love, it is essential that we each learn to keep our power, all of it, and primarily use it to study our direct, present, and repeatable by choice experience to identify the most important self-evident facts we turn into skills. We then use them as inside beliefs in our thinking to guide our daily lives. Like learning to ride a bicycle, it is primarily going to direct experience to learn smaller skills in the natural progression. This is using our skill of human self-consciousness in the mature way possible, as our sixth sense.

This is the most fundamental exercise of our ability and right of individual free choice, half of full mastery of the Teen layer. It is graduating into exercising mature free choice. As stated earlier, nothing else is true free choice.

They also allow us to consistently be truly free human beings, that is to not easily get fooled into thinking the priority of one of the lower layers is the highest priority, particularly a chosen outside belief at the Adult layer. This is only possible when we have mastered all seven of the smaller skills of the skill of human self-consciousness. Only then is our relating with the rest of the universe in full and freely chosen alignment with the operation of it. Only then are we also at all times fully aware of the appropriate ranking of the smaller skills of all seven layers. This is always giving priority to the most mature one we have learned. Only then are we free from the unconscious (without choice) inner conflict between giving our power to an outside belief and simultaneously seeking to use it to exercise our ability, right, and responsibility of mature free choice.

We then become happy people and appreciated by other partici-pants in nature's concert.

Here is the best part about being a personal scientist and giving priority in our thinking to inside beliefs. When we discover truths as self-evident in our direct, present, and repeatable by choice ex-perience, we can't ever fool ourselves into thinking we do not know them. They then *naturally, effortlessly, freely, easily, and permanently* become a part of who we are without the need of effort, force, or discipline. This is the beauty of living our lives based on using our sixth sense of self-conscious knowing to be a personal science.

We don't ever have to make ourselves do anything! And we love playing our instrument in concert with all the other instruments to consistently create together one beautiful sound, nature's maturation music.

There is now always a reason for doing one thing rather than another and it is always based on what we each judge to be our best action of self-conscious (by choice) participation in the maturation of us all, our true self-interest. We are going somewhere. We, both our physical bodies and the universe, are consistently maturing, now in the skill of Eldering.

Allow me to now guide you into keeping our power, all of it, and studying your direct, present, and repeatable by choice ex-perience to discover three more self-evident truths that are part of the mastery of the skill of human self-consciousness. Together they will allow you to master the smaller skills of the last two lay-ers of maturity of it, the Elder and Mature Elder layers. Eventually we will all be aware of them in the same way we are now all aware of sensations, differences and feelings, the skills of using a human language and being self-conscious, having the ability and right to keep our power—all of it—and exercise mature free choice, being aware and accepting responsibility for our shared responsibility to give priority to act for the common good, and choosing our fundamental inside beliefs. Each of these is knowledge and a skill that defines a layer of maturity in our skill of human self-consciousness.

By using personal science to answer the following three additional questions, you will be mastering the most important skills of the Elder layer.

Using personal science, the second question for us to answer is this:

Without the existence of a human language how did human beings invent the first word of a human language?

No one was there with an iPhone taking a video of it, and it certainly did not emerge in the direct way I will present. It was surely the result of much trial and error along the way, during the early years of the 200,000 years of the existence of the modern form of human beings. (Our ancestors have been around for six million years and civilization as we know it is only 6,000 years old.) However, what will be described is what we now know is how *fundamentally* it must have happened and, as you will see, it is self-evident in your direct, present, and repeatable by choice experience that this is the only way it could have happened.

The important thing to note is that without the reality of the oneness of nature, it would not have been possible.

First, for the few minutes while you do it, not permanently but just while you do this study, put aside all the beliefs you were born into and have chosen, even those living unconsciously (without choice) inside you as a result of your upbringing. As you did in the personal science study in *Chapter 1: The 7 Questions*, you can succeed in doing this by *very self-consciously* choosing to keep your power, all of it, and use it to study your direct, present, and repeatable *experience* to find the self-evident answer to this question.

Therefore, I invite you to keep your power, all of it, and primarily use it to join me in imaging, fundamentally, how the first word had to have been invented.

The question for our imagined story is this, "Without the existence of a human language, how did human beings invent the first word?"

Using Personal Science to Discover How Human Beings Invented the First Word

A long time ago, before there was a human language, imagine there were two human beings sitting in the shade of some coconut palms. It was a sunny day and their bellies were full. They were just lying around enjoying the day.

One was playing with a coconut and consistently making the sound "wacko wacko" while doing it. The other human being saw something she found interesting. She went over to him, put her hand on his hand on the coconut, and while looking at him directly in his eyes repeated the sound, "wacko wacko." He continued to look her in the eyes with her hand on his on the coconut and found it enjoyable to repeat back to her "wacko wacko."

Why did they both find this to be enjoyable? There was something *more mature* being experienced. They were discovering the first phase of being self-conscious, *knowing together* they were doing something while they were doing it. This is a more mature way to be with each other. Therefore, it was found to be enjoyable.

She then took his hand and put it on another coconut

and, looking him in the eyes again, said, "wacko wacko." Continuing to look her in the eyes he said "wacko wacko" back to her. She then did it with another coconut. Then another.

He then took her hand and put his on her hand on a coconut and, looking her directly in the eyes, said "wacko wacko" to her. She then said it back to him. He then did this with another coconut. And then another.

Without a human language, there is only one way they could have agreed to create the first word of a human language. They mutually experienced peace, something they enjoy, instead of conflict, something they do not enjoy. They registered this as the experience of agreement: as the two of them moving as one (peace) rather than moving against one another (conflict). Local agreement is the local experience of the oneness of nature where our attention is focused. In this case, the local self-conscious experience of moving as one by agreeing on the sound "wacko wacko" for a coconut.

When both options are equally available, we always prefer peace (happiness in a relationship) to conflict (unhappiness in a relationship).

In experience, it is self-evident that both options are always available.

When two of us are looking each other in the eyes, and we choose peace instead of conflict, *we experience it as self-conscious agreement—as moving as one and knowing we are doing it while we are doing it.* By choice, the two of us are moving as one instead of against each other. (It is what Lucy and I refer to as the experience of "local oneness.")

Agreement is moving as one with each other. Conflict is moving against each other. When looking each other in the eyes, it is the reality of the oneness of nature that has us prefer the experience of agreement to the experience of conflict, the experience of local oneness.

We still do this to this day. When we reach an agreement with another, we look each other in the eyes and mutually note the experience of local peace instead of conflict, often affirming this with a hand shake. The relative feelings present are peace and the absence of conflict.

We label this mutual experience, that is more mature than conflict, "agreement."

At this point these two human beings had created the first word of a human language, "wacko wacko" for a coconut. Using this eye-to-eye experience of *choosing* agreement rather than conflict (the experience of oneness rather than the experience of separateness), they created many more words.

However, they were still not able to be fully self-conscious. They had only unconsciously (without choice) created what we today label *"spaces"* or "places": *words for different parts of the universe that occupy one place and not another.*

Only later when someone came up with words for yesterday, now, and tomorrow did they unconsciously (without choice) create what we today label *"times": words for different times.*

They were now able to analyze the past, plan for the future, and consistently exercise their plan in the present. For instance, they could agree to get together to stack the coconuts floating in the ocean against a palm tree to dry.

Being in their village, that is without them being present, they did this by talking about the coconuts, palm tree, and ocean and their relationships between and among them. Instead of pointing and motioning, they could arrange the words that represent these places and times, either by talking with each other or writing them down in the sand or on paper. And they could know they were doing it while they were doing it. They could also exercise free choice to execute a plan to gather the coconuts from the ocean and stack them against a palm tree to dry. They could agree to have one person do it or for all in the village get together to do it.

This access to free choice also includes choosing their self-definitions, for instance, defining one's self as *primarily* a lover, family person, warrior, community person, coconut stacker, or the indivisible universe.

This is self-consciousness as we know it today.

It is the result of having words for both places and times, that is names for all the parts of the universe we now know are not really separate from each other and times. If they actually were separate from each other, we never could have invented words and be self-conscious. And we definitely would not be able to breathe!

Here is what is essential to understand: it was the reality of the oneness of nature that allowed us to invent the first words. In the process, we also unconsciously (without choice) invented the mutually agreed-upon illusion tool of assuming the universe operates as separate parts that allowed us to invent words for each part and time. This also allowed us to talk about them and the relationships between and among them without them being present. It also allowed us to exercise free choice in relationship with them, to be self-conscious parts of the universe.

Once some of these human beings *invented the mutually agreed-upon illusion tool* of the assumption the universe operates as separate parts, everyone began to use it. Using the words of a human language was a *more mature way* to relate with each other. Today there are over 6,000 human languages on Earth. Each is sounds and symbols that represent a part of the universe, or the entire universe. They are not what they are representing.

Priority was now able to be given to being self-conscious (choosing) over being conscious (reacting). When doing so life was experienced as more mature, as resulting in more consistent happiness.

Instead of only reacting, like lions, tigers, bears, dogs, and cats, they were now able to *primarily* be the watchers and choosers. They knew what they were doing while they were doing it and could easily choose to continue doing it or not *and know they were making this choice.*

They were no longer stuck in only reacting (being conscious)! They were now able to be self-conscious, to choose how to respond. (Don't we love this? If something crazy is going on, rather than react with anger we can choose to add love into the situation and reduce the craziness.)

They naturally began choosing mutually caring agreements with each other and their children. They learned they could sustain it as the container of their relationships as they got older, labeled "love." They joined with other families into villages based on agreements. And as they were ready, they gave high priority to Eldering their children up the mastery of the smaller skills of each of the layers of maturity of the skill of self-consciousness they knew.

Most important for us to note from this personal science study is this: without the oneness of nature they would not have been able to create the first words of a human language and thereby be self-conscious.

There is a hunter-gathering tribe deep in the jungles of Brazil that has created the mutually agreed-upon illusion tool of "space" (providing names for parts of the universe) but has not yet created the mutually agreed-upon illusion tool of "time" (providing names for different times). Their alphabet has only about half of our consonants and vowels. They live in lean-tos of palm leaves. When the wind blows them down, they laugh and simply create new lean-tos. [The wonderful Tom Wolfe, recently deceased, does a delightful job of telling the story of our maturation from Charles Darwin to the recent realization that human self-consciousness is primarily a skill as well as a biological ability in his recent book *The Kingdom of Speech (Little, Brown, and Company, New York)*. In it he thoroughly describes this tribe, the Priaha, the study of which has been very helpful in discovering that language and self-consciousness are the interplay of biological maturation, environment, and skills (nothing is separate from everything else). Daniel L. Everett is the linguistic scientist who lived with this tribe for many years and tells his story of discovering human language is primarily a skill in his recent book *How Language Began: The Story of Humanity's Greatest Invention* (Liveright Publishing Corporation, New York).]

Therefore, we can't say that all human beings on Earth have mastered both the *places* and *times* skill of a human language and self-consciousness, but I think we can comfortably conclude that today nearly all human beings have mastered this skill. We have matured. (As mentioned earlier, in 1800 less than 10% of humanity was literate. Today 86% are literate. This is an example of how maturation into skills, once known, are sustained and taught to our children and others around the world and rapidly become universally known. Maturation is the fundamental process in nature and can't be stopped.)

As described earlier, there are seven layers of maturity of smaller skills of the complex skill of human self-consciousness. Like the mastering of any skill, such as riding a bicycle, they build on one another in a natural progression and integrate together into the full skill of human self-consciousness. Each layer is defined by the discovery of the next smaller skill in the natural sequence. This is how a complex skill is learned.

With regard to cooperation for maturation of biology, environment, and skill, it is also important to note what the new science of epigenetics is discovering. Here is an excerpt from a recent article, *Epigenetics: The Evolution Revolution*, in the *New York Review of Books*, by Israel Rosenfield and Edward Ziff in the June 7, 2018 Issue (https://www.nybooks.com/articles/2018/06/07/epigenetics-the-evolution-revolution/):

> When the molecular structure of DNA was discovered in 1953, it became dogma in the teaching of biology that DNA and its coded information could not be altered in any way by the environment or a person's way of life…
>
> The structure of the DNA neighboring the gene provides a list of instructions—a gene program—that determines under what circumstances the gene is expressed. And it was held that these instructions could not be altered by the environment. Only mutations, which are errors introduced at random, could change the instructions or the information encoded in the gene itself and drive evolution through natural selection. Scientists discredited any…claims that

the environment can make lasting, perhaps heritable alterations in gene structure or function.

The developing literature surrounding epigenetics has forced biologists to consider the possibility that gene expression could be influenced by some heritable environmental factors previously believed to have had no effect over it, like stress or deprivation. "The DNA blueprint," Carey writes, "Isn't a sufficient explanation for all the sometimes wonderful, sometimes awful, complexity of life. If the DNA sequence was all that mattered, identical twins would always be absolutely identical in every way. Babies born to malnourished mothers would gain weight as easily as other babies who had a healthier start in life."

That might seem a commonsensical view. But it runs counter to decades of scientific thought about the independence of the genetic program from environmental influence.

It is the interplay and cooperation of our biology (genes), environment, and learning of skills that has us mature. The source of maturation is not solely one or two of them: we now know nothing can be separated from anything else. Also, as we just saw, to create a human language and be self-conscious we used three factors: places and times (the mutually agreed-upon illusion tool of assuming there are separate parts) and oneness (reality).

Here is another piece of important information in this area.

In a *New York Times Sunday Magazine* article on January 9, 2019 entitled "How Beauty Is Making Science Rethink Evolution" by Ferris Jabr (https://www.nytimes.com/2019/01/09/magazine/beauty-evolution-animal.html), the argument is made that beauty, not just survival of the fittest, plays a role in evolution:

The environment constrains a creature's anatomy, which determines how it experiences the world, which generates adaptive and arbitrary preferences, which loop back to alter its biology, sometimes in maladaptive ways. Beauty reveals that evolution is neither an iterative chiseling of living organisms by a domineering landscape nor a frenzied collision of chance events. Rather, evolution is an intricate clockwork of physics, biology and perception in which every moving part influences another in both subtle and profound ways. Its gears are so innumerable and dynamic — so susceptible to serendipity and mishap — that even a single outcome of its ceaseless ticking can confound science for centuries.

Even though they know beauty plays a role in our lives, later in the article it is revealed scientists do not know what beauty is. They do not know why we all like beauty so much. I think I do.

The scientists do go so far as to say everything is a participant in it, which is the assumption of oneness, but they do not know, as a result of this, they are close to assuming oneness is the fundamental fact in physics.

Cooperation for maturation, which is the obvious pattern of nature inside our skins, is the fundamental pattern of behavior everywhere. As stated earlier, life is not a contradiction where it is competition of each part for its self-interest outside our skins and the opposite inside our skins.

Beauty is witnessing in our perceptions the different processes of cooperation for the maturation of what we are perceiving as a sub-whole: a flower, a baby, or the only whole, the universe. We naturally enjoy it and encourage this perception. This is our love of beauty and the role through us beauty plays in maturation.

We enjoy a stream in the forest as beautiful because we are witnessing natures cooperation for maturation: we are experiencing the stream more as a sub-whole than as parts. We describe great art as having balance, coherence, and symmetry: we are experiencing it working as a cooperative whole more than as parts.

In human beings, direct participation in cooperation for the maturation of the whole results in self-conscious joy because it is the opposite of conflict that is pain. It is this pleasure that is forever pulling flowers, birds, animals, and human beings toward greater participation in cooperation for maturation, the fundamental process, priority, and activity of nature.

From the first personal science study in *Chapter 1: The 7 Questions*, we now know the universe operates as an indivisible whole. Also, therefore, what we each currently assume is the cooperation for maturation relationship among the parts within our skins we know is the same relationship among the parts everywhere. Also, we are going somewhere. Not in the mutually agreed upon illusion tool of separate parts but in the reality of oneness. Each of us, the entire universe and everything inside it, is maturing. Like it or not, everything is maturing to be maturing and for no other reason. Someday we may know why, but at this point I am not aware of anyone having resolved that riddle about nature. Fortunately, we do not need to know why. As long as we know how the universe operates, we can enjoy our lives by moving as one with it and not need to know anything we do not know.

To achieve the joy of full maturity in the *skill* of human self-consciousness, we do not have to know why the universe is *structured this way*, but it is necessary for us to know this is *how it is operating*.

Both competition and cooperation are processes. Neither explains why the process is occurring. Maturation does. We are going somewhere, not primarily in the mutually agreed-upon illusion tool of assuming there are places and times but in the reality of the oneness of nature. We, the universe, is maturing.

This is also easily self-evident. It is the answer to the third question:

Is maturation the fundamental process in nature?

Using Personal Science to Discover If Maturation Is the Fundamental Process in Nature

It is obvious that since coming out of our mother's womb we have been maturing. We first became aware of sensations; then differences and feelings; then learned a human language and were self-conscious. We next can discover we have the ability and right to exercise individual free choice. We can then discover mature free choice. Next, using it, we can discover the universe is an indivisible whole: we are first it that will not die and secondly our physical bodies that will die. Finally, we can discover we can know in direct experience the self-conscious experience of the oneness of nature. We can learn how to give that experience priority at all times and in all places (in the reality of the oneness of nature). Then, by having the priority of our behavior be self-conscious participation in maturation, the fundamental process, priority, and activity of oneness, we can sustain the feeling of contented joy we have intuitively known all along was our birthright. We also learned how to ride a tricycle, then a bicycle, and then drive an automobile. It is self-evident that we, as individual human beings, have been maturing in the skill of human self-consciousness as well as in many other skills.

Human societies, *our agreements with each other*, have also been maturing. We have matured from forging in the forest to forming tribes to forming villages to raising crops and livestock to building cities to living in geographically defined nations that are now the fundamental structure of our lives on Earth. Each was built on agreements we created that have consistently matured. For instance, nearly all nations on Earth have agreements to not kill, enslave, or steal (three still do not). In every other facet of human endeavor, such as discovering cures for diseases, the uses of computers and software, the inventions of printing, radio, television, and smartphones, and enjoyable methods of entertainment, we have also been consistently maturing (I like hot tubs). We have consistently matured from dictatorships toward democracy with a majority of nations now democracies. We have bicycles, automobiles, airplanes, and have sent a person to the moon and brought him back. (I still do not understand why it took so long for us to put wheels on suitcases and batteries in toothbrushes!) Also, all this maturation is permanent. Everyone in the future will know that electricity and computers are able to be used. Everyone in the future will know that people prefer democracy over dictatorship.

Thus, it is self-evident that the universe operates as an indivisible whole where all the parts are primarily cooperating with each other for the purpose of maturation, now primarily through our use of the skill of human self-consciousness and the making and keeping of agreements.

The theory that evolution is the result of only genes and environment will rapidly only appear in history books.

We are participants in evolution (now better named "maturation").

We are not outside it. We use our genes and environment to learn knowledge upon knowledge and skills upon skills and build agreements upon agreements in a consistent process of maturation. It is the indivisible universe that is maturing. Each generation builds on the maturation of the last one. This fundamental process of cooperation for maturation is moving inside everything, including inside each of us.

Therefore, everything you will read in this book is based on the following: we now know there are not two but three dimensions to the skills of human languages and self-consciousness: places, times, and oneness.

Up to now much of our human species has been only using the first two. This—giving names to different parts and times—is unconsciously (without choice) assuming the universe operates as separate parts. It doesn't. As we discovered in *Chapter 1: The 7 Questions*, it is obviously in plain sight an indivisible whole, as obvious as rocks are hard and fire is hot.

It is also self-evident that you have been and will continue to mature. Cooperation for maturation is the fundamental process in nature everywhere and at all times, not just inside our skins. (In understanding this, you are leaving the Material Age, each part giving priority to its self-interest as a separate part and in competition with all the other parts, and entering the Relationship Age, each part giving priority to the oneness of nature relationship of cooperation for maturation among the parts.)

This leads us into seeking the self-evident answer to the fourth question that defines the Relationship Age we are entering where our relationship with all things will be more important to us than our relationships with any particular things:

What is the activity of oneness?

Using Personal Science to Discover the Activity of Oneness

We now know the *most fundamental fact* the universe operates as an indivisible whole. We now know the *fundamental process in nature* is cooperation for maturation. We also know cooperation for maturation is the only thing that is real; everything else is within the mutually agreed-upon illusion tool of assuming separate parts exist.

This has us want to know the *activity of oneness*. How do we know it is what is occurring and the only thing occurring that is real? Let's now study our direct experience to find the self-evident answer to this question.

As described earlier, when we learn knowledge in direct, present, and repeatable experience, such as rocks are hard and fire is hot, it naturally, effortlessly, freely, easily, and permanently becomes knowledge in our thinking we label "true," a skill to consistently honor it as true, and a habit that is part of who we are *and no longer in need of our primary attention*. The rest of our lives we will not be able to fool ourselves into thinking rocks are not hard or fire is not hot.

The maturation in our thinking is permanent.

As asked earlier, where is this maturation? Can you point at it? Take a moment to see if you can find where it is and point at it? If it exists in places and times, you can point at it. Can you?

You will discover you can point at the words that name

it, but you can't point at it. Are you discovering this is true? Study your direct, present, and repeatable experience to determine for yourself if this is true. Only reach your conclusion from doing this, from giving priority to keep your power, all of it, and becoming a personal scientist: use your sixth sense to study your direct, present, and repeatable by choice *experience*.

Can you point at your maturation into the knowledge rocks are hard and fire is hot?

Take a few moments to look up from reading to see if you can identify where this maturation into this knowledge is and point at it.

Then go to the next page.

I think you will again discover you can't point at it because it does not exist in the illusion of separate parts, in the valuable mutually agreed-upon *illusion tool* that times and places exist. It only exists in the "place" that cannot be pointed at.

Maturation only exists in the cooperative process of the indivisible universe. The activity of oneness is maturation.

For us, it is primarily maturation in our thinking. This is the building of self-evident truths upon self-evident truths in any area of our attention. For instance, we know if we get a college degree it will be easier to get a higher paying job and earn more annual income the rest of our lives. This is identifying the *relationship* between getting a college degree and lifetime income. This maturation of our thinking is what has us decide to get a college degree.

The most important area of attention in our lives is the mastery of the skill of human self-consciousness. It determines how we experience the other parts of the universe.

Notice also that we can't get rid of any maturation in our thinking we discover to be self-evident. Once we know from direct, present, and repeatable by choice experience that rocks are hard and fire is hot and getting a college degree will increase our potential for more annual income, we can't ever fool ourselves into thinking we do not know it. If we ever doubt either is a fact, we can again turn our attention to a study of our direct, present, and repeatable experience to observe it is self-evident this is true. We can again give priority to being a personal scientist.

All maturation of knowledge is permanent, outside of being affected by times and places.

Thus, we can't ever fool ourselves into thinking we do not know the knowledge and skill of a layer of maturity once we know it. This is not only true for individual human beings but also for communities, societies, and the entire human species. Once we discover how to build a fire or stir fry vegetables, we can't ever fool ourselves into thinking we do not know how to do them. The automobile was invented near the end of the 1800s, and I do not think any future generation will be ignorant of its invention. The same goes for the invention of electricity, the telephone, computers, and nearly everything else invented in the past. Most maturations or inventions, especially today, are forever known and able to be used by humanity in the future. In fact, the Information Age connection of nearly all on Earth now means any discovery by any group will be forever known by the Earth community of human beings.

Cooperation for maturation is oneness in action. In us, it is primarily maturation in our thinking, in what we know as more mature self-evident facts and skills building on less mature self-evident facts and skills.

Next, this knowledge and these skills become part of who we are—habits. We no longer have to give our primary attention to them. Knowing rocks are hard and fire is hot or getting a college degree will allow us to earn more each year, have matured into being habits. We accurately relate with rocks and fire, and attend classes, without having to think about it.

This pattern is also true when learning the smaller skills of each layer of maturity of the skill of human self-consciousness. The mastery of each smaller skill in the natural sequence and turning it into a habit becomes a maturation that can eventually result in the mastery of the full skill that no longer needs our primary attention. It has become part of who we are, a habit.

This is the activity of oneness—maturation—moving inside us. We can't point at it because it is the universe that is doing it. Our maturation in the skill of *self-consciousness* is now the primary form of the maturation process of the universe.

Maturation has no location and it is permanent change, permanent maturation of an individual, a society, or the entire human species.

The action of oneness inside each of us is more mature self-evident facts building on less mature self-evident facts and our choice to include all of them at all times and in all places (in the reality of oneness) as a set of priorities. This way we value the information from the smaller skills of all seven layers of maturity of the skill of self-consciousness. We also respect their priority in relationship to each other, and we are also aware and honor our relationship to everything else.

One moment our judgment could be that what is most important for us to do for the maturation of us all is to elder a child. The next moment our judgment could be it is to negotiate an agreement between nations. The next moment it could be to take our Prius to the dealership to get repaired. The next moment it could be attending to the needs of an elderly relative. The next moment it could be driving to work. Each moment, what we do is solely determined by a Mature Elder's judgment of what is his or her best action that is direct self-conscious participation in maturation, the activity of oneness: Eldering.

For self-conscious human beings, the primary use of the *activity of oneness, of maturation,* is the mastery of the skill of human self-consciousness. It is the discovery of more mature self-evident truths and smaller skills that build upon less mature self-evident truths and smaller skills toward full mastery of this skill. Each smaller skill becomes a permanent skill, and we use all of the ones we know at all times and in all places (in the reality of oneness). We can even be maturing on our deathbed. (As mentioned earlier, in my next book, *Your and My Maturation Stories,* I tell the story of my mother maturing on her deathbed.)

I, like many of us, have spent most of my life thinking the exercise of free choice was primarily choosing between this or that in times and places. As mentioned earlier, I was fully living within the illusion that separate parts were real, even unconsciously (without choice) when I discovered the universe operates as an indivisible whole. For years afterwards, I was still unconsciously behaving as if oneness was *everything but me.* My Catholic upbringing had me *unconsciously (without choice)* stuck at including sacrificing myself for others as part of who I should be and therefore I was not part of oneness. It took me a long time to uncover this unconscious pattern deep inside me and to make sure my behavior included my physical body as part of oneness. Have any of you reading this discovered something similar about yourself? A particular personal blind spot? You might stop reading at this point and take a few minutes to see if you can identify particular blind spots you have as a result of your upbringing.

It is important to emphasize that skills are the same for everyone; therefore, the smaller skills of the seven layers are the same for everyone.

That is why all human beings are using the first three and why someday, before they leave home, all human beings will be eldered into using all seven smaller skills and be fully mature human beings. This is inevitable because maturation is the activity of oneness, is permanent, and it can't be stopped. Oh, we can at times regress into less mature behaviors, but just as we won't ever be able to fool ourselves into thinking we do not know how to ride a bicycle we won't be able to ever fool ourselves into believing we do not know the smaller skills of the skill of human self-consciousness when we have mastered them.

That is also why the articles arguing that all democracies have eventually reverted to some form of dictatorship are inaccurate. It is all part of the process of maturation in the skill of democracy. With the emergence of agreement nations, we will be taking a major step into having consensus building over time democracy based on accurate inside beliefs being a permanent part of human governance and replacing ballot box wars. Maturation does not happen in a straight line. And the mastery of all acting on the assumption the Earth is round was not happening at all, then some people got it, then more, and now nearly all on Earth are born into societies that know the Earth is round. It is the same with democracy. We do not yet know well how to do democracy. As we get better at it, particularly with the emergence of agreement nations as our priority over geographic defined nations, democracy will become a permanent maturation.

As individuals master each of the layers of maturity of self-consciousness and democracy as well, as has occurred throughout history, they will make sure they elder their children into the smaller skills of the layers they know. Most important, Mature Elders will make sure they elder their children into full maturity in this skill before they are twenty years old. They will know that this is their most important responsibility as parents.

They will also know that this is the only priority in a human society that is simultaneously best for their children and us all.

For this reason, they will also work to have it become the highest priority of the organizations, societies, and nations where they work and live. They will naturally, effortlessly, freely, easily, and permanently build mature human societies. Wherever they are, they will primarily Elder and assist all the organizations of which they are a part to also primarily Elder.

Mastering the smaller skills of a human language and basic self-consciousness (Child layer) only necessitates learning the first two dimensions of the skill of human self-consciousness: space and time. This is the awareness of different parts and times as if they are separate parts. The logical assumption is then that each part is in competition with all the other parts with his, her, or its highest priority being the self-interest of its part. We will now be leaving this Material Age and entering the Relationship Age where we know the first three layers—the Baby, Toddler, and Child layers—are the necessary first layers of maturation in the development sequence toward full maturity in the skill of human self-consciousness. They operate on the assumption separate parts exist to learn the skill of a human language and self-consciousness.

It is only at the Mature Elder layer, the highest layer, that we fully realize we have been doing this and discover we can know and choose as a skill the *experience of self-conscious oneness* as the container experience within which all other relative experiences occur.

From the inside, no one can move our arms and legs or think our thoughts but each of us. Therefore, from the mastery of the skill of this half of the Teen layer to the mastery of the Elder layer we can only live in the illusion we can give our power to a second thing that does not exist, an outside or inside belief (they are both words).

Also, once we have discovered our ability and right of individual free choice, half of the Teen layer of maturity, all later maturation occurs inside us as a result of individual or mature free choice. Each layer builds on the one before it. Also, we can be stuck not taking full responsibility for the second half of the Teen layer until we have achieved full maturity in this skill. Without Mature Elders edifying us there is this second half, accepting the responsibility for sharing in the ownership of participating in maturation for the common good, we will suffer the pains of serially giving priority to outside beliefs until we enter the discovery of the Elder layer.

The support of others can be helpful, but from the Teen layer on it is primarily a private activity, an inside job. From the Teen layer forward, only each of us can elder ourselves into the knowledge and mastery of the smaller skills of the remaining three layers. Also, the smaller skills of the layers build on one another and the skills of the lower layers cannot be negated to master the smaller skills of the higher layers. This is where understanding the importance of primarily using the priority pattern of thinking is essential. It is inclusive of all and never polarizes or negates. It only prioritizes.

Therefore, our mastery of the last three layers builds on honoring half of the smaller skill we mastered at the Teen layer, honoring our ability and right to keep our power, all of it, and exercise individual or mature free choice. Entering the Elder layer only begins to occur when we discover the importance of keeping our power, all of it, and using it as our sixth sense to study our direct, present, and re-peatable by choice experience to discover who or what is doing our breathing. This is the exercise of mature free choice, not individual free choice. This is giving priority to being a personal scientist. This is the beginning of maturation into the Elder layer.

Fundamentally, the Relationship Age is the ending of all self-consciously (by choice) and unconsciously (without choice) parent-child patterns of behavior. It is based on the discovery of the above four inside beliefs.

Hopefully, as a result of doing these four personal science studies, you now know the most important four inside beliefs to master the last two layers of maturity of this skill.

CHAPTER 6

Maturation Movement and 10 Recommended Priorities For 2020 US Presidential Candidates

Each day more people will realize we need a new movement.

A movement similar to the Civil Rights, Women's, and Environment Movements. We can call it the "Maturation Movement." In this chapter, I invite all 2020 US Presidential candidates to become participants in this movement.

A movement is an agreement that it is time for a change, a maturation, in one of our social agreements. If it has identified a change that we are moving toward and now able to understand and embrace, it will consistently grow in the number of people supporting it. It eventually results in a maturation in the thinking of us all, changes in legislation by governments, and changes in the operating policies of all other organizations to honor this maturation of our thinking in social agreements. As mentioned above, good examples of recent successful movements still in motion are the Civil Rights Movement, the Women's Movement, and the Environment Movement. All three are the identification of a more mature social agreement we are now able to embrace and, therefore, the number of people supporting them increases each day and with each generation.

It is time for us to create the Maturation Movement.

This is a movement that states it is time for us to embrace the obvious and self-evident fact, able to be directly witnessed as true by anyone, the universe operates as an indivisible whole. In addition, it is time for us to affirm maturation, not competition, is the fundamental process, priority, and activity of nature. Thirdly, this means there are two patterns of thinking, the separate parts pattern and the oneness pattern. While simultaneously using both, we need to learn to give priority to the oneness pattern and second priority to the separate parts pattern. Fourthly, for human beings who have matured into primarily using the oneness pattern of giving priority to priorities, the most important set of priorities are the layers of maturity of human self-consciousness. Therefore, our highest priority as a human society is to self-elder ourselves into full maturity in this skill so we can elder our children to full maturity in it before they leave home and marry. This is the worldview and mission of the Maturation Movement.

As stated twice before, when two or more people at the Teen layer or higher are living together, the other side of the coin of honoring each person's ability and right to keep their power and exercise individual free choice is the making and keeping of agreements. They are inseparable from one another and, as we mature, we discover both have to be fully respected and honored to enjoy living with other people.

Secondly and no matter its size or the number of people, all the people who happen to be living on the same piece of land will not share the same worldview. Our next layer of social maturity in democracy is respecting this and supporting like-thinking people to self-organize themselves into communities of friends based on their shared beliefs as long as they obey the rules of the geographic nations and do not harm others. In this book, associations of these communities are labeled "agreement nations." They are people who have joined one another for the purpose of meeting all of their individual and collective needs, the way nations behave. They will nearly always operate as democracies, and anyone in the world can join, or leave and join another, without needing to move one's residence. They are self-organized nations accepting full responsibility for living according to their chosen worldview. Those that have the most mature worldview and operate the best for the good of all will receive the greatest number of members. The geographic nations will increasingly give priority to nurturing the growth and maturation of agreement nations, letting a thousand flowers bloom and accept the responsibility for creating a safe place for them to emerge and mature.

The following *ladder of priorities*, not platform of planks where each is given equal value, are policies that honor both sides of this coin, individual freedom of choice and the making and keeping agreements that give priority to the common good, and the natural process of prioritization that cannot be escaped.

Fundamentally, we want to ask each Presidential candidate for his or her answer to this question, "What kind of human beings do you believe we are ready to become and what are your policies that will lead us to become them?" We want to know his or her worldview, where he or she would like to lead us, and how he or she plans to do it. Then, as members of a democracy, we can join him or her as partners in making it happen. We want to primarily be partners with him or her in a movement, not only for our social maturation but also as our collective participation in the maturation of humanity in our now global village.

Since cooperation for maturation is the fundamental process in nature, we want the answers to all other questions to be secondary in importance in determining our choice for a President.

Allow me to provide a recommended ladder of priorities for the 2020 candidates for President of the United States, or of any country.

I believe these kinds of agreements will eventually be as widespread around our globe as knowing and using a human language and honoring each person's ability and right to keep his or her power and exercise individual and mature free choice. Maturation is the fundamental process in nature, is always its priority and primary activity, and cannot be escaped or stopped. Throughout history, any experience of two steps back is always eventually followed with three steps forward. In my judgment, having the following policy priorities would be leading us into the next layer of maturity of social agreements we, as Americans, are now ready and able to embrace.

The following, in order of priorities, is the ladder I would like to recommend a candidate, or all candidates, consider embracing when running for President of the United States in 2020. They could appear under the motto of something like "Let's lead again and be worthy of it":

1. **The United States will take the lead to create a new global organization, for now we can call it United Nations Two. Its priority will be to end war and violence on Earth as a method of dealing with differences.**

   a. All wars begin and end in peace. Mature people skip the war part. They resolve conflicts with conversations that result in agreements they keep or re-negotiate. Yes, as in World War II, when an extremely immature person ended up in control of a powerful nation and sought to dominate other nations, war is necessary. However, we want to always do our best to avoid it through the making and keeping of agreements and the Eldering of all of our children into full maturity in the skill of human self-consciousness before the end of their teenage years.

b. Any geographic nation on Earth may join this new global organization.

c. If a nation joins it is committing to no longer allowing war, terrorism, or violence of any kind as a means of dealing with differences within, between, and among people in their nations.

d. They commit to making their militaries available to the other members as a police force, not a war force, to stop any war, terrorism, or violence as a means of dealing with differences.

e. Any war, terrorism, or violent actions within or between their nations will be treated as violations of these agreements. Therefore, they will be handled as a police action. War of any kind will never be used or allowed within or between member nations. Police action assumes the existence of agreements. War assumes an inability to reach agreements. This is establishing an association of nations firmly based on agreement, agreement to no longer participate in war or violence to resolve differences.

f. All groups of people with a cherished identify will be encouraged to create "agreement nations," defined by their agreements with each other to operate as an organization of people and not defined by geography. Locally like-thinking communities of friends can associate with other such communities, and others anywhere around the world, and operate as a transnational nation defined by agreement. As long as these agreement nations follow the rules within their geographic nations and do no harm to others, they will not only be allowed but actively encouraged by member geographic nations. This will be done in a celebration of the many different ways people will choose to elder their children and support each other's self-eldering. It will also be done to end the need for any community of like-thinking people to think the only way they can live their lives the way they choose is to get control of their geographic nation. Increasingly, the geographic nations will give high priority to encouraging and supporting the agreement nations as the next layer of maturity of democracy.

g. ***Commentary:*** When the United Nations was formed in the 1940s, Elenore Roosevelt, one of our US representatives, argued that it should be based on the honoring of human rights. She failed to win that argument. Instead it was based on primarily honoring the sovereignty of geographically defined nations. It will never be the case that the people who happen to be living on a particular piece of land will be operating at the same layer of maturity in the skill of human self-consciousness or share a religious, philosophical, or scientific belief accept, hopefully, to live in peace and honor each other's beliefs. The latter is the primary responsibility of geographic nations. What has happened is that democracies have become wars of the ballot box between and among groups to get control of a nation to gain the ability to force everyone to live according to that group's beliefs: an unconscious (without choice) continuation of the parent-child pattern in governance. This leaves no other option but to compete for power both to not have others impose their worldviews on us and to get the power to enforce our worldview on everyone or, hopefully instead, argue for a more mature model. The priority of the governments of geographic nations should be to arrange for safe and practical operations on the land, from fire and police departments to the provision of necessary utilities, schools, other agreed-upon social services; and secondly to support and encourage groups of people to form into agreement nations. This will end groups giving priority to seeking to control the geographic government (by force of arms or gaining political power) to make all live as that group thinks people should live. *This encouragement of the formation by all into agreement nations is the next layer of maturity of democracy on Earth.* Geographic governments will accurately treat agreement nations as free research and development programs. When they create and implement programs that work well for their people, the geographic nations will be able to point to their success to advocate that they become policies of the geographic nation. Being able to reveal its practical success could make it possible for the vast majority of the people in the geographic nation to easily support it. Also, and most important, those in the agreement nation no longer need to wait for the geographic nations to support any policy they determine to be wise. As long as they do no harm to others and follow the rules of the geographic nation, they are free to live according to their chosen agreements. The tendency toward a parent-child pattern by the group in power in geographic nations will also eventually end as all the agreement nations vote to make sure the geographic nations make it easy for different agreement nations to emerge and flourish. Finally, nearly 50% of the annual budget of the US Government goes to the military. This new global organization, especially as more nations join, will allow us to reduce the percentage of our annual budget that goes to militaries.

2. **Encourage the formation of agreement nations, nations defined by agreements rather than geography, the next layer of maturity of democracy.**

   a. This was already stated as a key piece of being able to succeed at ending war and violence as a means of dealing with differences. However, because of its importance also in the maturation of democracy it is appropriately the second priority of this ladder.

   b. The support and encouragement of the formation of agreement nations ends the need for one group to get control of a geographic nation to escape the dominance of others. Each agreement nation can organize their lives together as they judge best and join with all other agreement nations to be sure the geographic nation supports the emergence and flourishing of different agreement nations. The priority is for each of us to keep our power, all of it, and create with others the world we want instead of fighting for the freedom to do it by the only other means possible today, getting control of the geographic nation.

   c. As long as the rules of the geographic nation are followed and there is no harm to others, each group can organize its agreement nation as it judges best. In the laws of the geographic nations all must follow, there will usually be at least minimal respect for human rights and care for each other: no killing, slavery, stealing, child abuse, and other now universally recognized levels of maturity of human behavior required by all. As all the people in geographic nations mature, the standards they will require of all will also mature. For instance, nearly all nations on Earth have matured to respect the ability and right of individuals to keep their power and exercise free choice. This has resulted in the formation of many democratic governments, now at least a majority of the nations on Earth, and there are free market economies in nearly all nations.

d. While remaining even more responsible citizens of the geographic nation, primarily to protect their agreement nations, the priority of people in agreement nations will be their agreement nation. Like religions, as long as no harm is done to others, they can differ greatly, be fully allowed, and not need to get along with each other. However, many agreement nations will join in partnerships for common purposes. **Commentary:** The encouragement of the development of agreement nations is the next layer of maturity of globally organizing our lives together based on honoring both sides of the coin of our ability and right at the Teen layer: honoring each person's ability and right to keep his or her power to exercise individual free choice and to join with like-thinking people to make and keep agreements for the common good of all, not just the members of their agreement nation. It allows each group to create the lives they choose without interference by others. Agreement nations are easily possible in most nations today and can be encouraged. Agreement nations can tax or not tax their members. My guess is that most will not tax but cover all costs with donations, fees, and return on investments of capital donated to them. They will raise and mature their children as they judge best, creating their schools or using the geographic nation's schools and augmenting them with their maturation program. Finally, they will now be free to together organize their lives as they judge best without the fear of being forced to do so as others judge best. One of the new priorities of the citizens of geographic nations will be to provide a safe place for people to create and give priority to different agreement nations. Of course, this can greatly reduce terrorism, revolutions, and other violent means of getting control of a geographic nation.

3. **Eldering our children to full maturity in the skill of human self-consciousness before they leave home and marry.**

   a. Many of our schools are still teaching reading, writing, and arithmetic as if it is the nineteenth century. They also are not giving priority to teaching the most important skill for our children to learn: the skill of human self-consciousness, the skill of mutual mature love. We are now able to elder our children into discovering them as self-evident truths, as smaller skills that can accumulate and integrate together into full maturity in this skill by the time teenagers leave home and marry.

   b. We now know our invention of human languages was the result of an unconscious (without choice) invention of a mutually agreed upon illusion tool, the assumption the universe is separate parts (our mutual blind spot), that has allowed us to become self-conscious parts of the universe. We also now know the universe operates as an indivisible whole, operating the exact same way we experience the parts within our physical bodies cooperating for the health and maturation of our whole bodies. The fundamental assumption about how the universe operates is not the mutually agreed upon illusion tool of assuming it is separate parts necessary to invent a human language and be self-conscious.

c. We also know cooperation, not competition, is the fundamental process in nature. We know maturation is the particular kind of cooperation that is the fundamental process, priority, and activity in nature. We are going somewhere. We are maturing. What shape the universe will take at any point in the future is not most important. What is most important is that we know maturation is the fundamental process, priority, and activity inside and outside us at all times and personal contented joy lies in mastering the skill of self-consciously participating in it as a result of primarily being a personal scientist.

d. Therefore, this not only needs to be added to our school curriculums. It needs to be the highest priority in our schools. If not yet the priority in our local schools, then an augmenting program needs to be created by our agreement nations. There is nothing more important for a child to learn than the layers of maturity of the skill of human self-consciousness as he or she is biologically able to master each of them and into full maturity before he or she leaves home. Part of it is learning how to have our marriages be successful, how to have our parenting successfully elder our children to full maturity before they leave home, how to be a constructive participant in meetings, how to form agreement nations while fully honoring our responsibilities as citizens of geographically defined nations, and all other human relationship skills that are an extension of mastering the skill of human self-consciousness.

e. **Commentary:** There is nothing more important for a child than to be successfully eldered into each of the layers of maturity smaller skills when he or she is biologically ready to learn each and into full maturity before leaving home and getting married. If this is not accomplished, the child could remain at one of the lower layers the rest of his or her life and unconsciously (without choice) think it is the highest layer. When operating at the highest layer, the natural, effortless, freely, and easily chosen behavior priority at all times and in all places (in the reality of oneness) is moral behavior. It is this behavior in action each moment that has us experience the contented joy we have intuitively known all along is our birthright. This Eldering priority with each other and our children is also the only priority that is simultaneously best both for the child's happiness and the happiness of us all. It is important to point out human self-consciousness is a skill, not a belief. In this book we are only concerned with identifying the most fundamental facts about how the universe operates so we can learn the skills of relating with it correctly. We will not at any time focus on answering the most fundamental question in most of us nor should political candidates: "Why is the universe structured the way it is structured?" This answer is usually a religious, philosophical, or scientific answer. We are each free to choose our answer to that question. However, this proposed ladder of priorities is based on our known skills of relating realistically with the way the universe operates. Your answer to the above question will appropriately be more important to you than the mastery of this skill, or any skill.

4. **Managing Earth for the sustainability and flourishing of life.**

   a. We broke it. We have to fix it.

   b. We are the self-conscious (able to exercise mature free choice) parts of the universe. Therefore, by choice together we need to manage Earth the way we each manage our home, for the continuous safety, health, and happiness of all who live in it.

   c. Only those who still think the universe operates as separate parts cannot understand the importance of this. They believe we are each a separate part and, therefore, it is natural for us to each compete with all else for the self-interest of our physical bodies. They believe this is natural and to do otherwise is naïve. They are not aware that this is, indeed, our unconscious (without choice) priority up to our teenage years, the time when we are primarily learning a human language and the skill of self-consciousness. From the teenage years on it is possible for us to discover natural morality. It is giving priority to self-conscious participation in the fundamental process in nature of cooperation for the maturation of the universe (nature). This is our highest priority when we achieve full maturity in the skill of human self-consciousness. This behavior as our priority each moment is what results in the consistent inner feeling of contended joy we know is our birthright. It also results in accepting full collective responsibility for the wise management of our Earth home and all that exists. Throughout history, this priority in our behavior each moment has been labeled "Eldering." It is the only behavior each moment that sustains inside us contented joy, the most enjoyable joy.

d. Today the people on Earth are ready and able to join this Maturation Movement thereby entering the Relationship Age. It can rapidly happen as more each day self-elder themselves to full maturity in the skill of human self-consciousness and elder their children to full maturity in it before they leave home and marry. This will result in our self-definition changing to be "I am first the universe that will not die and secondly my physical body that will die." This is the maturation that will rapidly result in wise management of our Earth home.

e. **Commentary:** If we have achieved the knowledge and skill of the higher layers, our natural response to those who have not is compassion, the same loving compassion—without any sense of superiority but of oneness with them—we extend to our children when they are still not aware of the higher layers of maturity of the skill of human self-consciousness. We are not each a whole. We are all in this together as parts of the one indivisible whole. By nature, our primary intention is to cooperatively participate in their and our maturation. The problem is the innocence of immaturity. It is a result of not being aware of the oneness of nature and importance of self-eldering ourselves to full maturity in the skill of human self-consciousness. Therefore, their behavior is not to be attacked. It is not possible for a person who only has discovered some of the lower layers of maturity to operate at a higher layer. And we do not want to use force. Where compassionate care is appropriate, we extend compassionate care. Where non-cooperation with immaturity, especially in the face of the imposition of immature rules and regulations, the Mahatma Gandhi form of compassionate non-cooperation is appropriate. This method of stimulating further conversation will result in all parties eventually and genuinely agreeing on and keeping more mature agreements.

5. **Ending poverty on Earth.**

   a. Like it or not, Earth is now operating as one village. The highest priority of the Elders of a village is the survival, safety, health, and maturation of all of its members into full maturity in the skill of human self-consciousness. Ending poverty for all is therefore near the top of the list for Mature Elders on Earth.

   b. We would not let our brother or sister starve. Everyone is our brother or sister. Therefore, we want to make sure, as soon as possible and as rapidly as possible, for every person on Earth to have a basic monthly income to survive. People will still be motivated to have more income. The greatest cause of violence is poverty. Ending poverty is good for all, not just the poor. It is especially good for the business community: it creates more customers.

c. We now have the means to do this, if necessary, as a private-sector activity and with the assistance of geographic and agreement nations where they choose to participate. This way it is not necessary to wait for governments or any other organizations to do it.

d. Some people, such as the now richest man in the world, Jeff Bezos, have been able to become extremely wealthy, as he has, in twenty-four years using the stock market. That same means, investing conservatively in stocks and bonds, can now be used as a private-sector activity, with the assistance of any and all government and non-government organizations, to rapidly end poverty on Earth.

e. People can be encouraged to donate capital to a fund in a charitable organization, let's name it the "Common Good Fund," and receive a tax deduction. We can create a charitable organization for this and another purpose described below and name it "Trusts for All Children, Inc. (TAC)." Also, existing charitable organizations can create the following program as a project within their charitable organization. This capital would be invested in the stock markets, usually in an index such as the S&P 500 Index which is of the 500 largest and diversified companies in the USA and global indices. The annual net profits could be distributed to poor people as cash by responsible organizations already in existence around the world. The costs would be covered by other donations (see below) so none of the profits would be used to cover expenses. This way all contributors know that 100% of their capital's annual profits in this Common Good Fund will forever be used to end poverty on Earth.

f. Warren Buffett and Bill and Melinda Gates have created the Giving Pledge group, now with over 200 billionaires who have committed to donating at least half of their wealth to charity before they die. TAC, or similar programs in other charitable organizations, can become one of the main recipients of those donations and those of many others, including governments.

g. In addition, parents can be encouraged to create a trust fund at TAC for each of their children starting at birth. It will be the result of a $11 monthly donation from ten family members and friends for the first twenty years of each child's life ($132 a year per person). Throughout the child's life family members, friends, employers, and nations can contribute more to it. To keep the child above extreme poverty for his or her entire life, it could also be invested as above with a monthly distribution of a portion of its assets from the age of twenty years old. Thus, since the greater portion of the capital will usually be growing annually, it will also serve as a private-sector equivalent of US Social Security payments when elderly. Lastly, upon death the balance can be contributed to the Common Good Fund to end poverty. Using an existing IRS program, this will allow the capital to grow without taxation for the entire life of the child. An additional $1 to each monthly $10 will be used to cover the expenses of both this program and the above Common Good Fund and to fund other programs to assist people to get permanently out of poverty. Thus, participants receive a threefer: their monthly contributions solely supports the child they love his or her entire life, the balance upon his or her death will be used to permanently end poverty on Earth, and the additional US Dollar each month makes it easier for large and small donors to donate capital to the Common Good Fund because they know the expenses will be covered by these contributions.

h. **Commentary:** Private-sector programs like the two described above (with government participation welcomed) are now possible. The board members of Trusts for All Children can be respected people of integrity from around Earth. Not controlled by any government and with such a respected leadership, governments could comfortably participate in both programs to end poverty on Earth for every child of future generations. People and governments could also first focus on the children in their nations and secondly on children around the world. The wealthy on Earth would also now have a respected way they can participate in ending poverty on Earth forever by making donations, initially earmarked if they like for the children in particular areas of Earth they choose. They will also do so knowing it is a private-sector program and will not be part of any government's political football back and forth activities and strongly supported by the public. They will also enjoy the personal pleasure of ending poverty the way most of them made their wealth, through ownership of assets.

6. **Supporting the emergence of common good capitalism.**

a. The *primary essence* of capitalism is not giving priority to capital. That is secondary. It is giving priority to individual freedom and free markets. However, this is only one side of the coin of being members of a society. The other side is making and keeping agreements for cooperative maturation. Like the teams of a sports league, the voluntary freely chosen agreements could be cooperation for maturation and secondly for profit for a few or anything else. Giving priority to the common good is our priority as members of any society. Thus, the next layer of maturity of free markets is what I have labeled "common good capitalism."

b. This is where in the private-sector, and probably beginning with the competitors in each product market, like the teams in sports leagues they meet and agree on the common good agreements within which the competition will occur as second in priority. The competition is still as ferocious as before but now voluntarily second in priority. This is legal. They are reaching agreements mutually costly to them for the common good, not for collusion. This is our *primary responsibility* to which we have all agreed to as members of any society, now we are all members of our global society. And a government official could be present at all meetings to assure for the public only cooperation for the common good occurred, not collusion for self-interests.

c. The competitors could agree on a livable wage as a minimum wage in each location, other labor agreements, agreements to protect the environment, a percentage of contributions of annual profits to charity to reduced poverty, and on many other issues. The auditors can serve as the referees, reporting in easy to read annual reports posted online how, and to what degree, each company is keeping its freely chosen agreements.

d. In fact, cooperation among competitors is already happening only not for cooperative maturation. Today, the highest priority on Wall Street is the merger and acquisition of companies to have only two or three competitors in each product market. As described before, some visible examples of these are CVS-Walgreens, Home Depot-Lowe's, Visa-MasterCard, Pepsi-Coca Cola, FedEx-UPS, Google-Apple, Boeing-Airbus, and many more. In our modern communications system these companies do not have to directly talk with each other to give priority to being mutually profitable and secondly competitive, thereby making antitrust laws mute. This movement toward what can be labeled "duopoly monopoly" is occurring rapidly in every product market. In fact, simply because people do not want to have to go to more than one website on their computers to get what they want, some companies are achieving a near monopoly: Facebook, Amazon, and Google.

e. Private companies already cooperate for the common good. It is called "creating standards." The reason the same kind of plug can be used to plug any appliance into an electric outlet is because that standard has been agreed-upon. The Common Good Capitalism movement is simply proposing it be extended into reaching additional agreements for the common good.

f. **Commentary:** What is needed is for the general public to recognize that duopoly monopolies are occurring and insist upon maturation into common good capitalism. We already do the latter by governments making it illegal to kill, enslave, steal, and lie in business, all of which used to be acceptable in our distant history. It is now time, *in the private-sector*, for us to mature into common good capitalism where competitors in each product market openly, publicly, and freely, like the teams in a sports league, *reach agreements for the common good and secondly compete as ferociously as before* only now in a way that is not at the expense of the employees, community, and environment. It could also be agreements among companies in many markets as well, for instance within the entire tech sector. It is time for our business community to move into operating at the higher layers of maturity.

7. **Encourage the formation of People's Committees at all levels of societies within both geographic and agreement nations.**

   a. In communities, there needs to be an ongoing discussion of important current issues. It also needs to occur without a deadline. Instead, the goal should be eventually achieving a 70% majority vote in support of a resolution. The votes should be cast by elders selected by community groups from all walks of life. These decisions will not have legal authority. At the same time, they could have a powerful moral authority in the community.

   b. In-depth discussions of issues have little ability to get the attention they deserve by all forms of media because there is always something more exciting to hold the viewer's attention. Their priority is to sell their commercial slots at a high price. Therefore, another vehicle needs to be created that can hold the attention of the members in local communities. The People's Committee model can do this.

c. The People's Committee can be a non-profit organization that invites every major group—for-profits, non-profits, cooperatives, religious, and whatever to choose their most senior statesperson. The only people who cannot be chosen are those directly involved in electoral politics. Their priority is a competitive process and the priority of the People's Committees is a cooperative process for the maturation of the thinking of all. There can be town, state, and national People's Committees with each level taking into full consideration the agreements reached at smaller geographic areas. Representatives from the local People's Committees can serve on each next layer up Committees: county, state, and national. A similar program can be created in agreement nations.

d. The goal of each gathering is to create a safe space for all points of view to be presented on an issue and for mutually respectful discussions to occur. The goal is for all to experience together a genuine search for self-evident truths as the foundation of their chosen policy recommendations.

e. For instance, the difficult issue of a women's right to an abortion can be the focus of some meetings of the town's People's Committee on the same month each year. This will allow all to prepare their arguments well in advance. At the end of each session there is a vote. Until there is a 70% vote in support for a proposed policy, the discussion continues on the same month next year.

f. This consensus-building-over-time-on-issues important to the community will have no legal power. However, they will in actuality have the greatest power. It will become very difficult for a person to run for office and win if they are against the positions of the People's Committee that has received a 70% vote of support or is approaching that percentage.

g. Most important, there will now be an enjoyable, captivating, and very personal place for people in local communities to genuinely seek agreement together based on a genuine search for self-evident truths. If not able to participate in person, they can participate via their cell phones, computers, television, and radio.

h. Of course, geographic and agreement nations can both form People's Committees.

i. **Commentary:** We need a way for local people to meet face-to-face to discuss important issues to them both without a deadline and where the priority is on discovering together self-evident truths. This is the opposite of electoral politics that is a fight to win over an opposition with a deadline. When people with a sincere intention to find self-evident truths together remain in a mutually respectful conversation, they will eventually find some common ground upon which they agree and upon which they can then find additional agreements closer to their differences. More important, all can mature their thinking in the process. Finally, this is a way to escape the marketing strategies, tricks, and fake news of candidates to win elections. Instead, with friends and neighbors the focus can be on a genuine search for agreement on self-evident truths. As Mahatma Gandhi argued, the original inventor of this model, when people are eye-to-eye and a self-evident truth is well spoken, it is very difficult for anyone present to not honor it. This is the process that needs to be the foundation of democracy in both geographic and agreement nations.

8. **Formation of a Majority Supported Platform in each state.**

   a. Often, because of the marketing, manipulation of information, and fake and immature news, politicians are often elected who act against the positions on issues supported by a significant majority of citizens.

   b. Citizens in each state can be encouraged to form a Majority Supported Platform Committee, a non-profit citizens organization funded with donations. Here the word "platform," not "priorities," is used to signal that priority is not being given to one position more than another.

   c. Where polls show 60% or more of citizens in that state support a position, such as equal rights for women relative to men or we broke the environment therefore we have to fix it, they would appear on the Platform.

   d. No position with a polling of less than 60% support would ever appear on this platform. The public must know this, and this must be consistently adhered to.

   e. People in the state are asked if they support the list of positions. If they do, they are given a number. When more than 50% of the people in the state have committed to vote in support of this list of positions on the Majority Supported Platform, they know that if they all go to the polls and only vote for candidates who have committed to support that Platform of positions, those will be the only people elected to offices.

f. The more than 50% of the voters who chose a number signaling their support for these positions will then be sure they vote to maintain solidarity with all the others who have a number. Secondly, candidates will tend to only run for office if they genuinely at least support that Platform of positions.

g. People will know they will receive only one email a week before each election with the list of candidates from all parties who genuinely support the entire Majority Supported Platform.

h. For instance, no more than 318,236 people have voted in Vermont in the last three Presidential elections. Thus, if 160,000 or more voters made a personal commitment to vote in support of the Platform by supporting the candidates whom they judge genuinely support them, they know candidates who at a minimum support those positions will get elected.

i. **Commentary:** This is a way to successfully get beyond, at least at a minimum level, the manipulation activities in electoral politics and move toward what the majority support becoming what elected officials legislate.

9. **To get beyond our tendency in electoral politics to give priority to partisanship and instead give priority to cooperation for maturation, whoever is elected President commits to work with both major parties to identify their senior most respected morally based statesperson acceptable to**

the President to serve as one of three members of a Kitchen Cabinet with him or her.

a. The President would still have final say in all matters. However, he or she would welcome collaboration with the other two in a search for pieces of legislation that give priority to cooperative maturation. This would allow them to speak as one voice to more easily achieve support from both major and all parties.

b. The President would seek a consensus of the Kitchen Cabinet before coming forward with a proposal. However, if that was not possible, all three will speak at one time to explain their agreements and disagreements in the hope that the priority can remain seeking what is best for cooperative maturation. Then this responsible and respectful disagreement among these three people can become the major focus of the media.

c. The goal is for these three people to model mature, caring, mutually respectful, candid, honest, genuine, and sincere statesperson behavior when in agreement or disagreement.

d. **Commentary:** We are currently a very polarized and partisan society. This would be the institution of a process at the highest level to give priority to cooperative maturation and to have it be the context of responsible agreement and disagreement. Hopefully it would be seen as a model other polarized groups might imitate. Clearly, a bold action such as this is necessary to reveal a commitment to move beyond giving priority to partisanship or the self-interest of any person or group.

10. **To study all the other developed nations' health insurance programs and bring forward the best plan.**

    a. Every other developed nation has a universal health insurance program. This provides us with the opportunity to study all of them, learn from their experience, and identify the best plan for the United States.

    b. **Commentary:** No one should have to worry about adequate and quality health care. We can afford to provide it. Let's create a commission of well-intended people from all parties to do this study, bring forward a recommendation, and get this done.

CHAPTER 7

Maturation in Relationships and Organizations In the Relationship Age

Each day more people will become involved in one or more of the below activities that are, in my judgment, a maturation of how we will live our lives together.

Most were described in the last chapter and some additional information will be provided about each of those here. Others not described earlier will be described here.

We have both personal and social lives. It is essential that we also focus on cooperation for maturation of our social lives as well as the maturation of our personal lives.

We are all in this together as parts of one whole.

Romance

Knowing mature love in a romantic relationship as a *mutual* skill. Both people need to have achieved full maturity in the skill of human self-consciousness and be able to mutually experience it by self-conscious choice.

As stated a number of times, romantic love is not something between two noses. It is mutually knowing the *self-conscious experience of oneness* as a freely chosen and mastered skill. It is the chosen container of the relationship. Initially, as when doing the Mutual Mature Love Experience in the next chapter, *Chapter 8*, it can only be a mutually known skill for the minutes doing it.

A romantic relationship is usually the main place it is discovered and experienced as a mutually and freely chosen ongoing experience. It can then serve as one's base camp. It is where we know we can consistently and mutually experience it. It is also where we can return to confirm it is real and possible.

There is no relationship where it is more important to know full mutual maturity in the skill of human self-consciousness than in our most intimate relationship. It can assure both it will last for their life because it is a skill both have and know the other has it. It is also an essential skill to know to do a wise job of parenting children to full maturity by the time they leave home and marry. Finally, supporting each other's maturation in the skill of Eldering is *simultaneously best* both for each other and the maturation of us all.

This is mutual mature love in motion, the most enjoyable adventure in life.

Mature couples discover they have two self-conscious skills, the self-consciousness of being the indivisible universe and the self-consciousness of their physical bodies. They learn to give priority to the former. It is "the watcher and chooser." They give second priority to the latter, it is "the doer." They can then sit together and, while in appreciation rather than getting defensive, discuss the behavior of each in a genuine search for self-evident truths, a process of cooperation for maturation. In this case, mutual maturation.

Of course, this skill can be used in other relationships as well.

Historically, this skill has often been referred to as "acting according to one's conscience." That is how my father knew it. Whenever he had to sign a birthday card or left us a note of any kind, he always drew a rose with three leaves on its stem. He would then put two dots in the center of the rose for eyes. He then explained to us that the rose was always watching us to be sure we followed our conscience. One of his roses is on the cover of this and all my books.

Finally, it is knowing this skill as an eye-to-eye mutually known skill that is essential.

Mature love is mutually knowing, living in, and continuously giving priority *in our thinking* to the *self-conscious experience of oneness* and second priority to words. The highest priority *in our behavior* is Eldering. Only this has oneness become known as real. Being able to continually return to this primary relationship to affirm it as real, to serve as our base camp, allows us to consistently get better at unilaterally giving it priority when with people and organizations that are not operating at the highest layer of maturity in this skill.

This is why knowing this mutually known skill in our romantic relationship is essential to live the rest of our lives within its contented joy container.

Parenting

Parenting is *primarily* the skill of eldering children to full maturity in the skill of human self-consciousness before they leave home and marry. We want them to know how to invite another into a romantic relationship where they both know the skill of mutual mature love.

All during childhood we want to remind them, as they are able to understand it, there are layers of maturity of the skill of human self-consciousness. Then, when they are entering the teenage years, they will know they have mastered some and, more important, there are four more to master to achieve full maturity in the skill of human self-consciousness.

As described in *Chapter 2: Eldering Teenagers into the Teen Layer*, when it is judged they are maturing into the Teen layer of maturity it is essential that the relationship agreement be changed, *very officially and obviously changed*, to make decisions with them about their lives by consensus. It is also the time to guide them into answering the seven questions by giving priority to keeping their power, all of it, and studying their direct, present, and repeatable by choice experience. It is also the time to have them know the difference between choice, individual free choice, and mature free choice and, if they gave priority to mature free choice when answering the 7 questions, they were using their skill of human self-consciousness as their sixth sense to be a personal scientist. It is also the time to be sure they understand the seven layers of maturity of the skill of human self-consciousness and that the other half of mastering the Teen layer is accepting they now share with us all the responsibility of giving priority to the common good, cooperation for maturation.

They also have to be educated to know that whenever two or more people are together the other side of the coin of individual or mature free choice is the making and keeping of agreements. They are inseparable from one another or there is perpetual war. That is why from this point forward decisions of how we will relate with them need to be made by consensual agreements. They not only learn the importance of living with others by agreements, but also the skill of facilitating and achieving consensual agreements.

Also, now our teenager has to consistently talk with us to make or change those agreements!

This will reduce the possibility that the teen will float away from a strong relationship with us. Also, for the rest of his or her life the making and keeping of decisions made by consensus is a very valuable skill for him or her to learn.

The teenager is also informed that if agreement on any issue is not possible, we, the parents, will have to have the final say; but they also need to know we will try to never exercise that responsibility unless deemed absolutely necessary.

This is also a very important skill to learn for the rest of his or her life. In organizations it is important being comfortable allowing those to lead who have matured into full maturity in the skill of human self-consciousness and Eldering but only as long as they are respected as having those skills.

We then genuinely give priority to living with the teenager by consensus agreements. If it is ever deemed necessary to exercise our veto power, full explanation must be given. Hopefully it will be a rare exception, and the mutual respect relationship will be so strong it will never be necessary or respected if it has to be used. The teenager will then both trust this process and learn much about the skill of Eldering from us to use in life and when he or she has children.

What is most important is that cooperation for maturation is the priority when making, keeping, and renegotiating agreements. This will allow us, the parents, to remain in an ongoing Eldering relationship with our teenager.

The most important information to share with our children while children and particularly when teenagers is the layers of maturity of the skill of human self-consciousness. This will also allow us to assist him or her to understand the importance of giving priority to a study of his or her direct, present, and repeatable by choice experience. This is keeping his or her power and using it as the sixth sense of self-conscious knowing. This is being a personal scientist to identify the self-evident truths he or she will represent in words to use in thinking as inside beliefs. The teen can also be educated that if this personal science skill is learned, full maturity in the skill of the Teen layer can be learned and the Adult layer can be skipped, the choice of an outside fundamental belief on how the universe operates. The second part of the Teen layer is also described: sharing in the responsibility we all have of giving priority to cooperation for maturation and this can only be fully understood and mastered as a skill by mastering the smaller skills of the remaining three layers of this skill.

This can be the most powerful eldering activity of us as parents.

Maturation into the last two layers of maturity in the skill of human self-consciousness, the Elder and Mature Elder layers, can only occur by one primarily keeping one's power, all of it, and using it to study one's direct, present, and repeatable by choice experience to discover and master the remaining self-evident facts and skills that define those layers. Therefore, it is essential that the parent's eldering, except in drastic situations, always honors the teenager's ability and right to exercise mature free choice while assisting in the teenager's *self-eldering process* of achieving full maturity in this skill before leaving home and getting married. It will also allow this Eldering relationship with us to be available to the teen the rest of his or her life.

When our offspring have achieved full maturity in the skill of human self-consciousness, it is important for us to inform him or her that, in our judgment, that has occurred. Therefore, our responsibility of parenting is complete. This affirmation will be valuable for the teenager, now a Mature Elder, to know. This reveals to him or her that the parenting process is completed and there is not the possibility of unconscious parent-child behavior at least with us, the parents. This also means he or she is now fully responsible for his or her behavior as a Mature Elder. We can then enjoy the relationship of us all being Mature Elders and Eldering the rest of our lives.

As mentioned earlier, for more than twenty years I have been a member of a wonderful men's organization, The ManKind Project, whose main activity is a weekend workshop, New Warrior Training

Adventure. It initiates men into accepting full responsibility for their behavior (the Teen layer). I am consistently stunned at the number of men who are in their thirties and older who still do not judge they have been authorized to be adults. I highly recommend men of any age attend that workshop in your local area—www. mkp.org. Nothing is more important for men, and women as well, than to learn their innocence is behind them and they are now responsible for accepting full responsibility for being a participant in the cooperative process of the maturation of us all. That is not the priority of this workshop, but after attending it you can then more easily discover the next layer, the Elder layer. You can then also become part of this community of men who staff the future weekends to provide this Eldering process for other men.

Community

The experience of being a community member and a consumer are opposites. A consumer sees something. If he or she likes it, it is bought. If not, one walks away.

If a community member sees something and likes it, he or she declares, "Hey everyone! Look at this. It is beautiful. Let's have a celebration, ritual, party, or something to honor what it is. It is beautiful." Or, if he or she does not like it declares, "Hey everyone! This is broken. Let's get together and fix it."

The experience of a consumer and community member are opposites.

Everything about our current dominant society is focusing us on being a consumer. Every commercial is a scream at us to "Think only of yourself!" With the rejections of paternalistic systems, there is now little community left in our lives. Unless, that is, we create one. And given we are shedding being part of paternalistic systems, we need to learn how to create and operate one as a democracy, preferably a near consensual democracy rather than a majoritarian democracy.

As a result, we will freely choose to join with like-thinking people to create the lives we want. Next to our romantic relationship, this group of friends is our next most intimate relationships. We want it to be based on the making and keeping of freely chosen agreements based on a worldview we share. It is a self-created democratic organization. We want it to not be majoritarian democracy but a building toward consensus over time without a deadline democracy. We want it to build on mature free choice (half of the mature Teen layer) and have all at least be aware of the highest two layers: Elder and Mature Elder.

People will have to take initiative to find local like-thinking people. If you like what you are reading in this book, you can explore joining the nation we are creating called Chrysalis Nation (www.chrysalisnation.org). You can also search our website, and other websites, to find other communities and agreement nations that are forming. Or, create a constitution and set of agreements for the agreement nation you want to launch. Share it with friends and use social media and any other methods you can think of to find potential like-thinking people. Invite them to lunches, meetings at your home, and any other ways of getting to know each other you can think of to bring potential members into conversations with you to determine if forming a community is appropriate for you.

Be sure you do it using organic membership, the first person chooses the second person, those two choosing the third, those three choosing the fourth person, and so on. This is the way to be sure all both share the same worldview and ownership of each person being in the community.

Rather than primarily being part of our geographic nation, we will primarily be part of this self-created community of like-thinking friends with whom we can raise our children as we deem wise and enjoy each other in doing it. Think of it as a "re-villaging" of our lives by choice, not the giving of our power to another person, a group, or a set of outside beliefs that are a sustaining of the parent-child pattern of behavior.

We will remain fully responsible citizens of our town, state, and geographic nation. However, we will give priority to this mutually created community of friends based on democratic or consensual agreements that honor our chosen worldview.

Hopefully most of these re-villaging actions will be a full shedding of any parent-child patterns and the acceptance of full responsibility for creating our lives from scratch based on the discovery of self-evident facts, as personal scientists, particularly the ones that define the smaller skills of the layers of maturity of the skill of human self-consciousness as we understand them, not necessarily as I am describing them in these books.

It is important to point out the greatest power is with each individual, the second greatest is with his or her community of friends, the third with its association, and so on. The purpose of each association is to be in service to facilitating the needs, wants, and maturation of the individuals, communities, and associations in that order. This is the full honoring of mature free choice. Finally, there will usually not be taxation. Instead, all financial needs will be met by fees, donations, or return on the investment of tax-deductible donations to the community's endowment fund.

Much more, plus a description of the ups and downs and lessons from our thirty-six-year-old Friends and Lovers Community that was our attempt to re-village our lives, will be described in my next book, *Your and My Maturation Stories*. If you have a keen interest in this, I would also suggest you read another book by me available on Amazon, *Common Good Nation: It Is Time to Create a Parallel Nation Based on Agreement Rather Than Geography*.

Agreement Nations

These communities will associate with other like-thinking communities and form nations defined by agreement rather than geography, "agreement nations."

What is the possibility that all the people who happen to be living in a town or county will be operating at the same layer of maturity and with the same worldview? Not possible. (I am one of six children and even we have hugely different worldviews.)

Geographically defined nations are not the most mature form of nation.

As mentioned earlier, our next layer of maturity in nation formation will be to continue to be responsible citizens of our geographically defined nation. It has an important role to play of creating a safe place for agreement nations to flourish. However, we will give priority to our freely formed communities and agreement nations.

As described above, like-thinking people will create communities of friends for the joy of it and to do a good job of Eldering their children. These communities anywhere in the world will join with other like-thinking people into associations of communities. This will be their "agreement nation." While continuing to be fully responsible citizens of their geographic nation, they will give priority to their agreement nation.

This solves a major problem within geographic nations. Today our democracies are wars of the ballot box. The political party that wins often behaves like a dominant parent and treats the citizens as children, forcing everyone to live according to its worldview. Legitimatizing and encouraging the formation of agreement nations would reduce this. It will also allow all worldviews to exist as long as they do no harm to others and follow the laws of the geographic nations.

Most important, it will reduce the possibility for terrorism, rebellions, and wars. Instead, each worldview is supported in forming its agreement nation.

As stated earlier, each religion, philosophy, or science could form its agreement nation. The Bernie Sanders-AOC socialists could form theirs. The Tea Party could form theirs. Any group with a worldview could form one. The difference between these and all other groups is that they will behave like a nation, usually with a democratic process, and focused on providing all the needs of their members (participants can be described as "members" rather than as "citizens" to keep their difference from geographic nations easily clear).

Since people do not have to move their residence and can join or leave on any day, those that have a mature worldview and process and are doing a good job of operating as agreement nations will attract the most people and communities. Most will not have taxation but cover all costs with fees, donations, and return on investments of tax-deductible capital donated to the community or agreement nation's endowment fund. Most important, it will not be a special interest group. The members of each will relate with each other as members of a nation. They will take responsibility for meeting all of the needs of their members.

They will accept full responsibility for together managing, or not managing, every aspect of their lives as they deem wise.

This would also foster tolerance and mutual respect because no one will be able to tell anyone else in another agreement nation what to do. Also, all will want to make sure the geographic nation protects this right to form agreement nations rather than forcing all to live according to the worldview of the political party with the most power in the geographic nation.

The geographic nations will mature into giving priority to creating a safe space for agreement nations to flourish and voluntarily cooperate with each other, and all geographic nations, for the common good of all. For cooperation for maturation.

If you have an interest in learning more about the agreement nation we hope to form, the Chrysalis Nation, or creating your particular agreement nation, read my book, *Common Good Nation*, and go to our website, www.cyrysalisnation.org.

Ending Poverty

Ten percent of the people in the USA own 84% of the stocks. For the last 86 years, that includes the Great Depression of 1929 and the Great Recession of 2008, the stock market has had an average return of more than 10%. Both classical capitalism and neo-capitalism are based on companies giving priority to profits for shareholders, not the common good or cooperation for maturation. Also, adjusted for inflation, over the last thirty years employees have not had a significant increase in income.

Let's design a program in the private-sector to use the stock market to end poverty and welcome participation by any local, state, and national government. This will allow us to immediately create the Common Good Fund and Trusts for All Children program described in *Chapter 6: Maturation Movement and the 10 Recommended Priorities for the 2020 US Presidential Candidates.*

It is time we harnessed the way people have become wealthy to end poverty.

Those who are interested in helping us launch this program should go to our website, www.chrysalisnation.org, and send us a message stating that, including your phone number. If you are interested in making a substantial donation to make this happen, be sure to let us know that as well. This program is ready to go once we can receive the financing to do it.

Business

As also described in *Chapter 6: Maturation Movement and the 10 Recommended Priorities for the 2020 US Presidential Candidates*, in less than thirty years the Chinese have gone from wearing Mao suits and riding bicycles to soon being the largest economy on Earth. Napoleon was right: "China is a sleeping giant. Let her sleep, for when she wakes, she will move the world."

China has discovered the Achilles Heel of neo-capitalism: short-termism.

As described earlier, China has realized it is more important to be a corporation than a nation. It acts on the world stage as a corporation with 1.5 billion employees with a central bank, currency, and banking system as part of its tools. It realizes that as long as its priority is the long term, in the global economy they can do whatever is necessary to become the dominant company in every product market. All they have to do is make the best product and finance it being sold at the lowest price until all competitors leave that product market. Earlier, they accomplished this in the solar cell market and their goal is to do it in every product market, particularly focused on doing it in the next generation of technology: artificial intelligence, robotics, and advanced chip design. Their priority, like any corporation, is the shareholders, in their case the Chinese people. Their governance structure is, like most corporations everywhere, a parent-child structure.

The solution is to go them one better in maturity. It would be to, with their companies as partners, mature the global economy into common good capitalism.

Building on individual freedom and free markets, the foundation of capitalism, the competitors in each product market would act like the teams in a sports league. How common good capitalism would operate was briefly described in *Chapter 6: Maturation Movement and the 10 Recommended Priorities for the 2020 US Presidential Candidates*. It will be more fully described below.

We are now a global society with global companies. The goal will be for all the competitors in each product market, including the Chinese companies, to join in common good capitalism. This is where the overt priority is voluntary cooperation for the maturation of us all: the true common good. Like teams in a sports league, the secondary priority can continue to be ferocious competition, but now within a safe container, one that voluntarily gives priority to the good of all rather than at the expense of the employees, communities, and environment.

As stated earlier and worthy of being stated again, the priority of capitalism is not capital making more capital. It is the honoring of free markets. That is one of the reasons communist nations have finally embraced it. It is part of them honoring the Teen layer of maturity.

The only other way for common good capitalism to emerge is through nations taking the initiative. As we all know, that could take a long time to happen and to happen in the way we want. Something in that direction is currently being attempted by the Trump Administration and we hope it is successful. However, as the design of the now defunct Trans-Pacific Partnership Agreement (TPP) revealed, most such agreements do not give priority to the common good in a way that is similar to Common Good Capitalism. It would also easily be experienced as a paternalistic approach, a continuation of the parent-child pattern from which we want to escape. Since we give high priority to individual free choice rather than it in combination with an equal commitment to the common good, paternalistic is currently the way most businesses experience the laws of geographically defined governments.

The only way to escape this possibility is for the companies to do it themselves.

It is also the only way to end the growing fear of some we will all be working for the Chinese Communist Party in ten to twenty years. To some degree, this may not be an unrealistic fear given our short-termism blind spot. Our companies rushed into China, made great profits each quarter, and then discovered China's priority is to steal our technical know-how, use it to create similar companies, and use all the tools mentioned above to have them out-compete us in each product market over the longer term, not just in China but everywhere.

Only common good capitalism can stop this behavior by China. It is also best for the maturation of our economy and us all.

When CEOs and boards of directors of companies realize that relative to their competitors it will not cost them a penny, it will stop China's strategy, and it will strongly solidify their company's position in each product market, they will jump to do it.

As described earlier and also worthy of stating again, it is important to know what is occurring on Wall Street right now. Companies are rapidly merging to become the one or two dominant companies in each product market: CVS-Walgreens, Home Depot-Lowe's, Pepsi-Coca Cola, MasterCard-Visa, UPS-Fed Ex, Lyft-Uber, and Boeing-Airbus to name some of the visible ones to consumers. Ten years ago, there were ten airlines in the US and fiercely competing with each other, losing money, and their stock prices were crashing. They did not like that. They then took merger action to end it. Today four airlines control 82% of all the seats in the US market: Delta, United, American, and Southwest. They can now easily coordinate their activities, their profits are comfortably high, and the prices of their stocks are consistently higher. They are a "quodupoly monopoly" but may work their way into also soon being a duopoly monopoly. (It is not easy to identify the duopoly monopolies since, in 1981, the Reagan Administration had the Federal Trade Commission stop collecting industry consolidation data.)

In Gustov Grullon, Yelena Lorkin, and Roni Michaely's paper "Are US Industries Becoming More Concentrated?," written in October of 2016, (https://finance.eller.arizona.edu/sites/finance/files/grullon 11.4.16.pdf) they reveal the following: "More than 75% of US industries have experienced an increase in consolidation levels over the last two decades." As a result, they have had "higher profit margins, "positive abnormal stock returns," "more profitable M&A deals," "market value is a more important source of value," and "the average publicly traded firm is three times larger than 20 years ago." Further, "competition has been weakened" and "the US has lost over 50% of publicly traded firms (lower than in early 1970s when the gross domestic product was just one-third of what it is today.)"

Nearly all information is instantly available to all these days. This has throttled the ability of antitrust laws to work. Companies do not need to talk to each other to fully cooperate.

I remember well hearing the following exact words when sitting in a Ben & Jerry's board meeting a few Julys ago. I was listening to our CEO tell us this, at a time when in the US Ben & Jerry's and Haagen Dazs controlled 82% of the super-premium ice cream market: "In January, Haagen Dazs raised their base price and we matched it; and in June, we raised our base price and they matched it."

This is the new normal in our Information Age! This was duopoly monopoly behavior and fully legal because our executives at Ben & Jerry's had not spoken with Haagen Dazs. They just had access to the information necessary to execute this legal duopoly monopoly behavior and have the other witness it. This is legal and increasingly a common practice throughout our business community.

What is more disturbing is the nature of the Internet. People want to only click on one website to do each thing they want to do, not two or three websites.

Think of a small town in New England. It has a church or two, a post office, a fire department, a police department, a library, a movie theater, stores, a local bar, coffee shop, and automobiles. Today, on one website we can buy almost anything in the stores: Amazon. We can get almost any movie we want without commercials: Netflix. We can hang out with our friends without going to the bar or coffee shop: Facebook, Instagram, and WhatsApp all owned by Facebook. We can get any information the library could provide and more: Google. We do not need an automobile anymore because we have computers, iPhones, notepads, and watches that are all connected to each other: Apple. We don't need the Post Office anymore because we can communicate everything with others using our smart phones: globally Apple and Google are the duopoly monopoly controlling nearly 90% of smart phone operating systems.

My point is these are natural Internet monopolies simply because people do not want to go to two websites to get each of these needs fulfilled. Before governments come at them more aggressively to be treated as utilities and enforce regulations, they would be wise to get together and join the Common Good Capitalism Movement I will propose below by acting like sports teams in a league and agreeing on some voluntary cooperation for maturation rules of play.

This is not a foreign activity! Establishing "voluntary consensus standards" is a common practice in the business community. Here is some information from the *United States Consumer Products Safety Commission* describing voluntary consensus safety standards (https://www.cpsc.gov/Regulations-Laws--Standards/Voluntary-Standards/Voluntary-Standards):

There are thousands of voluntary consensus safety standards[1] ("voluntary standards") in existence and one may exist for your consumer product. There are many voluntary standard organizations (like ASTM, CSA Group, UL, and others) that facilitate the creation of these voluntary standards for individual consumer products. In many cases these standards bring industry groups, government agencies, and consumer groups together to agree on best consumer product safety practices.

Deciding on a living wage as the minimum wage, environmental policies, even the percentage of net profit to be donated to end poverty could be established among the competitors in any industry as new "voluntary consensus standards." This is an easy pathway already in existence for the private sector to mature into common good capitalism agreements. What is needed is the wisdom to do it and some bold leaders to lead.

Take notice that on August 19, 2019, the *Business Roundtable*, an association of the CEOs of 188 of some of the largest corporations in the US, announced a new *Statement of the Purpose of the Corporation*. Since its founding in 1972, its priority for the corporation has been "shareholder primacy." This was replaced with "While each of our individual companies serves its own corporate purpose, we share a fundamental commitment to all of our stakeholders," specifically pointing out their commitment to customers, employees, suppliers, communities, environment, and shareholders.

However, they avoided identifying a new priority.

It is self-evident that in any moment our behavior is determined by our priority. Ignoring we at all times, and for any period of time, have a priority is not being realistic. Therefore, since they were not willing to state a new priority, by default their priority is still "shareholder primacy."

In the 1970s, as a founder of the Calvert Funds, the first family of socially responsible mutual funds now with $17 billion under management, I was one of the pioneers of what was then labeled the "socially responsible business and investment movement." We argued corporations should "care more about all the stakeholders." Today, this movement has become part of the mainstream. This new Statement is simply acknowledging this has occurred, fifty years after the movement began.

"Caring more" is not good enough in 2019.

From the beginning the goal of our movement was what I am now labeling "common good capitalism," giving priority to the common good, something, by the way, that is not static and continually maturing. For instance, nearly all nations on Earth do not allow slavery.

As described earlier, our only two ways of relating with each other are competition or cooperation, war or agreements. Moving as one with nature (the universe) or moving against it. There is not a third option. A "society" is when a group of people *agree* to to stop fighting and give priority to the common good of all in the society and *second priority* to each person's or group's self-interest. This is a clear choice for giving priority to agreement instead of war, the only two options.

Therefore, the old as well as new priority of the Statement of the Purpose of the Corporation should be the same priority expected of all people and organizations in the US, and now on Earth since we now live in a global society: the common good. The fact they were not comfortable continuing to use prioritization as the construct for their new statement is noteworthy.

What they need to understand is if it is not the common good, they have left the US, and our now global society, and are in competition with it, as they previously were as well. They, like nearly all of the rest of us, were living in the illusion that separate parts were real and, therefore, giving priority to their physical body's and their company's self-interest was mature behavior.

They need to declare they are full members of our society and, therefore, their highest priority is the common good or own the fact they are now in competition with it.

In a society, an exemption from having this be one's priority is not possible. It would be a contradiction.

They were not comfortable stating their priority is the common good because it is still the financial interests of them as individuals and, by extension, to themselves and the shareholders of their companies. They wanted to avoid stating that. That was why they eliminated the construct of prioritization.

A *voluntary* Common Good Capitalism Movement is the loving way to begin our maturation from this immaturity in our corporate community. I and many are pleased they are moving in a positive direction, to be "caring more" about all the stakeholders. Since maturation is the fundamental process in nature, I am confident they will rapidly mature into joining the Common Good Capitalism Movement when they discover it can be a win-win in all directions, including for them and their shareholders. Today, however, we need them to not take fifty years to catch up to this movement. Today we need them to become the campions of it.

We are all in this together. It is time for our business community to take the lead to mature Earth into common good capitalism as their contribution to cooperation for maturation.

I have written a book on this: *Common Good Capitalism Is Inevitable.* It argues that the inevitable next layer of maturity of capitalism is common good capitalism. It is the only way to build on and sustain individual freedom and free markets that we do not want to in anyway negate. Voluntarily establishing new consensus standards would be adding to our right and ability to exercise individual free choice. That is the other half of our responsibility at the Teen layer: accepting shared responsibility for giving priority to the common good of our society, now our global society.

Also, and allow me to state it again, what is fundamental in capitalism is not capital making more capital. That is secondary. What is fundamental is the honoring of individual freedom of choice and free markets. The purpose of the Common Good Capitalism Movement is to change its highest priority from personal profit to the common good. This is the natural, effortless, and freely chosen priority of people who have achieved the Elder or Mature Elder layers of maturity in the skill of human self-consciousness.

Common Good Capitalism is where organizations voluntarily give priority to the common good—cooperation for the maturation of the universe, and second priority to profit or anything else. It is not against profit. It is only prioritizing the common good over profit.

For instance, and more specifically described than before, companies in a product market, like airlines, pharmacies, and home improvement, will come together like the teams in a sports league and reach agreement on the "common good rules of play." They will then continue to compete as ferociously as in the past. Like in sports leagues, whether the National Basketball Association (NBA) or a local girls' soccer league, there will be referees whose job it is to make sure the *highest priority at all times* is the voluntary agreements that give priority to the common good. The referees in these business leagues will be the financial auditors. They will report if or if not, and to what degree, a company is keeping these agreements.

If they agree, for instance, to have the minimum wage be the living wage in each location, they will all make the change on the same future day. Thus, relative to each other it will not cost the companies a penny.

This will make it easy for the multinationals and all companies to become good guys in our societies: their highest priority will now be the common good, cooperation for the maturation of us all. Rather than this change being a cost to the companies it will be beneficial because they and their brand name products will now be highly valued by the consuming public.

Nothing else will change unless they want it to. At the same time, they can reach any agreements for the common good they choose. It will all be visible to the public by the posting on the Internet of the agreements and annual audits in easy to read language. Elected or other government officials will also be welcomed to attend the meetings where competitors reach agreements. It will also no longer be acceptable to collectively give priority to the owners, shareholders, and/or employees at the expense of the rest of us. And the public will be able to participate in the discussions of what would be wise additional common good agreements for our times, particularly the balancing of the interests of the consumers, employees, suppliers, owners, environment, and society.

This maturation of capitalism using the sports league model is inevitable because there is no other economic maturation that builds on individual freedom and free markets, half of the Teen layer of human maturity. It also covers the other half, giving priority to the common good of all.

Finally, two things are happening that could rapidly bring this about. First, as described earlier, there is rapid consolidation of companies in each product market toward becoming nationally, regionally, or globally duopoly monopolies. Without ever talking to each other, this allows them to more easily match each other's fundamental price increases: to legally and quietly behave as duopoly, triopoly, or quadopoly monopolies.

In response to this, common good capitalism will emerge in one of the two following ways or, more probably, as a combination of both. First, some CEOs and boards will realize to build a better relationship with their customers it will be wise to be first in the marketplace to do this. That will begin a cascade of all companies doing it. Or, secondly, when the public becomes aware of this rapid growth toward duopoly monopolies, they demand our maturation into common good capitalism that becomes recognized as the only option that sustains giving priority to our ability and right of exercising individual free choice and, by extension, free markets.

In the US, CVS and Walgreens control 90% of pharmacies. Home Depot and Lowe's, UPS-FedEx, Pepsi-Coca Cola, MasterCard-Visa, Boeing-Airbus and many more companies control a high percentage of their product market. This makes it easy to match each other's fundamental price increases which is monopoly behavior through a duopoly back door. The latter is why this duopolization is quietly and rapidly occurring on Wall Street.

The main reasons for the high level of merger and acquisition activity today is the ease of quietly and legally doing this when the public is not aware of it. Also, since this legal backdoor way of monopoly behavior has been discovered, if your company is not seeking to be one of the two dominant ones, two other companies are. All companies now have to play this quiet game. Thus, it is only a matter of time before there is a movement toward common good capitalism, either by the companies themselves, through the demands of the public, or more probably both simultaneously.

A "movement" is a declaration that we have matured into knowing what is currently a socially acceptable behavior is no longer acceptable. The purpose of a movement is to assist us all to mature into the next layer of maturity in a social agreement area of our lives. Not just because there is a better option but because it is more than immature: it is immoral. It is not giving priority to the common good. Therefore, we have to stop doing it to continue on the path of cooperation for maturation.

Cooperation for collusion to increase profits is illegal. However, cooperation for the common good is not only legal but encouraged! It is expected! It is the assumed priority of all the people and organizations in any society where the choice is agreements rather than war.

It is time to move into common good capitalism. It is, therefore, time to build a Common Good Capitalism Movement. The companies will not be able to easily do it until the duopoly monopolies are known by the general public. That will be part of the social pressure of a movement that will result in public outrage. Such a movement will protect the companies from hostility from Wall Street investors that could lower the price of their stock. (A couple of years ago, I spoke with Paul Polman, when he was the CEO of Unilever, to make this argument. His response was, "You have to make me do it." He was keenly aware Wall Street would damage Unilever's stock price if he was the first mover without there being public acceptance of it.)

Also, joining this movement will provide duopoly monopoly companies the only way to protect their brand names from the public hostility toward them that will arise when it becomes aware of this widespread duopoly monopoly behavior. Therefore, it is important to both build the movement and find CEOs and boards, particularly of duopoly monopoly companies, willing to be the first to move into common good capitalism. Relative to one another it does not cost the companies a penny and it will do much to have the companies become loved by the public. Once this maturation process begins it could quickly turn into a hockey stick chart of rapid growth into common good capitalism product agreements around the world, new "voluntary consensus standards."

How do we build the movement Paul Polman says we need to build to provide a safe place for competitors to meet and reach agreements for the common good? With fun!

At Ben & Jerry's we learned people respond positively when we introduced social maturation ideas to them surrounded with fun. For instance, one of my fantasies is local groups of people all over the US rent a flatbed truck. On it they place a podium, a table with a trophy on it in front of a curtain, and a small musical band. They let everyone in town know they will be driving it into the Home Depot or Lowe's parking lot at a certain time, such as noon on Saturday. They also arrange with the local Ben & Jerry's or another local scoop shot for free ice cream to be passed out to all who attend. Fifteen minutes after most of the people have arrived, the band plays celebratory music while the truck is driving into the parking lot.

The purpose is to present a trophy to that local Home Depot or Lowe's for having accomplished becoming a duopoly monopoly with the other, together receiving in excess of 80% of all home improvement sales in the US. If it is not possible to get anyone to come out from the store, it is asked if anyone in the audience ever worked for it. That person is then invited to come onto the flatbed truck and is given the trophy to wild applause from the audience. Then before he or she leaves it is announced that if Home Depot or Lowe's joins into common good agreements with their competitors, the company will receive an even bigger trophy! The curtain is then pulled back and there on another table is a much larger trophy which brings another loud applause. This can then be followed by a speech by someone describing the wisdom of companies like Home Depot, Lowe's, True Value, and Aubuchon maturing into common good capitalism. Of course, the local media is notified in advance of this trophy presentation so they can have a reporter present.

This can also be done at CVSs and Walgreens around the country and in the parking lots of other duopoly monopolies. The purpose is to raise awareness in the thinking of the public to the possibility of voluntary common good capitalism. This will make it easier, as Paul Polman pointed out, for the companies to mature into common good capitalism.

Common Good Capitalism

In my book, *Common Good Capitalism Is Inevitable*, I suggest the emergence of an association to launch this movement, with the title "Common Good Capitalism Movement (CGCM)." It is my hope that this book stimulates its emergence. If you are interested in working on this, go to our website and send us a message stating that and include your phone number.

For businesses, there would be five options of participation. Companies or organizations can choose to participate in one, some, or all of them:

> **Membership**
> **Common Good Capitalism Certified Club**
> **1-10% Club**
> **Cap Club**
> **Sports League Model**

Membership

Any for-profit, non-profit, sole proprietorship, cooperative, or other organization around the world can become a member by going to our website, www.chrysalisnation.org, and clicking on the menu tab "Common Good Capitalism Movement." It is not necessary to become a member of Chrysalis Nations to participate in building this Movement. There will be a small annual membership fee ($1, or more as each chooses, by annual automatic renewal) to assure continued membership status in the Common Good Capitalism Movement.

By becoming a member of this Movement, a person or organization is declaring they are keeping the agreement, instead of going to war, we all make when we join a human society. It is to give priority to the common good, the maturation of the universe. This will expose for all to witness at our website both those who are publicly declaring they are honoring this natural highest priority and those who choose to not do so. The latter are then continuing to be comfortable being in competition with it. This will also allow those who do declare they give priority to the common good to easily find each other for the purpose of forging cooperative agreements for the maturation of us all.

There is no definition of "the common good." This is intentional. What is the common good is consistently maturing. There was a time when killing, theft, and slavery were acceptable. Today nearly all societies on Earth do not allow them. Laws against these are not yet universal, but we are confident that someday they will be universal (three of the nearly 200 nations on Earth still allow slavery). Also, given there are still the Civil Rights, Women's, and Environmental Movements reveals that in those areas the common consensus is continuing to mature.

Common Good Capitalism Certified

This is a certification that indicates an organization has become a member and has also been certified by B-Lab, Inc. (www.bcorporation.net) that it is operating at a certain level of common good behavior.

The only difference between being B-Corp Certified and being Common Good Certified is that the organization has also publicly declared that its highest priority is the common good, the maturation of us all.

B-Corp Certification is a checklist of responsible behaviors. Common Good Certification is an indication of the organization's highest priority.

Enron passed the screens of many socially responsible certifying organizations. Yet their highest priority, as later determined by the courts, was clearly not the common good.

The work that B-Lab is doing is extremely valuable, essential, and fully supported by the Common Good Capitalism Movement. A third-party certification process around the many particular areas of an organization's behavior is needed and that is what they are providing. However, at this time it is also essential that we go one step further to determine whether or not an organization has publicly declared that their *highest priority* is the common good or the financial self-interest of a few.

No organization that becomes a member of CGCM needs to acquire B-Corp or Common Good Certification. Both are options of participating at a higher level of commitment to this movement. However, if your organization is already certified as a B-Corp, do consider also becoming Common Good Capitalism Certified as well.

1-10% Club

Another option is to declare that somewhere between one and ten percent (1-10%) of annual net profit (or positive cash flow in the case of a non-profit) will be invested (not donated) in Common Good Investment Banking Firms (GCIBF). Their priority is to buy companies and convert them into Cap Club companies, described below. The return on these investments will endeavor to be a market rate return.

This is important to provide the capital necessary to build this movement. It is a way an organization can participate in doing so in a way that supports their organization by receiving a market rate return on its investment. Foundations could also be supportive by investing a portion of their endowment capital in CGIBFs. Many will emerge around the world and investors will be able to distribute their investment capital among a number of them to gain diversification.

It is also important to point out that, unlike all other investment banking firms whose priority is some particular investors, these CGIBFs have the same highest priority, the common good. Therefore, it will be easy to join with each other to each contribute a portion of their capital to buy large companies.

This is a very important feature of this Common Good Capitalism Movement. This will occur more and more as we go forward. This is how with strong public support bold moves in the private sector could eventually convert all of capitalism into common good capitalism, either by companies joining the movement or being bought.

Cap Club

This is for for-profit organizations that choose to put a cap on their annual return (total of dividend and stock appreciation) to equity investors.

The level of the cap is not what is important! What is most important is that it be made public. This will allow society to participate in deciding the appropriate cap in each situation.

For instance, if the company is a startup, the annual cap can be 1000%. As the company matures, it can lower its cap percentage. However, if the company is one of a near duopoly monopoly, it should appropriately be somewhere below 15% annual return to shareholders.

The principle is an ancient one. Rather than unlimited upside, investors deserve a financial return that is reasonable relative to their risk.

In this way, by choosing an appropriate cap percentage, the chosen priority is the common good, the maturation of the universe. The company will now be free to operate under these priorities and also free of pressure to give priority to seeking the highest return possible to shareholders, only the level to which they have committed. Each year any excess profit would be invested in CGIBFs.

The only use of the assets invested in CGIBFs would be as collateral to borrow money during difficult times or to grow the business. If borrowed on, the annual interest cost could be similar or lower than the market rate return sought with that capital. Thus, the capital is able to serve both purposes with no significant cost to the company. (Mondragon in the Basque Region of northern Spain has used this approach of having capital artfully go in two directions at the same time through this process of cooperation between the financing institution and companies. A comprehensive article on Mondragon is on our website: *Mondragon: 40 Year Later It Is Still the Best Example of an Agreement Nation.*)

Sports League Model
This is the fifth way members can participate in the Common Good Capitalism Movement. By the way, allow me to emphasize

again that members are free to choose to participate in any one or more of these five ways of participating in this movement.

The Sports League Model is when competitors in each product market voluntarily reach agreements that give priority to the common good and secondly continue to compete as ferociously as before. This sports league model was described above. I believe it will eventually be used to mature the entire global economy into common good capitalism.

Briefly, the competitors in each product market can meet, agree on the "common good rules of play," have their auditors report on how well they are keeping these agreements as well as on their financial performance, and then continue to ferociously compete as their second priority. Always their second priority. During sport events a referee blows a whistle and stops the play anytime someone breaks one of the voluntarily agreed upon rules of play. In the same way, the auditors will play the role of the referees and blow a whistle in the audit report on any company not keeping an agreement. This will have companies want to be sure the whistle does not blow at them. Also, the public will not only participate in the conversations on what could be some additional common good rules but also shame any company not willing to participate into either participating or going out of business as a result of a damaged reputation and the absent of public support. This is the kindness tactic of non-cooperation that can be used with companies not willing to give priority to the common good, cooperation for maturation. Of course, the companies could also agree there will be penalties for not fully keeping any agreements.

Now, as with sports leagues, the highest priority in the business community is the common good in a way all involved experience themselves as winning.

Here is how each stakeholder wins when the Sports League Model is used:

Shareholders	- public anger at duopoly and near duopoly monopoly behavior ends - a consistent and appropriate financial return is more easily achieved - they know their financial return is not at the expense of the common good - relative to one another it will not cost the companies a penny: any necessary increase in costs is raised by all competitors at the same time
Employees	- they know their contribution is primarily in the service of the common good - the minimum compensation employees receive is what is voluntarily determined by all involved to be appropriate for the common good and it is the same with all competitors in their product market association, usually including a livable minimum wage - they are equal participants with all involved in making the common good agreements
Consumers, Venders, And Politicians	- they know the freely chosen priority of all involved is the common good of all human beings and nature
Citizenry & All Involved	- the process is open and transparent; all are equal participants in the discussions of what

is giving priority to the common good for the entire society for our times, particularly not for just the shareholders and employees
- the third party common good audits provide verification that all participants are giving priority to the common good in their agreements and that their behavior is consistently honoring those agreements or, if not, how poorly they are keeping them

Let's focus for a minute on one example, Amazon. Here is what was reported in the June 29, 2018 *The Kiplinger Letter* (Vol. 95, No. 26, p.1):

15% of retail sales take place online now, once you exclude gasoline, restaurant meals and autos...things that are difficult to sell on the web. In 2013...it was just 9%. And there is no slowdown in sight.

Amazon nets 44% of those internet sales. 75% of households with yearly income of $100,000 or more have an Amazon Prime membership. Over 10% of Americans have Amazon's smart assistant, on a device ready and waiting to place orders by voice prompt.

This sports league solution will allow duopoly or near duopoly monopolies and monopolies to continue in existence with new competitors always free to join their product market association. If they choose to not join, they will be easily exposed to the public as not doing so. Increasingly this will not be acceptable by the public and, therefore, their business could have significant challenges or be shamed into joining the Common Good Capitalism Movement through non-cooperation with them by the public, by not buying their products.

Most important, the companies will no longer operate at the expense of the employees, community, and environment. Instead they will voluntarily make decisions that give priority to the common good of the society, now increasingly a global society, and secondly compete as ferociously as before.

The publicly shared common good audits, the equivalent of the referees in the sports league model, allow all to be in an on-going conversation on what is the appropriate way for our time to give priority to the common good. As the Civil Rights, Women's, and Environment Movements reveal, we will be continuously maturing in our understanding of what is giving priority to the common good.

It is important to point out again that no definition of "the common good" is provided. It is up to all involved to remain in an on-going conversation of what it is for our time. Maturation is a never-ending process.

Finally, this is voluntary action in the private sector. Competitors are free to do or not do any one of the above activities. And they create the process and agreements. It is also legal; all governments encourage giving priority to cooperation for the common good and government officials can attend the meetings to determine agreements to confirm for all the agreements are giving priority to the common good. What is illegal is direct collusion for self-interest. Also, sooner or later the current indirect way of building duopoly monopolies in the Information Age will eventually become publicly known. Because it is clearly giving priority to the common good, appropriate legislation in support of this solution will eventually be passed that nearly all will support. But it first has to emerge in the private sector, just as employee ownership had to prove itself in the private sector before the Employee Stock Ownership Program (ESOP) legislation could be pasted in the 1980s with the support of both the Republican and Democratic parties.

This forging of agreements among competitors can occur at the local level as well as at the national and international level. For instance, local businesses in a town, such as restaurants, can reach agreement to pay their help an agreed upon minimum wage that would end the low pay to undocumented workers in their kitchens.

Finally, and in summary, all non-profit and for-profit organizations could choose to establish an Elder Body, either with the ultimate operational authority above the board of directors, as described earlier, or as a committee of the board of directors. Its two sole responsibilities are to make sure the highest priority at all times and in all it does (in the reality of oneness) is maturation and that all are maturing in the skill of human self-consciousness. It can be thought of as an Internal Maturation Auditor. People determined to be mature in this skill and knowledgeable in the area of the organization's focus would be chosen to be on it. The existence of an Elder Body would go a long way toward having the public trust this is the priority of the organization.

By going to the Common Good Capitalism Movement tab on our website, www.chrysalisnation.org, and becoming a member of this Movement, individuals and organizations can publicly declare they are now committed to giving priority to the common good. This will not only be participation in building this movement. It will also let others in your product area know you are ready to reach agreements to be a participant in the Sports League Model.

This solution is the only solution that both honors and builds on individual freedom, sustains free markets, and gives priority to the common good, an honoring of the full Teen layer of maturity in the skill of human self-consciousness. Therefore, it will eventually be chosen. The primary purpose of the Common Good Capitalism Movement is to have it happen sooner rather than later.

China

There is a second important reason we will soon rapidly mature into common good capitalism: China.

As described earlier, China has discovered, economically, it is more important to be a corporation than a nation. This is also advantageous on a planet where now economic competition is more important than military competition. As stated earlier, China behaves as one corporation with 1.5 billion employees and control of the agencies of the state, its currency, banking system, and central bank. Unless we mature into the higher layers of maturity, China, Inc. could easily conquer the world economically. It is already implementing a trillion-dollar infrastructure plan throughout much of the world called the *Belt and Road Initiative* and investing substantial capital in research and development of cutting-edge technologies.

I was recently in China. Forty years ago, most people were living in villages. Suddenly, they are all part of the global capitalist economy. They have not had a Renaissance or Enlightenment. Most people have not discovered the importance of maturing into honoring individual freedom at the depth of people in the West. That is why most are comfortable living within a family and national paternalistic system. Communism is a dictatorship by a group rather than an individual. The nation is still comfortably operating at the Child layer, using the Parent-Child Based model of organization. That is why there is some but not a large demand for democracy.

Economically, China behaves as one corporation. It uses government money to succeed in particular product markets by providing financial assistance to its companies until they eliminate most of the competition and dominate that product market, as they accomplished in the global solar cell business. They will be able to continue to do this in every product market as we go forward. That is why they are now focusing on the markets of the future: artificial intelligence, robotics, computer chip technology, and their use in the production and distribution of consumer products, approximately 70% of Western economies.

Economically, there is only one way for the West to respond that builds on rather than negates individual freedom and free markets (half of the Teen layer). It is to use the Sports League Model. Short of uniting with other nations to isolate them that would be very difficult to do, it is the only response that will permanently stop China from dominating the global economy and instead operating on a level playing field with all competitors.

China has figured out how to do judo on capitalism, to use our power against us. Any company in the West will comfortably sell to the highest bidder; the highest bidder can always be China. But China has figured out a less expensive and obvious approach. Copy, steal, or partner with Western corporations and then use that knowledge to create a competitor. This is their priority and only common good capitalism can stop them from continuing to succeed as a result of our naivete.

If we are to protect our honoring of individual freedom and free markets, China gives us no choice but to mature into common good capitalism.

The only solution is to include in our thinking the existence of layers of maturity of the skill of human self-consciousness. As we now know, at the Adult layer we choose a fundamental belief on why the universe is structured as it is structured—Christianity, Islam, science, or another belief. We also choose a belief on how the universe operates. However, force, effort, and discipline are necessary to obey this latter outside belief because it is a negation of our ability and right at the Teen layer to each moment exercise not only individual but also mature free choice. As an Elder, we realize we are all in this together as parts of one whole, called the universe, and it is natural for us to mature to naturally, effortlessly and freely choose to give priority to the self-interest of that one whole. Throughout history this behavior has been called "moral behavior."

Now no force, effort, and discipline are necessary.

We have discovered our mature self-interest is giving priority to the totality of who we each are, the indivisible universe.

We in the West must at least mature to the Elder layer where we recognize it is natural for us each to mature to freely choose to give priority to the common good. We will then do it voluntarily in the business sector by using the Sports League Model. We either do this or China's dominance of the economy will become a step back in this global process of maturation in the skill of human self-consciousness. If immature leaders on just one of the two sides, it could lead to a military war that could be horrendous.

The Sports League Model, cooperative competition, is a fully voluntary and private sector activity. Maturing free markets to give priority to the common good was one of the agendas of the Pilgrims who came to America after 1492. You should know that the first corporation was created by a town meeting in New England to raise the money necessary to build a bridge. It was structured as one vote per shareholder, not per share. This was so it would operate in the exact same way as the town meeting, by a majority democratic vote. The story of how we got to where we are today is not the result of governments thinking it through and making wise decisions. It is not a pretty story. What is important now is that we make the sole important change necessary to correct the most fundamental mistake of what has evolved into being our current for-profit corporate structures that are free to give priority to a few, the shareholders. The priority has to again become the common good through voluntary action in the private sector. We need to continue to build on our now known maturity at the Teen layer. It is both honoring the right and ability of each of us to exercise individual free choice *and* accept shared responsibility for at all times and in all we do giving priority to the common good.

Our maturation into common good capitalism is inevitable. It is the only response to China that will succeed in keeping the human species on the course of cooperation for maturation without a major step backwards. Speeding up this inevitability is the primary goal of the Common Good Capitalism Movement.

Finally, when our economy begins to mature into common good capitalism, another phenomenon will begin to occur that is hard to imagine at this time. Companies will compete based on who is more loved as a result of doing good in the world. For instance, companies will create projects to mature entire economies in cities in poor nations so the public will love them and their brands. (You can read about this and much more in my book *Common Good Capitalism Is Inevitable*.)

This Movement can also be one of the causes taken up by Chrysalis Nation and the other agreement nations that emerge. It will also be fun. We will be direct self-conscious participants in the maturation of us all and we will know we are doing it while we are doing it. This is Eldering. There is nothing in our behavior that is more enjoyable than Eldering.

In the 1970s, there were only two things you could do with your extra money each year: invest it or donate it. Without being aware we were doing it; the Common Good Capitalism Movement actually began fifty years ago. It began with the many efforts to fill the space in between these two options, known as "the in between space." In it the priority was "investments prioritizing the common good." It was a combination of both with the priority being the common good. It included everything from foundations loaning some of their endowment (known as Program Related Investments or PRIs) at low interest rates where the investments were fulfilling their mission to give priority to the common good. It included investments in microloan programs around the world (small un-collateralized loans to poor people to start and sustain their small businesses). In the US, it included loans at low interest rates to community development financial institutions (CDFIs) that in turn loaned them at low rates for low income housing developments, to start cooperatives, and to invest in socially responsible businesses in low income communities. It also included Mohammad Yunus's loans to start socially responsible businesses around the world that provided zero return to investors. Finally, it included the "conscious capitalism movement" founded by John Mackey, the founder of Whole Foods. He labels a movement of "integral libertarians," people who give priority to individual free choice and recognize that at higher layers of maturity people freely choose to give priority to the common good.

What is being proposed here is simply an expansion of this movement that has already been emerging over the last fifty years on both the left and right sides of the political spectrum to include all for-profit and non-profit enterprises.

If you are interested in assisting us to expand the Common Good Capitalism Movement, let us know. Go to our website, www.chrys-alisnation.org, and send us a message stating that and include your phone number.

Common Good Investing

In the 1970s, I was one of the pioneers of what was then known as "socially responsible investing." Robert Swan and I created the *Institute for Community Economics* in 1974. I took the lead to facilitate fifteen leaders from all walks of life in meeting monthly at our offices in Cambridge for over a year to write one of the first set of social screens for investing. It later became known as "ethical investing," then "sustainable investing," then "ESG investing" (standing for "environment," "social," and "governance"), and now "impact investing." In 1982, this led to Wayne Silby, John Guffey, and I to create the first family of socially responsible mutual funds, now known as the Calvert Funds.

Today, this movement is going mainstream.

This is mainly the result of grade schoolteachers over the last couple of decades getting their students hooked on caring about the environment. Their students are now going to be inheriting $40 trillion. Goldman Sachs, JP Morgan, Morgan Stanley, BlackRock, and all the other asset management firms do not want their children to leave their financial management services.

Thus, the entire investment community has suddenly discovered that taking the environment into consideration when investing is a sound financial decision. It is taking social and governance issues along with it.

For the last three years *Barrons, Wall Street Journal's* weekly magazine popular with the investment community, has compared the 200 top socially responsible mutual funds with the top non-socially responsible funds and discovered that they consistently outperform by more than a couple percentage points. We knew back in the 1970s this would have to eventually be the case. Socially responsible funds invest in companies that have good relationships with their employees, the community, and the environment. They will be more loved by the consumers and their employees, have greater productivity, and have fewer conflicts with the government.

I believe the next chosen name will be "common good investing." It is investing in companies where their declared highest priority is the common good. They will also work with their competitors to use the Sports League Model. They will rapidly move toward the other options listed in this chapter to give this priority expression in all their behavior. (I am one of the founders of an impact asset management firm, Stakeholders Capital, www.stakeholderscapital.com, 888-785-4537, that specialized in this, particularly identifying private investment opportunities in this area for a portion of clients' portfolios.)

Maturation cannot be escaped or stopped, and it is fun. I ask all reading this to consider being a voice that publicly declares your support for the emergence of a movement, a bold and visible Common Good Capitalism Movement. It is inevitable. Be one of the first to join this winning team. Be the person in your community who rents the flatbed truck!

Politics and Governance

Basically, there are three forms of governments: Parent-Child Based, Agreement Based, and Oneness Based. Democracies are attempting to be Agreement Based, but as noted earlier, the political party in power often acts as if politics is Parent-Child Based. The main addition to corporate structure of Oneness Based organizations is described in the next paragraph.

Briefly, all organizations are encouraged to consider forming an Elder Body. It is above the Board of Directors in the organization chart. It has the ultimate power in the for-profit, non-profit, or co-operative organization. However, it delegates full responsibility for managing the company to the Board of Directors. The Elder Body maintains the right to veto any decision which it commits to try to never do. It has two representatives at all Board meetings. If they deem a decision is being made that is not in the best interest of cooperation for maturation, they can call for a meeting of the two bodies. The Elder Body then facilitates discussions toward a resolution all agree honors that priority. In this way, by the addition of an Elder Body, the primary responsibility of making sure the highest priority at all times and in all places (in the reality of oneness) is cooperation for maturation and it is institutionalized in the organizational structure.

Obviously, the goal is to have the most mature people both in the skill of human self-consciousness and the affairs of the organization on the Elder Bodies.

There are layers of maturity of the skill of human self-consciousness. We need to now integrate our awareness of this into all we do, including the organizational structures of all of our organizations.

I am doing this in another way with a company I am creating at this time. All of its common shares are owned by a private foundation we have created. It serves as the Elder Body. We, the foundation, plan to own other companies as well. This is another way of institutionalizing an Elder Body's relationship with a company or many companies. The for-profit companies can issue securities of any kind, additional equity without voting rights with restrictions on upside returns, preferred shares, or debt securities. We see ourselves institutionalizing giving priority to the common good both in the operation of the companies and with the returns on our common shares. Earning from the common shares will be donated or invested with the priority continuing to be an *institutionalized commitment* to give priority to the common good, cooperation for maturation. They could be allocated for charitable purposes or they could be invested in Common Good Investment Banking Firms that buy companies and convert them into common good companies with a cap on the return to equity investors.

Honest Global Currency

If no government will do it, it is time to create in the private-sector an honest lobal currency equivalent. It is also time to create a parallel currency to be used solely to cover the costs of our global social needs, such as ending poverty and meeting our sustainable environment goals to reduce the greater costs later of not doing so. The latter will be briefly described at the end of this section.

Inflation (that results in a reduction in the purchasing value of a national currency) is a hidden tax that is only paid by those who live paycheck to paycheck or close to it. Those with wealth can use their accumulated assets to earn income that is usually greater than this hidden tax. This is not fair. The people who can least afford it are paying this hidden tax.

Either a nation, all nations, most nations, or a private institution needs to create an honest currency or equivalent, one that by design does not inflate or deflate in value. This is possible by having it designed as follows. The below design will assume we are creating a privately issued honest currency equivalent since it is the quickest way to prove its value. We can label it "the Bart," in honor of the fact that with barter there was no inflation or deflation:

Foundations of an Honest Currency Equivalent

1. For every debit there is an equal credit and vice versa.

2. No one can create Barts out of thin air. They only come into existence by being bought by current national currencies.

3. The initial value would be tied to the value of the current dominant national currency on a recent date in the past (a value that can't be changed), such as the value of the US Dollar on December 31, 2018 or, better, a date just before it is launched.

4. Each day or month the value of all Barts are automatically increased by the rate of inflation or decreased by the rate of deflation of the dominant national currency (US Dollar).

Therefore, since nearly all national currencies are always losing value because of inflation, this privately issued currency equivalent will seek to maintain its value by an agreement of all using it. Here is how it will do that.

The US Dollars, Japanese Yen, European Euro, and all other currencies used to create an account in the privately issued currency equivalent mutual fund or other legal vehicle will be conservatively invested solely for the purpose of increasing the value of Barts to offset inflation in US Dollars. At the end of each day or month the value of Barts would automatically be increased relative to the US Dollar by using a percentage of the return on investments to offset inflation. Any percentage above that and a small amount necessary to cover costs not used is set aside to facilitate a slow and consistent increase in the monthly value of the Bart with the goal of at least consistently offsetting inflation. Thus, not only would the currency equivalent endeavor to offset any lose from inflation but also potentially provide an even better return.

A currency should not favor some individuals or groups. That is not the case with our current national currencies. Those who have wealth and are able to borrow benefit relative to those without wealth and unable to borrow.

A nation, nations, or group in the private-sector needs to step forward and provide the world an honest global currency or the equivalent thereby at least ending the hidden tax of inflation that is mainly suffered by those with lower incomes.

The above private sector plan would be fully legal and multinational corporations would be the most interested in using it because it could become the equivalent of an honest global currency, something the world badly needs. This would greatly reduce their costs of dealing with many national currencies and make it easier for everyone else to use it as well by increasing the amount in circulation.

There is already an effort to create such a currency equivalent in Greenfield, MA, the Common Good Payment Card. Members use a credit card to make purchases that saves the businesses the 2.75% or more charged by other credit cards. More than 80% of the assets never leave the account because depositors keep enough money in their sub-accounts of the program's account at a bank to be available to use for payments. We are now in the process of arranging for some of the deposits that are not loaned to projects in the local community to be invested in liquid investments so together the income will approach or exceed the offsetting of inflation.

It is time for the creation of an honest global currency or a usable equivalent. Inflation (reduction of the purchasing power of a currency) is a hidden tax only paid by those who live paycheck to paycheck or close to it. Those with wealth can cover this cost with the income on their wealth. Therefore, this hidden tax punishes the most those closest to being poor. This is immoral.

International companies hate having to deal with over a hundred currencies and would be the first to use it and insist upon all who do business with them using it when relating with them. This would create the liquidity that would make it easy for all to use it. It is remarkably easy to do and, as also mentioned earlier, one way of doing it is being piloted in Greenfield, a small town in Massachusetts. Once proven there it could be rapidly copied around the world.

You can learn more about this in my next book, *Your and My Maturation Stories.* And, by the way, the Libra currency, recently announced that will be launched by Facebook, uses a basket of national currencies to establish its value. The money lost by the depositors to inflation is distributed as profits to the 100 planned participating large companies. This is a sustaining of the immoral pattern of national currencies, not an ending of it.

Finally, some friends have also postulated the creation of a parallel currency that would solely be used for ending poverty, meeting our sustainable environment needs, and perhaps some of the other Sustainable Development Goals (SDGs) of the United Nations. It is best launched by central banks. Using blockchain, chaincode, and hyperchain technology, it could keep track of all transactions to assure it is only used to provide capital to poor people, accomplished using qualified non-profits and government agencies, and to pay for the costs of putting our environment back onto a sustainable pattern. They call it "pre-distribution." It is paying for these costs now rather than the greater costs of not dealing with them until later. For instance, we will need $5 trillion to accomplish the environment needs of our planet. Our current economic system cannot provide it: it would be too slow and it is skewed in the wrong direction, toward profit. A parallel "green currency" launched by central banks could provide this capital quickly and the priority would be solving the problem using public private partnerships of all kinds. This green currency would not disrupt the current financial system, provide the large capital needed quickly, and meet these needs. More on this another time. However, it is important for you to know these kinds of solutions are being explored.

Science

We now know the self-evident truth that the universe operates as an indivisible whole and that the assumption it is separate parts is a mutually agreed-upon illusion tool we invented to create human languages and, thereby, be self-conscious parts of nature. All scientists will eventually fully embrace this as the container of all of its thinking because it is a self-evident truth, easily observed in plain sight when we use our skill of human self-consciousness as our sixth sense.

Therefore, it is time to assist science to embrace as fundamental the fact the universe operates as an indivisible whole.

It will not negate anything science has discovered up to now about the relationships between and among the parts. It will only create an accurate container for our scientific research: the universe operates as an indivisible whole.

It is easily self-evident to anyone who keeps his or her power, all of it, and studies the question, "Who or what is doing my breathing?" by answering the 7 questions near the beginning of this book, the universe (nature) operates as an indivisible whole. All of its parts operate everywhere the way we currently assume all the parts within our physical bodies operate.

Yet many still behave as if the fundamental process in nature outside our skins is the opposite, competition by each part with its self-interest as its highest priority. Reality is not a contradiction, believing that cooperation for maturation is the fundamental process within our skins and competition for self-interest is the fundamental process outside our skins. We are now ready to embrace the fact, easily experienced as self-evident in our direct, present, and repeatable by choice experience, the universe operates as an indivisible whole.

Also, doing so not only allows us to experience our lives as meaningful. It also results in the mature free choice of moral behavior, the experience of natural confidence, and the consistent inner self-conscious feeling of contented joy.

The voices of our scientific community are some of the most respected voices in our societies. Many now agree with what is being stated in this book, but it is not fully and overtly embraced by the entire scientific community. It is time they accepted their responsibility to do so.

Psychotherapy

The highest priority in all psychotherapy will be the introduction of, and eldering the client up, the mastery in the natural progression of the smaller skills of the layers of maturity of the skill of human self-consciousness. Returning to health from suffering from immature behaviors and mental illness will be geared toward the mastery of this skill. It is primarily the ending of the unconscious (without choice) inner conflict between giving priority to an outside belief we obey and exercising our ability and right of individual free choice, the primary source of the experience of inner conflict.

The focus on working through issues *in words* is not the highest priority in what can be labeled "maturation psychotherapy." It is *mastering the layers of maturity of the skill of human self-consciousness.*

Peace on Earth

As also described in the last chapter, *Chapter 6: Maturation Movement and the 10 Recommended Priorities for the 2020 US Presidential Candidates*, it is time to end war and violence as an option of dealing with differences on Earth.

This can only be done by making, keeping, and monitoring agreements.

Therefore, it is time to create a new global organization of nations who commit to never participating in wars or violence to resolve differences and make their militaries available for police action, not war action, to stop it wherever necessary. If war or violence emerges within or between any member nations, the militaries of all member nations will be available to stop it *as a police action, as an action of keeping our agreements.*

This organization will be married with the nurturing of the emergence of agreement nations within each member geographic nation to allow each group to create a community of people based on their worldview as long as it does no harm to others and follows the laws of the geographic nation. This is our next step toward assuring continuous global peace for member geographic nations and, hopefully, eventually for all nations on Earth.

Any time two or more people at the Teen layer or higher gather together, the other side of the coin of honoring the ability and right to exercise individual free choice is the making and keeping of agreements. If we want to have permanent peace around the world, it will be necessary to create this new international organization based on agreement to do it. It is accepting full responsibility we all have at the Teen layer, sharing in the responsibility of giving priority to the common good, cooperation for maturation. It is also the choice of agreements rather than war from those only two fundamental choices possible in human relationships.

I have shared just enough of what is in my next book, *Your and My Maturation Stories,* that you will know the essence of each proposal. If you have greater interest in any one of them, I encourage you to read my next book, *Your and My Maturation Stories,* my book *Common Good Nation, a*nd go to www.chrysalisnation.org to become involved with those seeking to create Chrysalis Nation or another agreement nation. Or, if that is a more substantial activity than you are interested in at this time, only participate in the programs that interest you.

There is a Maturation Movement emerging that will define the new Relationship Age into which humanity will eventually mature. Your participation at any level you choose is welcomed.

CHAPTER 8

Mutual Mature Love Experience

In this chapter, with a friend you choose, the two of you will be guided into the *mutually known self-conscious experience of the oneness of nature.*

You may at first think this is not possible and shy back from wanting to do it. If the oneness of nature is real, it has to be able to be experienced in direct experience. The reason you may not until now experienced it is because you, along with the rest of us, have been living within the mutually agreed upon illusion tool of the assumption of separate parts that allowed us to invent words and be self-conscious.

You may still unconsciously (without choice) be doing that and not aware of it. Since nearly everyone else is doing it, sustaining operating on that illusion has been easy to do.

The purpose of this guided experience is to reveal to you it is possible to know the experience of oneness as a direct self-consciously chosen experience.

Yes, you can know it alone, without learning to know it with another person. That is possible, but very difficult to accomplish.

The reason is for it to be a self-consciously known experience a mutually known human language has to be present and given second priority to unable-to-be-broken-up-into-parts experience.

It is the mutually agreed upon words of a human language that allow us to be self-conscious. Without them present, we cannot easily know it as a self-consciously known and able to be chosen experience within which we can experience everything else as secondary.

You can read through this chapter now. However, if you do not do this exercise with another, whether or not you are aware of it you are still giving priority to words. You are still unconsciously (without choice) living within the illusion separate parts are real. They are not real. To begin living in reality you need to know *experientially* the difference between operating on the assumption of oneness and operating on the assumption of separate parts. This experience with another is the two of you choosing to do both fully and simultaneously *and giving priority to the experience of oneness and second priority to words.* This has you living in reality self-consciously. You will immediately notice you feel safe, without any experience of fear, there is contented joy, and you do not want to leave it. This is being in reality. It is being self-consciously in the reality of the oneness of nature.

You will then know this "wavelength," as I like to name it. You will learn you can be self-consciously participating in it with people who also know it or, privately, with people who do not know it. It is the oneness wavelength that is always present, and you are now able to be a self-conscious participant in its process of cooperation for maturation.

While fully doing both, it is giving priority to unbroken-up-into-parts-experience, the oneness wavelength, and second priority to the words we use to be self-conscious parts of the indivisible universe.

Why choose to do this experience with another? You could just read through it, get the main idea, and move on.

There is a very important reason to do it.

As a result of you knowing in direct experience rocks are hard and fire is hot, they naturally, effortlessly, freely, easily, and permanently become self-evident facts you use in your thinking and can't fool yourself into thinking you do not know them. No effort, force, or discipline is necessary. Allow me to repeat that: no effort, force, or discipline is necessary. In the same way you know rocks are hard and fire is hot, you want to know in direct experience you can choose the mutual self-conscious experience of oneness with another person.

Until you choose to do it in direct experience with another, you will not know it is possible in direct experience with another.

Because the mutually agreed upon illusion of separate parts (human language) is present, you can know it as a self-conscious direct experience. This is why you want to make sure you do this experience with a friend you choose. Like knowing rocks are hard and fire is hot in direct experience, it is a permanent maturation into the knowledge and skill of the Mature Elder layer, the giving of priority to the experience of the oneness of nature and second priority to the words we use to talk about it.

Like the discovery and mastery of each of the smaller skills of the lower layers of maturity, this seventh smaller skill will also eventually become a habit and no longer in need of your primary attention. Then at all times the highest priority in your behavior will be Eldering, being, wherever you are sitting or standing, a direct self-conscious participation in the cooperation for maturation of the universe. Because you know it in direct experience, by using your skill of human self-consciousness as your sixth sense, you will be able to consistently know the experience of natural confidence and the feeling of contented joy, the most enjoyable joy, or how to find your way back to it when you lose awareness of it. You now know where this wavelength is and can choose to participate in it again.

However, if you do not exercise mature free choice by being a personal scientist and discovering this in direct experience, you will remain stuck at the Elder layer or lower until you do.

If you have not mastered the smaller skills of the six lower layers, you will still be able to experience this self-conscious oneness when you do this exercise. However, not having mastered the smaller skills of the lower layers, afterwards you will be vulnerable to unconsciously (without choice) giving priority to one of them, fundamentally the only mistake we can make in life. However, knowing what is possible by having this experience will stimulate you into turning your attention to fully mastering the smaller skills of the lower layers. So do not hesitate to do the below exercise if you judge you have not yet achieved full maturity at the Elder layer.

In the first personal science study in *Chapter 1: The 7 Questions,* you were guided into keeping your power, all of it, and studying your direct, present, and repeatable by choice experience to discover it is self-evident the universe operates as an indivisible whole, as one thing. That was guiding you into the discovery of the smaller skill of the Elder layer, awareness of the oneness of nature as obvious and self-evident. This allowed you to represent it in words not only as your most fundamental inside belief but also to discover your accurate self-definition. It also allowed you to discover the importance of giving priority to the oneness pattern of thinking and second priority to the separate parts pattern of thinking. This was all part of the mastery of the Elder layer, the layer where we get all the words in our thinking to accurately represent the way the universe operates as inside beliefs. When this is fully accomplished, we are no longer distracted by trying to get our words to accurately represent reality. That job is done. We can then turn our full attention to discovering the *smaller skill* of the seventh and final layer of maturity of the skill of human self-consciousness: giving priority to the self-conscious experience of the oneness of nature. That is what you will be doing in the exercise below.

It is an exercise. With another, the two of you will be guided into the self-conscious experience of oneness so you will know it is real, can be chosen, and is enjoyable. However, it will be occurring for a period of time and in a particular place. Full maturity in this skill is only easily sustained when we know it in our most intimate relationship, usually our romantic relationship. Having this base camp to return to after the challenges each day of relating with people operating at all different layers of maturity is extremely valuable to consistently get better at knowing it, choosing it as our priority, and maturing in our skill of Eldering. The possibility of this consistent mutual skill is the main attraction of romantic love.

You can read through the guidance into this self-conscious experience and then read through it again, step by step, when choosing this experience with another person. If possible, it is best to have a third person guide you and another in choosing this experience by reading the following. However, it will be written as if one of the two of you choosing to have this mutual self-conscious experience together is reading this section-by-section as appropriate. If a third party is available, he or she will easily be able to adapt the guidance into that process as he or she reads through it for the two of you.

Choose to do this with a friend, lover, or adult child. Sit in straight chairs, knees to knees almost touching, with your eyes as level with each other's eyes as possible. A couple of pillows can help make this happen. Be sure to be in a place where there will not be interruptions; and, if you have them, turn off your cell phones. Make sure no lights are shining directly into the eyes of either person. If they are necessary to see another clearly, it is fine to leave on your eyeglasses; but it is best if you do not need to wear them. If one of you needs to wear your eyeglasses, be sure the other can easily see your eyes.

One of you will read the following piece by piece as appropriate to guide the two of you through each section.

Repeat each set of guidance as needed.

The purpose of choosing to do this exercise is to have the two of you mutually know the self-conscious experience of oneness in a relationship with another person. Each of you do whatever you each judge necessary to continue allowing yourselves to be fully available to your study of this experience to see if you can discover this mutual experience together, including stopping the process for a bit to take a breath or asking for the directions to be read again. There is no need at any time to hurry or not be fully comfortable you understand the directions.

Now, with the out loud reading from the beginning of this chapter by the one who will be doing the out loud reading, begin this experience together. I will let you know when the experience is completed. There will then be additional out loud reading necessary to share with anyone with whom you do this experience or was witnessing it. (Reading copy out loud is a way to be sure both or all people present have heard the information and know all the others have also heard it.)

Let's now begin the guiding of the two of you into mutually knowing the direct self-conscious experience of the oneness of nature:

Guidance of Two People into the Mutually Known Self-Conscious Experience of Oneness With Words Second in Priority

Throughout history it has been discovered there are only two ways this thing we call "the universe" or "nature" could be structured: as one thing or as two or more things, that is, as separate parts.

The person not reading this can hold out between the two of you their two fists separate from one another as the symbol of separate parts. He or she can do that now.

When we are assuming the universe operates as separate parts, one of us is one of these fists and the other is the other fist, two parts separate from one another. Each does not know what the other is thinking. Each cannot tell the other what to do. We are assuming each is fully separate from the other.

When we first come upon the other, we will, on the surface, be pleasant; but our *priority* is to check out the other to see if he or she can be trusted. The other could be a Jack-the-Ripper type person. We are *privately and primarily* cautious until we know it is safe.

Now the one not reading can clasp his or her fingers on two hands together to create a ball and hold them between the two of you as a symbol of oneness. Do that now.

When we are assuming the universe operates as one thing and come upon another person, we are *primarily and publicly* open and trusting. We know the other person and our self are like a finger on each hand. He or she is as much a part of me as I am of him or her. We know that whether or not the other is aware of it, his or her natural primary intention is good, just like ours. Also, whether or not he or she is aware of it, it is to be a participant in the maturation of us all, to participate in having all the parts of the universe cooperate in more mature ways. We know that about this neither one of us has choice. This is the nature of oneness: co-operation for maturation that is its fundamental process, priority, and activity.

Thus, fundamentally there is nothing to fear.

The other could still be a Jack-the-Ripper type person; but, if necessary, we know we can handle that as a second priority. We also know we will have a better ability to do so if we are primarily open and trusting and see the other as his or her primary good intentions. Why that is so is a discussion for another day.

At this time, we just want to know in our thinking the difference between assuming oneness is true and assuming separate parts are true. One is the *experience* of being separate parts. The other is the *experience* of being parts of one whole.

Now let's turn our attention to our actual physical bodies sitting in the chairs facing each other. Let's study the difference in the *behavior* of the assumption of oneness and the *behavior* of separate parts.

If assuming we are separate parts, each of us is only our physical body and not the other's physical body or the air in between us. Therefore, the behavior of each of us is either going toward the other or, because our attention has become focused elsewhere, away from the other.

The primary behavior of separate parts is of each of us going toward the other or away from the other.

To indicate in motions the behavior of assuming separate parts, the person not reading this can twirl their hands a number of times toward the other and then a number of times in another direction that is away from the other. The one not reading can do that now. Then read the next sentence.

Since there are only two fundamental ways the universe could be structured, the *behavior of oneness* has to be the exact opposite of the behavior of assuming the universe operates as separate parts.

If one person has not read this book, the other person asks that person to provide his or her best answer to this question: "What is the behavior of oneness?" or "What is the opposite of going toward or away from one another?" Only after an answer has been presented, read the next sentence. (If both of you have read this book and know the answer, go to the next paragraph.)

Don't worry. I have guided people into this experience hundreds of times and no one has ever found the accurate answer. You will eventually understand why.

Here is the answer: the opposite of going toward or away from another as if there are separate parts is to "define self as all that is." Now there is no place to go toward or away from where one is not already.

The behavior of oneness is to be fully receptive because we are each *first* the indivisible universe. There is no second thing to move toward or away from or, therefore, to fear. This receptiveness is the *behavior* of operating on the knowledge the the universe operates as an indivisible whole. It is knowing that *fundamentally* there is not a second thing to fear. Secondarily, within the perception of times and places, of separate parts, there may be, but fundamentally there isn't. In the reality of oneness, there is not a second place. Therefore, there is not a second thing to fear.

You will now be guided into the *mutually known experience* of this behavior of oneness with each other as your *primary choice* with words remaining present and second in priority.

To have a strong experience of contact with each other, as much as possible while one of you is reading this, hold each other's hands. Also, *in silence and while consistently looking into each other's eyes,* choose in your thinking the following three things one at a time. You will eventually settle into a place together of comfortably, not staring but receptively, looking into each other's eyes.

While you both continue to choose to remain in that comfortable experience with each other, what is occurring will then be described so you can become familiar with it and able to choose this experience with another as a skill when it is a mutual choice. Or, when with others who do not know this experience, to unilaterally and privately choose to give priority to participating in it, "the oneness wavelength." It is always present and able to be given priority as the chosen container experience of everything else you are experiencing and doing.

I will now describe what I will below guide the two of you into doing with each other.

In silence, one at a time in your thinking and while resting in, not staring but receptively resting in, each other's eyes, you will choose to do the following three things. Once you have each chosen in silence to do them in the order presented, just choose to be receptive the rest of the time. It will have the other two experiences also be fully present.

First, privately in your thinking you will **define "self" as "all that is."** There are two ways this can be done. You can take on the self-definition, "I am the universe, all that is." Or you can say, "I am (the name of the other person)." This also works because if we define "self" as where our attention is focused, we are in the pattern of oneness in our thinking with where our attention is focused, in this case in the relationship with the other person. Either one will have your thinking be in the pattern of oneness.

Secondly, privately in your thinking **be totally receptive** to whatever comes into your thinking. It could be the shape of the other's nose, the color of the other's hair, your guess of what the other is thinking. Whatever it is, let the thoughts come and go as they please. The universe operates as an indivisible whole. Fundamentally, it is all me relating with me. In oneness, there is nothing to be afraid of. Being receptive is the opposite of being afraid.

Thirdly, **know you are doing this while you are doing it. Be at choice each moment.** There is the possibility that you will float into having your primary attention on the words in your thinking about what you are doing. That is primarily being in the experience of separate parts, primarily focused on words that are separate parts.

Instead, each second be at the choice of choosing this *self-conscious experience* by choice with the other.

While you choose to be silent and continually rest your eyes in the other's eyes, in your thinking choose to do the above three things one after the other. Once you have done all three, choose to be receptive the rest of the time. The two of you will eventually settle into comfortably resting your eyes in the eyes of the other without a desire to leave.

That was the explanation of what the two of you will be doing. You now know exactly what the next paragraphs will guide you into doing with each other.

Now let's do this exercise.

While **being silent, continuing to hold each other's hands,** and **continuously resting in each other's eyes,** each in your thinking do the following three things in this order:

- **define "self" as all that is or the two of you.**

- **be totally receptive, let whatever thoughts come into your thinking come and go. And,**

- **each moment know you are doing this while you are doing it; be at choice.**

When, while in silence and each in the privacy of your thinking have chosen these three things in order, choose to be receptive for the rest of the time. You will eventually both settle into comfortably and steadily resting your eyes in the other's eyes with no desire to leave. Resting receptively in each other's eyes, not staring into each other's eyes. Be sure to give it enough time, usually three to four minutes. When one of you is confident that the two of you have settled into being comfortably receptive eyes-to-eyes with each other for a period of time, one of you can break the silence.

If it feels good to read the last eight paragraphs one or more times before beginning, do so. The first one begins with, "In silence, one at a time in your thinking…"

Be sure you are both fully comfortable and know the directions. Then go silent for a few minutes and do it. When it is obvious that the two of you have settled into being comfortably receptive while looking each other in the eyes for some period of time, one of you can break the silence.

Now be silent and choose to have this mutual experience. Briefly, here are the directions again.

In silence, and while holding hands and resting in each other's eyes, in your thinking choose to do the following three things in this order:

- **define self as all that is or the two of you,**

- **be totally receptive to all that comes into your thinking, let whatever thoughts come into your thinking come and go. And,**

- **know you are doing it while you are doing it; be at choice each moment.**

When you have chosen to do all three in your thinking in order, **just choose to be receptive.** When you know you have both settled into comfortably looking each other in the eyes for a period of time, in a few minutes, one of you can break the silence.

Then turn to the next page.

Now, become silent, and be sure to stay silent while you are doing it, and do it.

Remain comfortably resting in each other's eyes while one of you breaks from it *only to read each following section* and then always return to remain in this mutually receptive eyes-to-eyes experience when not reading, even in silence for a minute or so just to be sure you confirm you are both choosing to be in it together.

It will be easy to remain eyes-to-eyes with each other. There is no more enjoyable experience to have with another person than the *self-conscious experience of oneness.* By choosing this experience together, it was possible for the two of you to mutually experience it in your relationship.

If you are resting comfortably in each other's eyes, that is what you are doing. You are mutually agreeing to give priority to the experience of oneness and second priority to words. For instance, you are secondly listening to these words as they are being read.

I will trust that the two of you settled into this shared experience with each other. If so, there are three important experiences present. First, there is an absence of fear. Secondly, you like it. Thirdly, there is no desire to leave it. Note whether or not these are true for the two of you.

Is there an absence of fear? (Each answer.)

Do you both like it? (Each answer.)

Is there any desire to leave? (Each answer.)

Also note, you can comfortably remain in this mutual experience while you listen to this reading, talk, or do anything else as a second in priority activity.

You are both *giving priority* to the self-conscious experience of oneness in a relationship with another human being.

If this is what you are experiencing, this is how the two of you confirm for yourselves you are mutually experiencing in your relationship the self-conscious experience of oneness. If the two of you are not having the experience I am describing, at another time simply choose this experience again, with the same person or another person, until you discover it.

When you discover it, **here are three specific things you are both experiencing** that will reveal it to be self-evidently true that you are experiencing the skill of *choosing with another* the mutual self-conscious experience of oneness.

First, notice that you are continuously and comfortably looking into each other's eyes. There is full comfort in doing so. It is so comfortable and enjoyable you have no desire to leave this mutually known experience. This is not a foreign experience for each of you. You each do this each day in your relationship with your reflection in a mirror. It is really a shiny piece of metal on a wall eighteen inches from your nose that reflects your face. Since you think of it as a reflection of yourself, *you are comfortably in the experience of oneness with it.* There is clearly nothing to fear. You are *experiencing* your reflection in the mirror as another part of you even though it is, in physical terms, separate from you.

The only difference here is that you are now doing this with another person. You are experiencing the other person as another part of you, as you experience your reflection in the mirror as another part of you. Since you are both doing this at the same time, you are in the mutually known self-conscious experience of oneness with each other. Therefore, there is no second thing to fear.

It is the exact same experience of oneness with the mirror only with another person. The point being made here is that this experience is not foreign or new. Like seeing your reflection in a mirror, it is an experience with which you are both familiar. You are just having this experience of oneness *self-consciously with another person* instead of with a shiny object on a wall.

Second, what has actually happened is the two of you have chosen to be on what can be described as the same "wavelength"

together, the same field of energy, the same vibration, the same container experience within which everything else is occurring as second in importance.

It is a wavelength that is everywhere at all times and able to be *self-consciously (by choice) participated in* by any human being. It is the mutually known self-conscious experience of oneness wavelength.

You are now both self-consciously experiencing oneness together while words are present but second in priority.

You can, for instance, look away from each other and then look each other in the eyes again and notice you have not left together giving priority to this wavelength. Go ahead. You can both do that now. Look away from each other for a few moments, even get up and walk around the room if you like, and then come back to looking into each other's eyes. You will find you are still giving priority to this *mutually known self-conscious experience of oneness*. Do that now. Then read the next paragraph.

This experience is enjoyable and there is no reason to leave it. Thus, you do not easily leave it even if not looking each other in the eyes.

There was not a change in the experience with each other when not looking each other in the eyes. Now that you know this self-conscious experience of oneness wavelength exits and can be a chosen experience in relationship with another, one of you could be on the telephone here and the other on a telephone in Tokyo. The two of you could choose, and mutually be aware of participating in, this *self-conscious experience of oneness wavelength* as the container of all you talk about on the telephone.

It is not primarily the result of sitting your physical bodies next to each other and looking each other in the eyes. That is how you have come to mutually know it together—in a direct, present, and repeatable experience. You have first come to know it in a mutually known experience when sitting with another human being.

This is necessary to learn it is possible! This is actually the two of you self-consciously choosing to give priority to the oneness wavelength that is always present and available for your participation. You both now know it exists, the experience of it, and have the ability to mutually choose it as your priority with words fully and comfortably present and second in priority.

Also, now that you know it there, the other person is not necessary. You both now know it is a wavelength that is present everywhere and you both know you can participate in it. You both know you can together tune into it by mutual choice when on the telephone now or next week or next year. It is the mutual experience of oneness self-consciously known together in relationship with each other. You also now know the two of you can choose to be on the oneness wavelength together if you at any time mutually choose to do it.

What is important to know is that you both could not have had your first experience of this *as a self-conscious experience* accept in a relationship with another person such as you are having now. This experience is only *initially* possible by having two people choose to have this experience of self-conscious oneness the top priority and words second in priority. Now that you have each been initiated into the knowledge that this wavelength exists and have experienced it, from this point on you each will be able to learn to *unilaterally* choose it as your experience container at all times and in all places (in oneness). To do so is now a skill you know and can turn into a habit.

Once the two of you know it you will never be able to fool yourselves into thinking you do not know how to go here with each other or another person. You know how by mutual choice to tap into the wavelength of self-conscious oneness that is always present and able to be mutually experienced as the experience container of all you are doing together.

Thirdly and lastly, and while continuing to look each other in the eyes, turn your attention to identifying the feeling you are each experiencing. Each share with the other the word you would use to describe what you are feeling. "What is the particular word that represents for you the feeling that is present?" Share it with each other now. Then read the next paragraph.

It doesn't make any difference what word you each chose to label the feeling you are each experiencing. Notice, however, they are both positive words. That is what was important. It was the word you each chose to identify the positive feeling you are each experiencing. Some words often chosen are "calm," "peace," "love," "contentedness," "warm," "grace," and "serene."

Now while comfortably and receptively continuing to look into each other's eyes, notice something very interesting about this feeling: it is different from every other feeling you have ever had. There are no degrees of feeling it. This is the mutually known self-conscious experience of the oneness of nature while words are present and second in priority.

There are no degrees of the feeling of oneness. We are either fully experiencing it, or we are not experiencing it. Therefore, we can't get better or worse at it. All we can do is hang out in it. We are either moving as one with the rest of the universe or we are not. There is not a third choice.

We can learn to hang out in it as the experience container within which we secondly do things in the mutually agreed-upon illusion there are separate parts. If there are no degrees of oneness, all we can do is hang out in it, this wavelength, or not hang out in it as the experience container choice of everything else we experience and do.

There are degrees of every other feeling we could have.

All other feelings are *relative feelings*, a feeling relative to another person or part of the universe. If we are friends, on a scale of one to ten, with ten being the best of friends, we could be at a seven. If we do not see each other for a long time, we could slip to a six in closeness of the feeling of friendship. If we again spend enjoyable times together, it could become a nine.

There are not degrees of the self-conscious experience of oneness. We can't get better or worse at it. All we can do is choose or not choose to hang out in it as the chosen experience container for all sensations, differences, wants, experiences of individual and mature free choice, beliefs, and conversations with each other. This is the self-consciously known fundamental feeling of contented joy we have been seeking since we were each a Toddler and entered the path of mastering the skill of achieving full maturity in this skill of human self-consciousness.

The difference is we now know it as a mutually known and self-consciously chosen experience of oneness in relationship with another person. The purpose of our maturation up the mastery of the smaller skills of the seven layers of maturity of the skill of human self-consciousness was to master this smaller skill of being able to choose to give priority at all times and in all places (in the reality of oneness) to the self-conscious experience of the oneness wavelength. To be able to self-consciously participant in the fundamental process, priority, and activity of the universe, cooperation for maturation.

Notice something.

You are still comfortably resting in each other's eyes. You are enjoying doing so. You are also experiencing no desire to leave this mutual experience.

These are the three behavioral experiences that confirm this is the mutually known self-conscious experience of oneness in your relationship with each other: you are fully comfortable looking into each other's eyes without any experience of fear, you are enjoying it, and you do not want to leave it. The universe really is an indivisible whole. The two of you are now *self-consciously* in the experience of that reality with each other: you know you are self-consciously participating in it while you are doing it. Words are fully and comfortably present but always secondary to what you are giving priority: *the mutually known direct experience of the oneness of nature.*

This concludes the pointing out of the three important experiences you are having. The reader should continue reading.

Now, whether or not the two of you have mastered all seven smaller skills, hopefully through this guided study into this experience with another you have each discovered the mutually known self-conscious experience of oneness in relationship with another person. It will now be easier to master the smaller skills of the layers of maturity of human self-consciousness you still have not fully mastered. You now know that when they have been mastered, and as the result of free choice, this can be the continuous mutually chosen container in a relationship with another person, often called "romantic love," "friendship love," "mature parent-child love," "community love," "nation love," or "love of all." Every kind of love is the experience of this wavelength, the experience of *primarily* choosing alone or mutually with another to hang out in the experience of the oneness wavelength as the chosen container of everything else. In this book, this activity is labeled "mutual mature love." The mutuality is with all that exists.

There are many flavors of love but at the bottom they are all this *experience.* My friends and I call this "the mutual mature love place" or simply "the love skill."

Self-consciousness needs to use the mutually agreed-upon illusion tool of separate parts. Doing this exercise with another is essential to be able to experience oneness as a self-conscious experience. Only by honoring that this mutually agreed-upon illusion tool of words is present, and you are both giving priority to the self-conscious experience of oneness without any experience of conflict between the two, can the two of you easily come to know eye-to-eye the direct experience of self-conscious oneness is real, always-present, and able to be participated in.

It is something we can know, choose, turn into a skill, and turn into a habit.

That concludes this study of your experience together to discover in relationship with another mutual mature love, the mutually known direct self-conscious experience of oneness as the priority with words present and second in priority. Be comfortable choosing this experience many times and with many people so you get to know it well. And if for whatever reason the two of you did not come to know it together this time, choose to do this exercise together at another time or with another person. It is not mysterious or magical or special. Mastering this skill is easy to get to know, easier than learning to ride a bicycle. You just need to yield into giving it a sincere try. Like riding a bicycle, it may be experienced as difficult to learn at first. But once known it is experienced as easy to do.

There is one other piece of information that needs to be mentioned and read after choosing this experience with each other. When doing this experience with someone who has not read this book or when others have witnessed it, *it is important that the below is read out loud for that person or those people*. However, it is also important for it to also be read out loud as a reminder for the two of you of the importance of not accidentally imposing the oneness worldview upon others:

To Be Read Out Loud to All Who Participated in Or Witnessed the Mutual Mature Love Experience Between Two People

If tomorrow, you go up to another person and act as if that person and you are one, the other could easily feel threatened. The other would experience you as demanding he or she change to behave as you are behaving, to be behaving as if you are two self-conscious parts of a whole. If so, this could easily be experienced by the other as "you are invading my space."

That experience of the other will be accurate. You would be demanding the other join you there. One can only discover and know this with another as the result of the exercise of individual free choice.

The knowledge of the higher layers of maturity of the skill of human self-consciousness build on the Teen layer that in part, and initially at least honors individual free choice. As I trust you just did, one can only voluntarily choose the above experience. Another cannot to any degree be forced into it nor do we ever want to attempt to do so: that is not honoring that person's ability and right at the Teen layer of individual free choice. They will naturally and appropriately rebel.

Most of us live in societies where most people are still unconsciously (without choice) giving priority to the assumption that separate parts are real. They do not know it is a *mutually agreed-upon illusion tool* that has us mutually act as if separate parts exist, at least not until we discover doing so is a mutually agreed-upon illusion tool. They do not know we can *mutually* experience ourselves as self-conscious parts of the indivisible universe. If so, they are operating as if the sixth (Adult layer) or a lower layer of maturity of the skill of human self-consciousness is the highest layer. These are the layers where they are unconsciously (without choice) operating as if separate parts are real. Or, and this is a possibility, they also know what you have just learned and are only acting as if separate parts are real to be honoring that is the current socially acceptable relationship container.

The kind and compassionate way of relating with another is to always accept them exactly as they are and do our best to add love to the equation. It is to operate as if the layer they are operating on is the highest layer while *inside* giving priority to the highest layer we know. It is the way a parent is with a child, talking as if Santa Claus is real when the child still believes he is real, *while inwardly giving priority to parenting.* Or it is honoring a teen's or older person's need to give priority to exercising individual freedom of choice. We know it is most important that each person keep his or her power, all of it, and use it to solely study direct, present, and repeatable by choice experience (use personal science) to identify the self-evident facts one chooses to guide one's thinking. Each person does have equal access to choosing, with another, the mutual experience of self-conscious oneness and giving second priority to words. However, it must be a free choice to choose it. Until this is freely chosen, a person does not know he or she has access to it.

While making sure we do not impose our worldview upon another, there is still a difference in our behavior. We now know we are primarily as much the other as ourselves.

Therefore, there is no experience of superiority in our compassion.

There is only the feeling of oneness experienced as compassion, kindness, and love toward another part of ourselves. Fundamentally, it is the same way our right arm experiences our left arm. Only the other person, unlike the arms, has the ability and right of exercising individual free choice.

The other is then experienced as a part of us operating at the highest layer of maturity he or she knows. We remember well when we were thinking it was the highest layer. There was no way we could have discovered a higher layer without once believing each lower layer was the highest layer. It is part of mastering the smaller skills of human self-consciousness in the natural sequence. This knowledge has us only experience a feeling of *oneness compassion* with another, not separate or superior compassion.

We then operate within the assumption that the layer of maturity at which the other is operating is the highest layer while giving priority in our behavior to Eldering actions.

In summary, be sure you do not unilaterally behave with another as if we are all one unless the other has verbally or non-verbally invited you to do so. The former would be imposing our worldview on the other. The other will experience it as an invasion of his or her space, as us imposing a worldview upon him or her. It is usually best to outwardly give priority to the assumption there are separate parts while inwardly living as if they do not exist. You can then read to what extent the other knows the experience of oneness as real and only invite a *mutual recognition of it* as you read the other is ready to go there with you.

Finally, hopefully you now know that the choice of giving priority to the direct self-conscious experience of oneness is a skill, a skill you can at all times and in all places (in the reality of oneness) choose to self-consciously experience as your chosen container of everything else that is occurring. You will learn to experience everything you used to think was outside your skin as now inside who you primarily are, the indivisible universe. It is this that makes compassion occur that has no experience of superiority in it.

This is the end of this out loud reading. Now be comfortable discussing your experiences of choosing to do this Mutual Mature Love Experience with each other. When you are done with sharing your experiences with each other, reading the next few paragraphs out loud can be an enjoyable way for the two of you, or all of you, to complete this mutual experience you have just had.

As many times as you like, let yourself do this exercise to discover this direct and mutual self-conscious experience of oneness with others. I want to most strongly encourage you to do it with your lover. If you are not married, before you marry be sure your mate to be has mastered this skill and is able to live in mutual mature love with you. This is your most intimate relationship and will be the foundation of being able to live in the joy of being Mature Elders and Eldering the rest of your lives.

The above was only an exercise at a particular time and in particular place to allow you to know this is possible. It is essential that you have an ongoing relationship with another person of *consistently living within this direct and mutual mature love as your base camp.* After the challenges of being with people operating at different layers of maturity during our days, we each need a place to which we can return to affirm this is real. This is the main desire for and attraction of romantic love.

Then you can do as Lucy, my lover, and I do. Each morning, once we have breakfast on the table, we hold each other's hands. We then look into each other's eyes in this fully receptive way and enjoy knowing this self-conscious experience together. While we are doing it, we sometimes state what is going on: "We are giving priority to the mutually known self-conscious experience of the oneness of nature. We are being fully receptive. We know we are doing it while we are doing it." Then, before we eat our breakfast, often having a hard time leaving it because we know the food is getting cold, for a few moments we continue resting our eyes in each other's enjoying the experience of mutual mature love with each other. When we cuddle in bed at night, before falling asleep we do similar things in the joy of the dark and the strong tactile experience of touching each other's physical body.

If you are in a romantic love relationship, I encourage the two of you to establish traditions like these. You will then also come to know the joy of mutually giving priority to Eldering the rest of your lives. Mastering the seven smaller skills of human self-consciousness is only the beginning of our lives. It allows us to then know the never-ending joy of mutually maturing in the skill of Eldering.

Each of us is not alone, never have been, and never will be.

In our daily actions, nothing is more enjoyable than Eldering. It is each moment giving priority to what we each judge to be our best action of participation in the maturation of the rest of who we each are, the indivisible universe. Eldering is the only activity that is simultaneously best both for us and the rest of the universe.

Doing it consistently as a habit, mutually from within our most intimate relationship, is what allows us to self-consciously *know together* the inner feeling of contented joy, the most enjoyable joy.

Remember, the oneness of the universe is always present, or we would not be able to breathe. Think of it as in the air that surrounds everything. It cannot be escaped and its process of cooperation for maturation cannot be stopped. Contented joy is self-consciously knowing we are at all times and in all places (in the reality of oneness) primarily participants in it, the activity of Eldering. Only this as the priority in our actions sustains the feeling of contented joy.

CONCLUSION

If when answering the 7 questions near the beginning of this book you kept your power, all of it, and used it to *primarily* study your direct, present, and repeatable by choice *experience* and discovered the universe operates as an indivisible whole, you are now a personal scientist. If this is true for you, I would like to suggest you consider doing the following five things. They are my best suggestions on how to have your life be an expression of this knowledge. If you like, you can become a member of Chrysalis Nation, even if only to monitor how this Maturation Movement is developing, both in that organization and elsewhere.

The five following suggestions are what you could do, some or all of them, if you choose to Self-Elder yourself, and your community of friends as well if you like, into full maturity in this skill:

Five Ways to Participate in the Maturation Movement

1. Accept Full Responsibility for Your Maturation Being an Inside Job.

Achieving full maturity in the skill of human self-consciousness is an inside job. The mastery of the smaller skills of the layers after the Teen layer can only occur through the exercise of mature free choice, by using our skill of human self-consciousness as a sixth sense to be personal scientists. From the inside, we each have sole and complete control of our physical body and, from the inside, none anywhere else. Therefore, each of us must accept full responsibility for this Self-Eldering process. It is an inside job.

2. Create a Base Camp.

Our most intimate relationship, usually our romantic relationship, is our base camp. If possible, we want our mate and us to know full maturity in the skill of human self-consciousness and the joy of mutual Eldering. This can begin by inviting your partner to read this book and doing the exercise in *Chapter 8: Mutual Mature Love Experience.*

If achieving mutual maturation into full maturity in this skill in your romantic relationship does not appear to be currently possible, there are many reasons why remaining in the relationship can be appropriate for you. This is fully your decision. However, do your best to assist your partner to discover the joy of full maturity in this skill both out of love for him or her and your relationship. This will be one of your Eldering responsibilities. Doing it skillfully, where your partner experiences no pressure or demand but only an attractive invitation, is one of the most important Eldering skills to learn. Operating at full maturity yourself, and in terms of time giving priority to eternal time, will make this Eldering activity easy to do.

3. Re-Village Your Life.

For support in this maturation process, as well as that of our spouses, families, and friends, we want to not just have friends here and there which is fine. We want to also form a self-consciously chosen and organized community of friends based on agreements of how you want to live, enjoy, and mature together. That is, we want to re-village our lives. We want to accept full responsibility for creating the lives we want in our most intimate relationships.

Form your community using organic membership. The first person choosing the second person, those two choosing the third, and so on. This has all fully share ownership with each other of choosing the person and genuinely choose to be in community with each new person. Your community could also have sub-groups of all kinds emerge, such as your dearest friends group, personal growth support groups, couples' groups, men's groups, women's groups, music groups, party groups, business groups, environment groups, ending poverty in our community and around the world groups, and many more. Do your best to legitimize sub-groups as part of your community rather than having them break away into new communities.

4. Join an Agreement Nation.

Have your community group join in association with other like-thinking communities to form an agreement nation for broader mutual support and to make your agreement nation available for other communities to join. The emergence of agreement nations is the next layer of maturity of democracy.

5. **Be a Fully Responsible Member of Your Geographic Nation.**

> While giving priority to your agreement nation, become a fully responsible and active member of your geographic nation with your priority having them move toward providing a safe place for agreement nations of all kinds to flourish. Having our geographic nations create a safe place for agreement nations is part of our maturation into this next layer of maturity of democracy.

The following is a summary of the most important insights I think you would like to keep in your thinking as you finish this book.

Since the invention of the words of human languages, and definitely up to the early teenage years in each person's life, nearly all of us have had a blind spot. We are all unconsciously (without choice) assuming the universe is separate parts. It isn't. It is an indivisible whole. However, to invent words that allows us to be self-conscious parts of the indivisible universe, it was necessary to also invent the assumption it is separate parts. Only then could we invent a sound and symbol, a word, for one thing that is different from those invented for all the other things. If beginning in the early teenage years, when we are first biologically able to do so, we are not eldered into the mastery of the smaller skills of the remaining layers of the skill of human self-consciousness, we can spend the rest of our lives unconsciously (without choice) operating on the assumption the universe is separate parts. As a result, we think we are each only our physical body, one of them. This will have us assume the self-interest of our physical body is our natural highest priority and, therefore, competition is the fundamental process in nature. Neither is true. Assuming the universe (nature) is separate parts was a *mutually agreed upon illusion tool* we were not aware we were inventing when we invented words for things: our mutual blind spot. Most on Earth are still unconsciously (without choice) operating as if this is the accurate fundamental assumption. It is not. It is obvious in plain sight, particularly when answering the 7 questions, the universe operates as an indivisible whole or each of us would not be able to be consistently breathing.

Since for most of us the above Eldering has not happened, we are unaware we have been using the skill of human self-consciousness these inventions allow in an immature way. We have been choosing our most fundamental belief from the smorgasbord of *beliefs in words* we come upon, herein labeled an "outside belief." In doing so, we are unconsciously (without choice) sustaining the pattern of relationship of childhood, when our parents had our power. When choosing an outside belief, we are giving our power to a second thing, those words, and treating it as a parent-substitute. Now, whether or not we are aware of it, our only option of relating with it is again to obey it, as we obeyed our parents.

It is easy for us to unconsciously (without choice) sustain this pattern of behavior. Until we discover this *mutual blind spot* we all have when children, it is the only pattern of thinking we have used.

We are unaware we are continuing to give priority to the fundamental assumption about reality necessary to invent the words of a human language, the assumption the universe is separate parts. It is not separate parts. Therefore, there is no second thing to give our power. By continuing to give our power to what we unconsciously (without choice) assume is a second thing, we are unable to know the experience of natural confidence and the feeling of contented joy. These are only possible when we discover the assumption of separate parts is a mutually agreed upon illusion tool we invented and there are not separate parts. We can then confirm the latter by keeping our power, all of it, and using it as our sixth sense to study our direct, present, and repeatable by choice experience to discover the reality of, and direct experience of, the oneness of nature.

The oneness of nature is real and can be directly experienced.

It is most easily done when mutually chosen with another human being. Then the invention of the assumption of separate parts is fully present, allowing us to know it as a self-conscious experience, *while we are giving priority to the direct mutual self-conscious experience of the oneness of nature.*

There are two steps to this process. First, we need to keep our power, all of it, and *primarily study our direct, present, and repeatable by choice experience*—to use our skill of self-consciousness in the mature way, as a sixth sense—to discover the universe operates as an indivisible whole (the beginning of mastering the Elder layer). This is now our most fundamental inside belief on how the universe operates, it is accurate, and we can at any time confirm it is true in direct experience. This can be accomplished by answering the 7 questions near the beginning of this book and giving priority to finding the answers in a study of our *direct experience.*

When being self-conscious, words are always present. It is human languages that allow us to be self-conscious, to know what we are doing while we are doing it and to exercise individual, or mature, free choice. Therefore, when we are being self-conscious, they are always present and between us and whatever we are thinking, observing, or doing. Having our words accurately represent reality is essential to keep inaccurate thoughts in words preventing us from knowing, and being able to consistently choose, the experience of oneness as the container of all else. This is the mastery of the Elder layer, the sixth of the seven layers of maturity of the skill of human self-consciousness.

The second step is to do the exercise in *Chapter 8: Mutual Mature Love Experience.* This is discovering we can most easily know the direct self-conscious experience of the oneness of nature in a relationship with another person. This is just an exercise to reveal to you it is possible. To know this as our chosen priority in an on-going relationship, particularly with our romantic lover, and as a choice possible at all times and in all places (in the reality of oneness) is the mastery of the seventh and highest layer, the Mature Elder layer.

What is important about eventually doing this exercise with your romantic partner is for the two of you to know this eyes-to-eyes mutual experience of mature love is possible.

This is the beginning of the mastery of the highest layer of maturity of the skill of human self-consciousness, the Mature Elder layer. The two of you can then learn to give priority *at all times and in all places (in the reality of the oneness of nature)* to the experience of the oneness of nature. Knowing and being able to choose this experience with another will eventually lead us to mastering the skill of having it be our chosen priority at all times, as if it is a wavelength always present in which we can participate. It is in the air the is always present and around everything, as well in all things. We can then more easily give it priority when relating with someone who does not know it. We now know where it is and can always choose to give priority to participating in it as the container of everything else.

In both cases, we have shifted from primarily using in our thinking the assumption of separate parts to primarily using the assumption of oneness. We do this by giving priority to the oneness pattern of thinking, giving priority to priorities. We now use this pattern of thinking to choose our mature self-definition, "I am first the universe that will not die and secondly my physical body that will die." We simultaneously continue to use the separate parts assumption because it allows us to know the experience of oneness in a relationship with another person *as a self-conscious experience.* As stated above, we sustain using this pattern of thinking, now as our second priority, because it is a mutually agreed upon illusion tool, called "a human language," that allows us to be self-conscious. However, we give priority to the oneness pattern of thinking because it accurately represents the reality the universe operates as an indivisible whole.

Mastering the skill of using this accurate fundamental inside belief, our mature self-definition, and both patterns of thinking and prioritizing them correctly is the mastery of the Elder layer. Knowing how to *give priority to the self-conscious experience of oneness*, whether with someone with whom we can mutually know it or someone who does not know it, is the mastery of the Mature Elder layer.

This results in us giving priority to Eldering each moment the rest of our lives. Wherever we are each sitting or standing, this is giving priority each moment to whatever we judge to be our best unique action of participation in the maturation of the universe, the fundamental process, priority, and activity in nature. We now know this as our "true self-interest," our "mature self-interest."

Our maturation into full maturity in this skill was, hopefully, only the beginning of our lives. The remaining part of our lives we primarily Elder. It is the only priority in our behavior each moment that sustains inside us the experience of natural confidence (Elder layer) and the feeling of contented joy (Mature Elder layer) as the container of all else we experience.

When full maturity in this skill is achieved, in our actions only the priority of Eldering is living in reality. Now whatever is occurring in times and places is always secondary in importance, important because it is participation in maturation, but always second in importance. We now know our priority in nature is self-conscious participation in maturation, our responsibility as human being parts of it and our mature self-interest.

At this point it is important to note to master the choice of giving priority to the self-conscious experience of oneness at the Mature Elder layer it is necessary to have mastered the most important inside beliefs at the Elder layer. Each smaller skill of the next layer of maturity builds on the skill of the previous one. Without the words in our thinking being accurate we will be distracted from focusing on mastering the skill of the Mature Elder layer. We will still be trying to get the words to be the correct ones in our thinking. This is why the contents of this book can be very valuable for you, particularly very valuable for mastering the smaller skill of the Elder layer.

There are three uses of our ability of choice. The first is the one we use when children. It is the *exercise of choice* when others have invented the options from which we can choose, like offering us the choice of chocolate, vanilla, or strawberry ice cream. The second is the exercise of *individual free choice*. This is where we discover, as teenagers, we are capable of inventing the options of choice. For instance, should I choose to try out for the football team or the debate team. *Mature free choice* is when we use our skill of self-consciousness as our sixth sense. It is keeping our power, all of it, and use it to study our direct, present, and repeatable by choice experience to identify the most fundamental belief we will use in our thinking, what is herein labeled an inside belief. When we do this, we discover it is obvious, as obvious as rocks are hard, fire is hot, and the Earth is round, the universe operates as an indivisible whole.

It is this experience that from that point forward has us naturally, effortlessly, freely, and permanently use in our thinking this accurate fundamental assumption about reality: the assumption of oneness and all that is an extension of that assumption.

Simultaneously using the two patterns of thinking is the equivalent to playing a piano with two hands instead of one hand. The left hand, the rhythm, is the equivalent of the oneness pattern of thinking (always the same over and over again). It is given priority. The right hand, the melody, is the equivalent of the separate parts pattern of thinking (always different). It is always second in priority. Music is one of our most ancient rituals of honoring the relationship between the oneness of nature and separate parts. When we are singing together, we are all singing the same words in the same way. This makes it easy for us to give priority to the experience of oneness, what we most enjoy about the *experience* of singing together. This is local oneness. It is experienced as over the top sensational when it is experienced as universal oneness, the real oneness. This is why singing with others can be more enjoyable than watching a singing performance.

My hope is the reading of these books and the doing of the mutual mature love experience exercise is just the beginning of you mastering the skill of being a Mature Elder. If you accomplish the mastery of this skill, the rest of your life will be experienced as meaningful because you will know each moment what to do. It will always be what you judge to be your unique participation in maturation. In your unique way you will always be a social activist. You will no longer experience yourself as alone, a physical body competing to survive with no other recourses other than those of your physical body. You will instead experience yourself as *primarily* the entire universe without regard to how big or small you may think it is. You will know, whether or not others are aware of it, the highest priority of every other human being is to achieve full maturity in the skill of human self-consciousness and be primarily Eldering. About this they do not have choice. This is nature. You will then learn to primarily speak to that priority in everyone, both because that is who they primarily are and who they know in their own way is who they primarily are.

You will then join with another in a romantic relationship where you are both fully mature in the skill of human self-consciousness so you can enjoy mutual Eldering the rest of your lives, particularly in the mutual Eldering of your children to full maturity in this skill before they leave home and marry. You will also accept full responsibility for creating the life you want by joining with some of your friends who share your worldview in the re-villaging of your lives together for the mutual pleasure of it, mutual support in managing your romantic relationships, and mutual support in the Eldering of all the children. You will have this community join with other like-thinking communities to become an agreement nation, the next layer of maturity of living democratically that is making decisions as close as possible by consensus based on identifying accurate facts about the operation of the universe. As you judge best, you will become active, both locally and globally, to end poverty, participate in maturing capitalism into common good capitalism, and whatever other activities you choose. You will not shrink from playing your role in this fundamental process of maturation. Rather, each moment you will extend yourself into it in whatever ways you determine are appropriate for you. Nothing is more enjoyable than Eldering.

We are all in this together as parts of an indivisible whole. Our priority is no longer our pains in the past or our fears about the future. We now give priority to the eternal now, all the past, present, and future as one experience. While here as a self-conscious part of the indivisible universe, our priority is each moment being a self-conscious participant in the cooperative process of maturation that will never end.

Each day more people will give priority to the unbroken-up-in-to-parts-experience-of-oneness that is always present, or we would not be able to breathe, and second priority to Eldering. In doing so, they will also see themselves as part of the Maturation Movement on Earth, the maturation of all human beings, and the agreements in our organizations, into full maturity in the skill of human self-consciousness.

The above five suggestions are ways you can choose to be an active part of this maturation process. The more we engage with others in ongoing agreements to do it the easier it will be for us to be consistently maturing in our Eldering skills.

It is the mastery of this skill of human self-consciousness, the skill of being a Mature Elder, that will allow us to mature capitalism into common good capitalism. Therefore, I ask those reading this book who are leaders in the private-sector to take the lead in maturing our economy into common good capitalism and to invite, in particular, Chinese companies to participate. There is no need to wait for geographic government leadership or approval.

You are already doing it! As mentioned earlier, it is called "agreement on standards."

Common good capitalism is simply agreements on additional standards of behavior for the common good, the "voluntary rules of the game." They will eventually be supported by geographic and agreement nations, but there is no need to wait for leadership from others. It is also important we begin this process as quickly as possible.

This priority, the making and keeping of agreements that voluntarily give priority to the common good, is the natural fundamental priority of any society of people that has chosen agreements rather than war in their relationships with each other. We are ready for it to be the voluntary priority of our now global society.

Our business community has the easiest ability to take leadership here. In common good capitalism, everyone wins instead of some winning at the expense of others. Respect for and the honoring of skills and abilities and a hierarchical organizational structure for efficiency remain, but they are now second in priority to love, to cooperating for maturation.

The leadership is best taken in the private sector. It can be quickly and legally accomplished there. Therefore here, at the end of this book, I call on the leaders of companies in the private-sector to find the wisdom and courage to lead us into common good capitalism.

This is an extremely important time to do it! It is the only action that, by inviting Chinese companies to participate in it, will end the conflict for economic world dominance that is emerging. Immature people on both sides will believe achieving success is most important rather than cooperation for the common good, for maturation. They will still be unconsciously (without choice) operating as if one of the lower layers is the highest layer. Immature people easily do immature things. Therefore, the potential for military conflict is great and for the second time it would be between two nuclear powers. It is essential we not let this happen by voluntarily initiating common good capitalism policies with each other.

We only have two choices when relating with others, war or agreements. Moving as one with the universe or moving against a part of it, and therefore, all of it. Let's initiate agreements wherever we can.

Secondly, I ask our politicians, particularly the 2020 US Presidential candidates, to seriously consider the 10 Recommended Priorities presented earlier.

It is time to end war and violence the only way possible, by agreement. It is time to create United Nations Two.

It is also time for all people to be encouraged to re-village their lives. Next, to join other communities of like-thinking people to form their agreement nation. It is also time for all democratic geographic governments to encourage agreement nations as one of the next layers of maturity of democracy. It is also time for non-democratic geographic nations to encourage them also as their first layer of maturation toward democracy. This is a very safe way to orchestrate the eventual maturation of the geographic nation into all of its citizens being capable of executing well democratic processes.

The emergence of agreement nations can go a long way toward ending war and terrorism as the only way some people believe they can live the way they want to live. The formation of an agreement nation provides them a peaceful option.

It is time for us to accept responsibility for managing Earth well for the health of us all and sustainability. It is time to give high priority to ending poverty on Earth, beginning with bold private-sector programs to do it in which governments can then participate if and when they choose to do so. To rapidly accomplish this, it is time to create the Common Good Fund and Trusts for All Children programs described earlier. It is time to have the most important curriculum in every educational system at every level be the mastery of the skill of human self-consciousness. It is time to have all of our marriages grounded in the mastery of this skill so couples can enjoy mutual mature love together the rest of their lives, know they will, and raise their children to full maturity in this skill before they leave home and marry.

Hopefully, you now know, as a result of keeping your power, all of it, and from a study of your direct, present, and repeatable by choice experience when answering the 7 questions, the universe operates as an indivisible whole. *Operationally,* this is now your most fundamental fact about the universe.

As stated a few times, it does not answer the question, "Why is the universe structured the way it is structured?" But it does answer the question, "How does the universe operate?" This allows us to learn the *skill* of operating as a part of it. This skill, like all skills, is the same for everyone. This will allow us to easily enjoy using it with each other. It is a skill, not something in conflict with anyone's religious, philosophical, or scientific answer to the question, "Why is the universe structured as it is structured?" The answer to this question by each of us is appropriately given priority over mastering this or any skill.

The smaller skills of the seven layers of maturity of human self-consciousness are the same for everyone. This is what makes it such a joy to mutually know them with your lover, children, friends, workmates, and all in the other organizations of people where you are a participant.

I love playing basketball. What makes it fun is everyone knows the agreements, the rules of the game, and everyone gives priority to them while we enjoy competing for the fun of it, for the exercise we get, and the skills we continue to mature. We can now all be playing the game of Eldering. What makes it fun is everyone in our communities can know the agreements, the rules of the game, and everyone can give priority to them while we enjoy competing for the fun of it, for the exercise we get, and the skills of Eldering we continue to mature.

You now also know that the skill of human self-consciousness, the skill of mutual mature love, is a complex skill. That means, like learning to ride a bicycle, there are layers of maturity of smaller skills you need to learn in the natural sequence. Each time you learn one you need to integrate it into unity and full cooperation with the smaller skills you have already learned and turn that into a unified skill and then a habit before you can focus on mastering the next smaller skill. You can eventually master all seven smaller skills to achieve full maturity in this most important skill to learn before the end of your teenage years. Or, if necessary, as soon afterwards as you can accomplish it through Self-Eldering, the only way you can master the smaller skills of the last two layers. It is an inside job.

This process, by the way, will expose to your awareness all the immature habits that will need to be replaced with mature ones. This is also an inside job. You will need to accept the responsibility of identifying in words the immature patterns in your behavior so you can choose how to relate with them. Some you may choose to keep, some you will replace with more mature patterns you now know, and sometimes you will choose to do some of both. For instance, as a Catholic I had a clear agreement with myself to never even have a thought about romantic interest in a married woman. When I ceased being a Catholic, I judged it was a good choice and kept that pattern.

I was not as successful at changing one of my immature patterns. My unconscious (without choice) actions to get attention I decided to change. I am still working on that one. As a butcher in my father's meat market, and as an actor, I used this to my advantage by identifying the exact way to fill the particular space of the meat market full of people or each particular theater. Jettisoning it from my unconscious (without choice) behavior in my daily life and only filling the space of my physical body with my energy, rather than sometimes filling the room with it, has not been an easy change for me to make.

Between full maturity in this skill and death, Eldering is *at all times and in all places (in the reality of oneness)* the habitual priority in action of Mature Elders, those fully mature in this skill. There is not a higher layer. Between mastering it and death, our highest priority in action each and every moment is doing this, labeled in this book what it has been labeled throughout history: Eldering. Life is now simple and enjoyable, regardless of what is occurring around us.

We know that, fundamentally, mastering this skill is mastering the relationship between our human languages and the reality of the oneness of nature. Not understanding this is why nearly all on Earth are still operating on the assumption it operates as separate parts, competition is believed to be the fundamental process in nature, and the self-interest of our physical bodies is assumed to be our natural, healthy, and mature priority. None of this is true. Only recently have some of us discovered the mature relationship between our human languages and the obvious in plain sight oneness of nature. Correcting this blind spot is the beginning of the Relationship Age, the beginning of us having access to full maturity in the skill of human self-consciousness.

If raised by Mature Elders, mastering this skill can be near the beginning of our lives. From then on, our priority is not personal enjoyment as if our physical body is a separate part. It is *each moment* participating in the maturation of the universe in the best and unique way of which we each determine we are capable.

We are not a whole. We are all in this together as parts of one whole. Up to the teenage years we assume everything not inside our physical bodies is outside them. If then guided into keeping our power, all of it, and giving priority to a study of our direct, present, and repeatable by choice experience when answering the 7 questions, we can discover everything is inside *who we primarily are*, the indivisible universe. It is then obvious that, just like the parts inside our physical bodies, the natural highest priority of all the parts of the indivisible universe are cooperation for maturation, what we may label when we freely choose to do it "natural moral behavior" or "natural loving behavior."

And the only mistake any of us can make is to give priority to the priority of a lower layer of maturity. If we have mastered the smaller skills of all seven layers, this is not something any of us would intentionally do.

This is why only the mastery of this skill by everyone in our now global society will end the choice of violence or war to deal with differences.

Therefore, compassion, forgiveness, and Eldering care are our natural response to both ourselves and others when behaving in immature ways. We know we could not be operating at a higher layer of maturity without previously operating as if each of the lower layers was the highest layer. And we all have immature habits that have not been fully replaced with mature habits. They will have us do immature things. This will also make it easier, with no experience of superiority, to be compassionate. We are, indeed, all in this together as parts of one whole and by nature our primary intention is always to be a participant in its maturation. To add love to whatever is occurring around us. About this we do not have choice. This is the nature of oneness and the process of maturation moving inside each of us.

Finally, I awoke in the middle of the night last night and realized that reality is three dimensional. I also realized the importance of directly experiencing its three-dimensionality, everything having a shape and colors and in relationship with everything else as parts of one thing. When I fully woke up and looked around, *I realized giving priority in experience to three-dimensionality is the choice of the direct self-conscious experience of oneness.* I was amazed at how obvious it was once I gave it a try and how easy it was to experience it as a self-conscious choice experience.

The following was my important new insight. Being self-consciously aware of the experience of three-dimensionality is being self-consciously in the experience of oneness. Everything was then occurring inside it. The natural confidence and contented joy it provided confirmed it is the choice of the direct self-conscious experience of oneness.

We each become aware of the first dimension at the Toddler layer. It is *differences.* They are experienced as *places* or *things* or *spaces*, the words we use to label this dimension. We became aware of the second dimension at the Child layer when we learn a human language and are self-conscious. It is becoming aware of *changes*. They are experienced as, and labeled, *time*. It takes time for a seed to change to become a sprout, then branches, leaves, flowers, and apples. We discover the third dimension at the Mature Elder layer.

It is the self-conscious experience of oneness. In experience, I realized, it is awareness of three-dimensionality, giving priority to the direct awareness of three-dimensionality.

In our thinking, it is then realizing this is the oneness within which the relationships between and among the *things* and *changes* (places and times—the other two of the three dimensions) are occurring as secondary in importance.

If you, right now, simply look up from reading and, looking around, experience three-dimensionality as your primary experience, *that I realized is the direct self-conscious experience of oneness.* It is, of course, in plain sight and I was just not mature enough in the skill of human self-consciousness to see it as such until last night. That last statement is important. Without having mastered the lower six layers, particularly the sixth layer, experiencing this may not be easily possible.

It is turning our attention to experiencing everything we see, such as chairs, lamps, tables, other people, our physical body, and the building, existing inside and secondary in importance to something else. That something else is the oneness of nature, un-broken-up-into-parts experience. Focusing my attention on the chair being different from the table is focusing it on the *experience* of the first dimension, place (space, things). Focusing my attention on the water coming out of a faucet is focusing it on the *experience* of the second dimension, time (change). Focusing my attention on the three-dimensionality of everything in relationship with everything else is focusing it on the *experience* of the third dimension, oneness.

Without being able to see it, we know there is three-dimensional reality: places, times, and oneness. And without all three being present, we would not be able to self-consciously know we are breathing. More important, simply being aware of three-dimensionality is the direct *experience* of oneness. If when we give priority with the focus of our attention on it we have the *experience* of natural confidence and feeling of contented joy, we know we are in the direct *experience* of the oneness of nature Without being able to see it, we know the air is everywhere or we would not be able to breathe. Without being able to see it, we know from answering the 7 questions oneness is everywhere or we also would not be able to breathe.

This is the mastery of the smaller skill of the highest layer of maturity of the skill of human self-consciousness, the Mature Elder layer.

Giving priority to three-dimensionality is the skill of choosing to give priority to self-conscious oneness.

This is what I realized when I awoke from my sleep last night. The reason this has not been described earlier in this book is because I only last night became aware of it. This book was already being prepared for publication. I am sneaking it in here at the end of the *Conclusion* so you can have the opportunity to practice keeping your power, all of it, and studying your direct, present, and repeatable by choice experience to see if you agree with what I believe I have just discovered: how to choose in any moment to give priority to the direct self-conscious experience of oneness by giving priority to the experience of three-dimensionality.

If it is true that as the chosen container experience within which we experience everything else is experiencing three-dimensionality, it will be easier for you and all other readers to master the last smaller skill of human self-consciousness: it will be known in each moment there is the option to choose to operate within the direct experience of self-conscious oneness as our chosen priority experience. Of course, this necessitates knowing the wisdom of using the priority pattern of thinking.

Check this out for yourself right now. Do recognize, if you have not mastered the smaller skills of the lower six layers, you may not be able to have the direct experience of oneness: you will have difficulty primarily focusing on experience instead of words. As perhaps you, this skill is new for me as well. However, give this a try and if you do not recognize it as the direct experience of oneness, you can always come back to it later when you have mastered the smaller skills of the lower six layers.

Look up from reading for a few moments, or minutes, as long as you like, and **simply turn your attention to the experience of three-dimensionality of whatever you see across the room such as lamps, tables, and including people if they are present.** That is all. Nothing more or less than that.

From where you are sitting, turn your attention to the experience of three-dimensionality. And stay in awareness of it for a while.

Then turn to the next page.

First, you probably noticed it was easy to do. It was easy to turn your attention to the experience of three-dimensionality. It should be.

It is choosing to self-consciously experience the reality of oneness. It is and always has been in plain sight. It is three-dimensionality.

Secondly, you were instantly aware all the things you noticed were existing inside the experience of three-dimensionality, *experienced as second in priority*. It was obvious in your direct experience three-dimensionality was more important than any of the *things* you noticed, including your physical body and other human beings if they are present. It was also obvious any *changes* you witnessed, such as other people walking in the room or perhaps the leaves on a tree outside a window moving in a gentle breeze, were also second in importance.

Giving priority in experience to three-dimensionality is experienced by me as giving priority to the self-conscious experience of oneness. I experience myself as actually moving in and self-consciously doing oneness. As walking around inside myself. Inside *three-dimensionality* or *oneness*, they are two words for the same thing. Also, it was experienced as natural, effortless, and freely chosen self-conscious participation in oneness, who we each primarily are and have been since birth.

It is the mutual mature love experience without doing it with another human being.

Perhaps more important, it is now a skill, a choice of how to be. Words are not necessary. That is the wonderful thing about knowing it as more accurate knowledge. It can now become a *skill* to always give priority to the experience of three-dimensionality, as the container of everything else, then a habit, and then part of who we are. Words are not necessary, definitely valuable to be self-consciously aware of what we know, but not necessary for the *priority of mastering this as a skill, habit, and becoming part of who we are.*

Where the accurate words about mature self-consciousness at the sixth layer become important is when we lose our way or are depressed. We then need them to know how to again choose this container experience. This is why having mastered the six lower layer smaller skills and having turned them into habits and skills is essential. This was immediately obvious to me.

If you are not having the experience of three-dimensionality as the self-conscious experience of oneness as I am describing it, as an exercise to know it is possible you need to do the three things you did to experience it with your friend when doing the mutual mature love skill experience exercise. First, be comfortable defining "self" as primarily "all that exists." Secondly, be fully receptive because in oneness there is not a second thing to fear. And, thirdly, know you are choosing to do these things while you are doing them, each moment be in choice to be doing them. Lastly, once you have done these three things, choose to be receptive. Then all three will be operative.

Again, look up from reading for a few moments, or minutes, as long as you like, and again **turn your attention to the experience of three-dimensionality.** That is all. Nothing more or less than that. If you got it the first time, just do it again here to reinforce your knowledge of this option of choice.

Define "self" as "all that exists."

Be totally receptive, letting thoughts come and go.

Be at choice each moment to be doing this.

Then just be receptive and all three will be operative.

Once you have done this, turn your attention to the experience of three-dimensionality. And, stay in awareness of it for a while.

Then turn to the next page.

If you experienced everything as second in importance to something, that something was oneness, experienced as three-dimensionality. If so, that is it. You choosing to know and experience oneness and give it priority. Everything exists inside and second in importance to it.

Notice also you are primarily using the oneness pattern of thinking: giving priority to priorities and second priority to the separate parts pattern of thinking: this or that in times and places such as lamps, chairs, tables, walls, pictures, and people.

Now that we know how to choose to be in the direct self-conscious experience of oneness, we can discover our lives are more enjoyable when we choose this three-dimensionality experience as the container experience of all else we experience. We also can confirm all things are other parts of ourselves rather than in any way polarize ourselves with them because we know the former is a more accurate and enjoyable relationship with them. And we can confirm that knowing we are doing this while we are doing it is also more enjoyable than not knowing we could choose to do it. This knowledge and choice is then a truth and skill we can't ever fool ourselves into thinking we do not know it.

This morning I was able to confirm in a study of my direct experience the three things described in the last paragraph were definitely more enjoyable. I also became aware I was *experiencing natural confidence*, that my insight was being confirmed as accurate in direct experience. I was also aware of the *feeling of contented joy*, the most enjoyable joy. Both were the result of *giving priority* in experience to three-dimensionality, the self-conscious experience of oneness.

My guess is you and I now have access to the experience of full maturity in the skill of human self-consciousness. We know we can in any moment choose to execute the smaller skill of the highest layer of maturity of this skill by giving priority in experience to three-dimensionality. Once we master it as our primary skill at all times and in all places (in the reality of oneness), our lives will be enjoyable by choice and skill. *In our behavior,* each moment our priority will be Eldering, the self-conscious activity of oneness that sustains the inner experience of natural confidence and feeling of contented joy.

There is one other important thing you may have noticed.

It is now easy for you to keep your power inside your skin, the only place where you have sole and complete access to the power of the universe (I think you now know there is only one power). You will now neither seek power over others nor give your power to others. The first does not make sense because only each of them can from the inside execute their power. Thus, any power over them would necessitate effort and force on our part, neither of which we want to do, except when parenting where it is a joy. Secondly, we also do not want to give our power to others, particularly by allowing what others do to determine how we respond (reacting instead of choosing our response). Not having our power by us giving it away and having to obey where we have given it is also not enjoyable. In the experience of three-dimensionality, it is obvious we only have power over our physical bodies, from the inside none anywhere else, and from the inside no one else can execute our power. Stunningly obvious.

Again, look up from reading for a few moments and notice this. First, focus your attention on the experience of three-dimensionality. Once you have done that, **become aware the only location where you have the ability to move and think is your physical body. Secondly,** *from inside you* **no one else has access to do those things.**

Then turn to the next page.

When I do this, what is to me obvious, and I found so enjoyable to notice, is from the inside I had absolutely no power to move or think except in and with my physical body; and from the inside no one else has that power. At the same time, I knew I was first the indivisible universe I was experiencing as real by being aware of three-dimensionality. I was secondly my physical body able to move and think. Not only are all the things I see second in priority to oneness, but so also is my physical body.

We are each a self-conscious part of the indivisible universe and only have sole and complete responsibility for our physical body, the only place where *from the inside* we have sole and complete control and none anywhere else. It now makes no sense to try to get power over others. Or to give our power away because then we don't have it anymore and now have to obey where we believe we have given it.

From the inside no one can execute it but each of us.

Our access to the power of oneness is solely in each of us and that access can't be used by anyone else. Therefore, we want to keep our power, all of it. Then by being a personal scientist both use it to end any unconscious (without choice) giving it to others and instead accept full responsibility of having it. We then use it first to Self-Elder ourselves to full maturity in the skill of human self-consciousness and secondly in cooperation with others for the maturation of the universe, our mature self-interest.

We are each the whole enchilada! Our primary responsibility is being a participant in cooperation for maturation of the indivisible universe, the only thing that is real. Everything else is only real as a perceived part of it and, therefore, important but second in importance.

In conclusion, the purpose of this book was to introduce as many readers as possible, and as quickly as possible, into knowing in direct experience it is obvious in plain sight the universe operates as an indivisible whole. Secondly, to assist you to learn the smaller skills of the seven layers of maturity of the skill of human self-consciousness necessary to consistently live self-consciously in the reality of the oneness of nature. Defining one's "self" as "first the indivisible universe and secondly, my physical body" is not an easy thing to do in cultures focused on each person exercising individual free choice (not mature free choice) with the natural highest priority assumed to be his or her physical body's self-interest. Being aware of the above option of each moment giving priority in experience to three-dimensionality will, I think, make it much easier for you and others to master the smaller skill of the highest layer of maturity of the skill of human self-consciousness, the Mature Elder layer.

Up to now I have used words to stimulate me into the experience of oneness. Now, I just realized, I can use choice, the choice of the direct experience of oneness by choosing every moment to experience everything occurring in three-dimensionality. No intermediary is necessary! I can now know it as the result of choice. I can't express how much I love this. How much I love being aware of three-dimensionality (oneness) as an option of choice.

If what I have just described is not something you have done before, then we are both in the same boat on this one. It was only last night that I became aware of the value of this insight and skill as I hope you now value both as well. Let's each of us, you and all reading these books and me the writer of them, *keep our power, all of it,* and study our direct, present, and repeatable by choice experience to see if this last insight, and the direct experience choice I am sharing with you, is an inside belief and skill. That it is an experience we can confirm in direct experience is real because our lives are more enjoyable as a result and a skill we can master.

If so, learning at all times and in all places (in the reality of one-ness) to give priority in experience to three-dimensionality can be for each of us the known and able to be chosen self-conscious experience of oneness. It can also confirm *experientially* that from the inside we each only have sole and complete control over our physical body and, therefore, sole responsibility for Self-Eldering ourselves to full maturity in the skill of human self-consciousness: it is an inside job.

I now know, as of last night, giving priority to the experience of three-dimensionality as the container experience of everything else (at all times and in all places) is the choice to give priority to self-conscious oneness. It is giving priority to living in reality the universe operates as an indivisible whole.

Try this on and let me know if you discover this to be true and in plain sight. We are going somewhere. We are maturing. I think last night and this morning I matured more. Hopefully, as a result of reading this and studying your direct experience to check out what I have just shared, you did as well.

This is why cooperation for maturation between and among human beings *using agreements instead of war* is mature human behavior. It is also why giving priority to Eldering each and every child to full maturity in the skill of human self-consciousness is the natural highest priority of our now global society. Only fully mature, or at least close to fully mature, human beings know the wisdom and joy of choosing agreements instead of war in any of its forms.

EPILOGUE

With regard to our 2020 Presidential candidates, we need to remind them that, anytime two or more people operating at the Teen layer or higher are together, the other side of the coin of honoring our ability and right to exercise individual free choice is making and keeping agreements, preferably with the priority being the common good of all.

Fundamentally, our only two choices are continuous war or agreements. We are all stuck together as parts of one whole. Therefore, our only two choices are moving against or moving in unity with the rest of the universe. There is not a third option.

Those who have chosen to not do war have agreed to live by agreements. When people choose to do this, they have chosen to be what we call a "society." Their highest priority while members of the society is to make, keep, and negotiate agreements that give priority to the common good of all in it.

The following may sound harsh, but it is true.

Any person or organization whose priority is not the common good of the society has left it and is now in competition with it. No exceptions are possible.

One is either a member of the society and giving priority at all times and in all places (in the reality of oneness) to the common good, or one has left the society and is in competition with it. There is not a third choice, and there are no exemptions possible.

In addition, whether or not we like it, we now primarily live in a global society.

Therefore, here are what I think are the three most important agreements we, as a human species, are now ready to make with each other. We need to ask our 2020 US Presidential candidates if they will give priority to them in this order:

Three Most Important Priorities to Ask of Our Presidential Candidates

1. Form a Global Organization to End War and Violence as a Way to Deal with Differences

It is time for the United States to take the lead in creating a new global organization of those nations willing to agree to end war and violence as a means of dealing with differences within, between, or among them and to deal with any emergence of it as a police action, not war action. For this purpose, and only if necessary, the member nations will make their militaries available for these police actions to end any emergence of violence.

We, the United States, have by far the largest military on Earth. Therefore, it is a moral imperative we provide this leadership.

2. Encourage the Formation of Agreement Nations.

To end all parent-child patterns of thinking, we want to encourage all to re-village themselves into communities of friends based on a shared worldview. They then want to join with other like-thinking communities into agreement nations. They will have their geographic nations be second in priority and be fully responsible citizens of both. This is the next layer of maturity of democracy that will allow people in both democratic and

non-democratic geographic nations to fully and immediately live within their worldview without having to get
control of the geographic nation. And,

3. **Encourage All Parents and Educational Organizations to Elder Children to Full Maturity in the Skill of Human Self-Consciousness Before They Leave Home and Marry.**

We want to encourage all parents, educators, and
others to give priority to eldering our children into full
maturity in the skill of human self-consciousness before
they leave home. This is the only priority that is simultaneously best for them and us all. This includes the skill
to marry within the known skill of mutual mature love.

All else will fall into place if they give priority to these three most
important policies, including taking aggressive action to respon-
sibly manage our environment for sustainability, end poverty on
Earth, and mature into common good capitalism. As a human species, we are ready to mature into choosing these three agreements.
Therefore, those of us who understand this have a moral responsibility to advocate instituting them.

It is similar to walking along a river, seeing a small child drown-
ing, there is no one else around, and we know how to swim. The
moral imperative is for us to jump into the river and pull the small
child to safety. We are now ready and able to choose the above three
agreements. Therefore, if they want to lead, our candidates have to
be experiencing a moral imperative to lead us into reaching these
agreements.

Cooperation for maturation is the fundamental process, priority, and activity in nature. It cannot be stopped. Like saving the
small child, the next possible layer of maturation for us cannot be

ignored. Since we are ready for them, we will experience much social pain until we embrace these three agreements. The current social suffering we are experiencing is a gift. It has forced us to see that these three agreements are part of defining the next layer of social maturation for human beings on Earth.

To end the suffering, we need to stop standing on the shore deciding if we should or should not jump into the river and save the child. We can now reach these three agreements. Therefore, it is time for all, and in particular our leaders, to jump into the river and lead us into this next layer of maturity for humanity.

We need to insist that the people we choose to be our candidates for President of the United States, or any nation, are at least ready to take the lead to move these three programs forward.

MATURATION MOVEMENT

If you are for agreements instead of war,

If you are for cooperation for maturation instead of competition for self-interest,

If you are aware, we, as human beings, are all in this together as self-conscious parts of an indivisible whole,

You are a member of the Maturation Movement.

Our symbol is an umbrella, our maturation into cooperation with the sun and rain for the right amount of each. When we march for agreements not war, we bring an umbrella. When we open them at the same time, it is a declaration we are all in this together and seek agreements instead of war.

We each accept full responsibility for ourselves and stand firm for agreements and not war. We invite others to stand with us. It is the numbers standing with each other that will end war as an option on Earth.

All wars begin and end in peace, in agreements. We stand for skipping the war part.

We stand for the maturation of our children to full maturity in the skill of human self-consciousness before they leave home and marry.

We stand for agreement nations as the next layer of maturity of democracy.

We stand for common good capitalism as the next layer of maturity of capitalism.

We stand for managing our Earth home for health and sustainability for all future generations.

We stand for ending poverty on Earth for the common good of us all."

We stand for Eldering, each moment giving priority to the unique action we can each take of participation in the maturation of us all, the universe.

We stand for giving priority to love, the self-conscious experience of the oneness of nature, and second priority to moving as one with all that exists that sustains the inner experience of natural confidence and feeling of contented joy.

We stand for Eldering in all of our actions

CHRYSALIS NATION

I am in the process of creating a website to continue sharing my insights. If there is enough positive response to this book, I will join with others to create an organization called Chrysalis Nation. It is for the individuals and communities that hopefully will emerge around the world based on the self-evident truths described in this book. People are encouraged to join as an individual. If they wish, they can also invite their friends who share this knowledge to form a community. These communities are then encouraged to join in association with other like-thinking communities into an agreement nation, called "Chrysalis Nation." Its Constitution, Bill of Rights, and operational procedures are fully described in my book *Common Good Nation: It Is Time to Create a Parallel Nation Based on Agreement Rather than Geography.*

If you want to create an agreement nation different from Chrysalis Nation, you can also use that book to create it.

It is my hope that many different agreement nations emerge.

I hope you consider getting involved in this way as part of your participation in the maturation of us all. While being fully responsible citizens of both, it is time to mature democracy into giving priority to agreement nations within safe places to do so created by geographic nations.

To learn more, go to chrysalisnation.org. If you so choose, it will also guide you into creating a support group with friends to nurture each other in mastering the smaller skills of each layer and changing your habits to be in alignment with it. If you also so choose, you could re-village your life by creating a community of friends that could become a community in Chrysalis Nation.

For the last nineteen years, I have mainly isolated myself in the woods of Western Massachusetts to discover our mutual blind spot and the insights as a result that have been presented in this book. The emergence of the organizations proposed herein will be dependent on enthusiastic people showing up and ready and able to do them. Therefore, if you are interested in building a Maturation Movement, a community of friends, Chrysalis Nation, Trusts for All Children, Common Good Capitalism Movement, or any of the other organizations described herein, go to our website, become a member of Chrysalis Nation, and send us a message revealing your particular area of interest. From this point on I will primarily teach and support others in creating and running these organizations. Therefore, I will happily go anywhere to speak and run educational workshops to assist people to learn what has been presented herein so they can become inspired to join this Maturation Movement and participate in it in any ways they choose.

Let a thousand agreement nations grow and flower! And let a thousand agreements between and among agreement nations and geographic nations flower! This can lead us out of all the parent-child relationships we no longer need or want. As personal scientists, it is time to self-consciously live into the Relationship Age with each other.

We are all in this together

THE ROSE ON THE COVER

The rose on the cover is what my father, Hienie Mollner, would draw next to his name each time he signed a note or card with a gift.

When anyone asked him what it meant he would say, "That rose is always watching you to be sure you are following your conscience."

The three leaves represented the Father, Son, and Holy Spirit in his Catholic tradition. For me they represent the three dimensions of the skill of self-consciousness: recognition of differences, the mutual illusion tool of a human language that allows us to become self-conscious, and the oneness of nature. For all we know, since nothing was written down for over 60 years, the following may have been the original symbolic meaning of the Son (recognition of differences), the Holy Spirit (the mutually agreed-upon illusion tool of human language that allows us to self-consciously participate in the maturation of the universe), and the Father (the oneness of nature). They are the three dimensions of the skill of human self-consciousness.

ACKNOWLEDGEMENTS

My father, Hienie, knew love. He didn't know how to talk about it or even directly show it with affection, but he knew how to be it. I eventually knew that we primarily ground every pound of hamburger meat fresh for each customer in Mollner Meat Market primarily as an expression of love. Everything we did in the meat market was primarily an expression of love. Thanks Dad.

My mother's primary intention was always love. I couldn't see that while we, her six children, were growing up. Her priority was always to have us do the right thing so we could escape the poverty she knew as a child. This had me feel dominated by her, and I developed a grand strategy over many years to escape from it. In her older years I was able to clearly see that her primary intention was love, and I am sure glad I saw it before Margaret died so I could directly appreciate her for it. We became extremely close in her last years. Thanks Mom.

In my judgment, my brothers and sister, Hank, Monica, Larry, Mark, Greg, and I, understood little of what was going on at any depth as we grew up together at 1412 Vinton Street in Omaha, in Saint Joseph's Parish, the Mollner clan, and Mollner Meat Market; but we knew love was present. Thanks to all of you.

Without the adventure Marybeth Home and I took in my first marriage I definitely would not have learned much of what I have learned about life. And without the adventure of raising Jaime with her into adulthood, and now raising Stella, my thirteen year old daughter with Lisa and Andi, toward adulthood, I would not have been able to write this book.

A gigantic thanks to Lucy Blakeley, my mutual mature love partner. Without Lucy having the courage to join me in this love adventure I never would have learned the final pieces necessary to write this book.

Wow! Thanks Lucy!

ABOUT THE AUTHOR

Terry Mollner, in the 1970s, was one of the earliest pioneers of socially responsible and impact business and investing. A founder with Bob Swann of the Institute for Community Economics (ICE), he guided fifteen leaders from around the country in the writing of one of the first set of social screens for investing. In 1982, with Wayne Silby, one of those leaders, we used those screens to establish the Calvert Family of Socially Responsible Mutual Funds the first family of such funds. Today the Calvert Funds (www.calvert.com) are one of the largest family of such funds with $17 billion under management and its management company is now owned by Eaton Vance Funds that allows for international distribution.

In the 1970s, the team at ICE were also the creators of one of the first "community development financial institutes (CDFIs)" that make loans to low income housing projects, social and cooperative enterprises in low income communities, and microloan programs in poor communities (small uncollateralized business loans around the world). Today similar funds exist in communities throughout the US and are supported by annual funding from the US Government.

In the early 1990s, Dr. Mollner took the lead to create Calvert Impact Capital (www.calvertimpactcapital.org) a charitable organization, to raise donations and investment capital to fund this industry. It has raised over $2.5 billion to reduce poverty around the world and is one of the largest contributors of capital to the growth to this movement. Dr. Mollner continues to serve on the board of Calvert Impact Capital and was on the board of the Calvert Funds since inception until he retired. He continues to serve on the Advisory Council of the Calvert Funds that is focused on the honest maturation of this industry as it increasingly becomes mainstream investing.

In 2000, he stepped up to assist Ben & Jerry's (www.benjerry.com) in its need to be bought by a multinational to deal with its distribution needs as it was becoming a global brand. As part of its purchase by Unilever, he and the board arranged for a contract that allowed Ben & Jerry's to both continue to operate as an independent company and have a contract that obligated Unilever to allow it to continue to spend forever the same percentage of its annual budget on social activism as of the year it was bought. Ben & Jerry's is the only socially responsible company from the last half of the 20th century bought by a multinational to sign such a contract. Terry was on its board since its purchase in 2000 to 2018.

Dr. Mollner is a founder and chair of Stakeholders Capital (www.stakeholderscapital.com), a socially responsible asset management firm with offices in Massachusetts, New York, and California. Since 1973, he has been the founder and executive director of Trusteeship Institute. Its current main project is exploring the potential for creating Chrysalis Nation (www.chrysalisnation.org), an agreement nation. He is also the author of *Common Good Capitalism Is Inevitable, Eldering,* and *Common Good Nation,* and a book and many articles on the Mondragon Cooperatives in the Basque Region of northern Spain, the first large association of cooperative companies to give priority to the common good rather than the financial interests of its members. It is the best example of an agreement nation. He is also a Co-Founder of the Foundation for Climate Restoration, and on the board of CoolCap Fund and PCI Media.

As part of his experiments to learn more about re-villaging our lives in a modern context, he is one of the founders of three modern intentional re-villagings that in some form continue to exist: Spanish House, Hearthstone Village, and Friends and Lovers Community